BADGER™
SAVES THE WORLD

IDW®
IDW Publishing • San Diego, CA

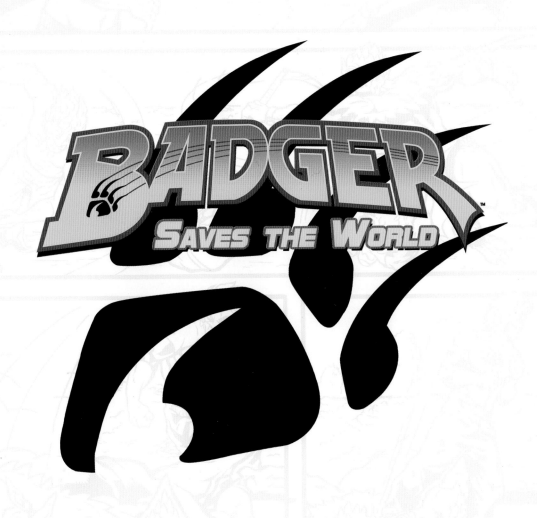

BADGER
SAVES THE WORLD

BADGER CREATED BY MIKE BARON AND JEFF BUTLER

Bull!

Written by
Mike Baron

Art by
Kevin Caron

Ink assist by
Scorpio Steele

Colors by
John Hunt

Letters by
Chris Mowry

Badger Saves the World

Written by
Mike Baron

Art by
Kevin Caron *(pgs. 4-96)*,
Alberto Dose *(pgs. 97-140)*

Colors by
John Hunt

Art and color assist by
Lynx Studios *(pgs. 75-96)*,
Mario Boon and **Jason Jensen** *(pgs. 119-140)*

Letters by
Chris Mowry and **Neil Uyetake**

Original series edits by
Andrew Steven Harris and **Tom Waltz**

Collection edits by
Justin Eisinger

Collection design by
Neil Uyetake

IDW Publishing
Operations:
Moshe Berger, Chairman
Ted Adams, President
Clifford Meth, EVP of Strategies
Matthew Ruzicka, CPA, Controller
Alan Payne, VP of Sales
Lorelei Bunjes, Dir. of Digital Services
Marci Kahn, Executive Assistant
Alonzo Simon, Shipping Manager

Editorial:
Chris Ryall, Publisher/Editor-in-Chief
Scott Dunbier, Editor, Special Projects
Justin Eisinger, Editor
Kris Oprisko, Editor/Foreign Lic.
Denton J. Tipton, Editor
Tom Waltz, Editor

Design:
Robbie Robbins, EVP/Sr. Graphic Artist
Ben Templesmith, Artist/Designer
Neil Uyetake, Art Director
Chris Mowry, Graphic Artist
Amauri Osorio, Graphic Artist

ISBN #: 978-1-60010-186-1
11 10 09 08   1 2 3 4

www.IDWpublishing.com

Originally published as BADGER: BULL! and BADGER SAVES THE WORLD Issues #1 to 5.

UF-DA!

Commentary by Mike Baron

THE LEGEND OF THE EXPLODING DOG

I have been polishing *Badger Saves the World* for years. It's a story that starts small and grows and grows. It's about everything, including string theory. It begins with a bang. And therein lies the problem. Therein lies the tail that wagged the dog. The exploding dog. The exploding dog that appears on the first page of *Badger Saves the World*.

My trusted agent gave the scripts to his trusted amanuensis to read. His trusted amanuensis wrote: "In this the dogs don't talk but our villain, aptly or perhaps too cleverly named Pavlov, has trained dogs to be suicide bombers. This is A BIG PROBLEM... exploding dogs are neither funny nor clever. Exploding dogs belong in a horror movie. In addition, there is a huge sequence with a demon. It would be interesting to explore Badger's sanity, but to do that we need to keep our villains grounded in reality."

I want a movie sale as much as the next guy, but trying to guess what a movie producer wants is a mug's game. You put out your best stuff and hope somebody bites. The reader did not get beyond the first issue and did not see how the story grows. I don't see exploding dogs as a deterrent. In fact, it's only a matter of time before terrorists try to use them in that way, given the terrorist mind-set and their attitude toward dogs.

Plus the exploding dogs were already drawn. Twice! (**Nick Runge** drew the first page before we became involved in another project.) The purpose of the exploding dog is to define the villain—and again, if I may be so bold, to foreshadow something that is bound to happen.

Kevin Caron had already begun illustrating the series in spectacular fashion. With **Chris Ryall**'s approval, I decided to substitute a one-shot for the first issue to entice producers. My trusted agent's reader said, "For a movie version. We wanted to see a *Fight Club* version of this in that we explore the levels of Badger's sanity. *12 Monkeys*, *Mulholland Drive*, and others are good examples of this aspect of the storyline. "

Okay. I kinda sorta think I know. So I put it through the *Badger* meat grinder and a lotta "Bull!" came out. It's also an easier entry point because of its presentation of Badger's condition.

There's a jail scene in "Bull!" There's also a jail scene in the next issue, "Dog Killer." The sharp reader will descry that the scenes are similar, but different. Variations on a theme. The jailhouse scene in "Dog Killer" was written long before the scene in "Bull!"

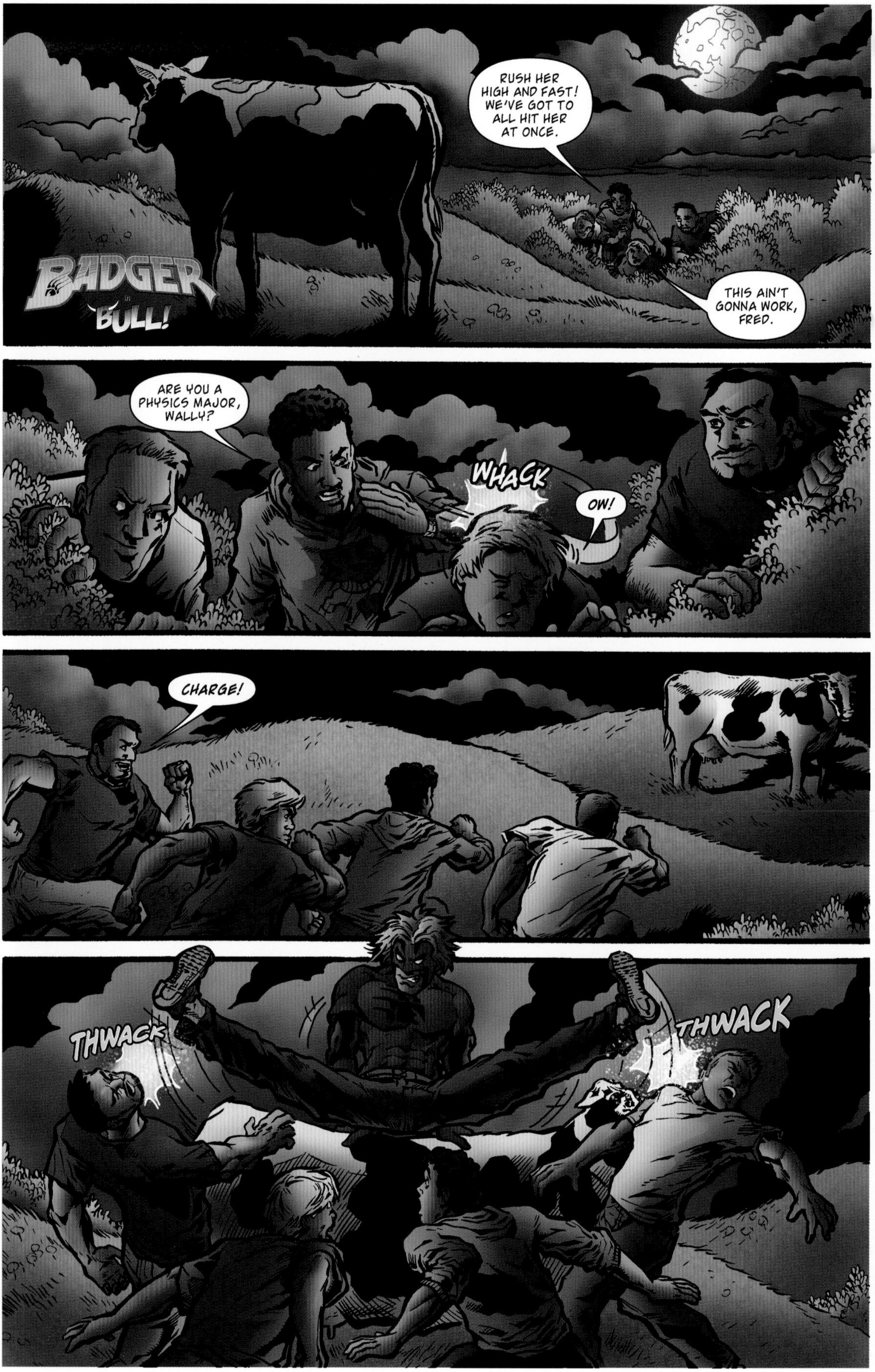
RUSH HER HIGH AND FAST! WE'VE GOT TO ALL HIT HER AT ONCE.
BADGER
BULL!
THIS AIN'T GONNA WORK, FRED.
ARE YOU A PHYSICS MAJOR, WALLY?
WHACK
OW!
CHARGE!
THWACK
THWACK

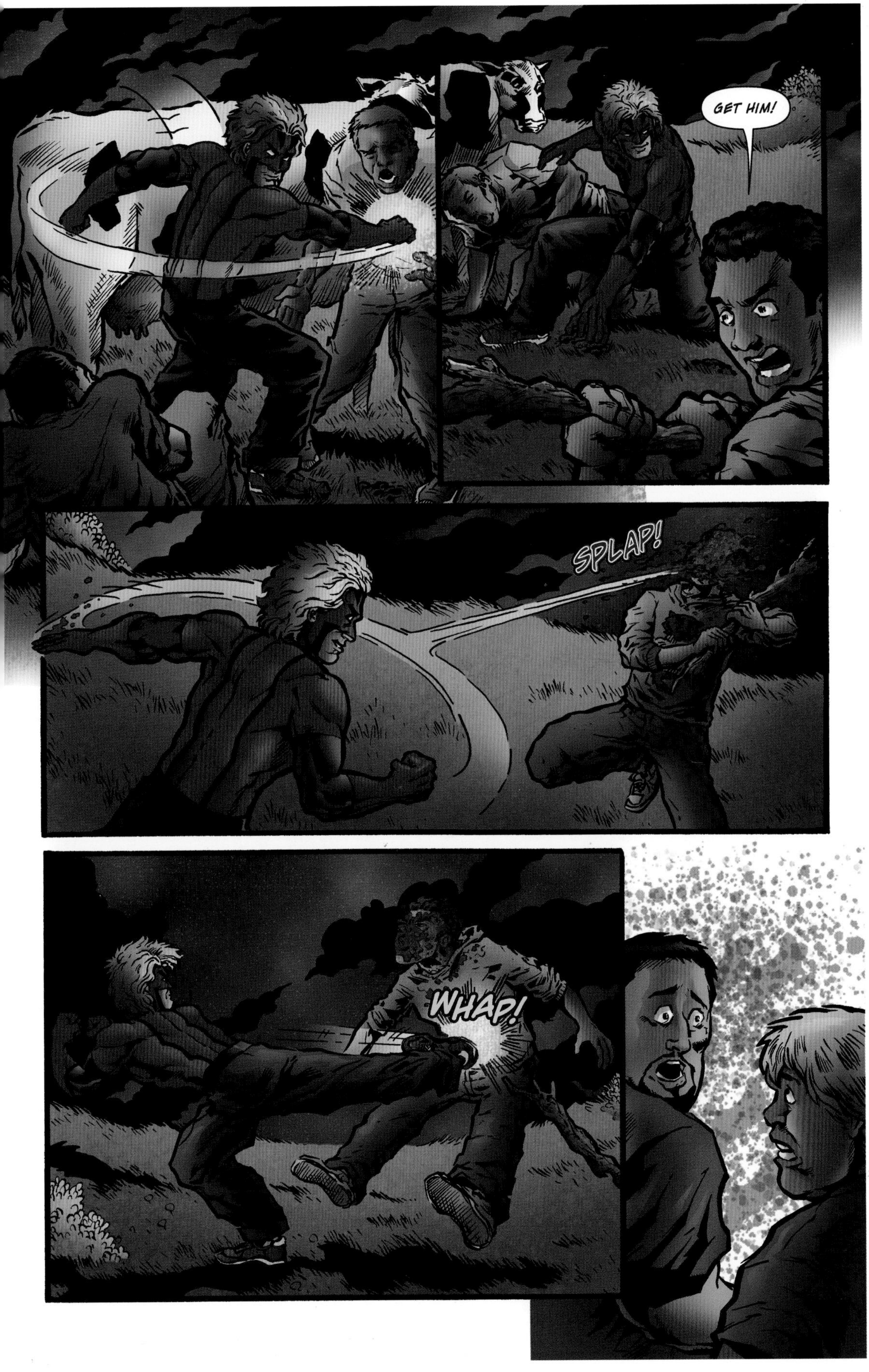
GET HIM!
SPLAP!
WHAP!

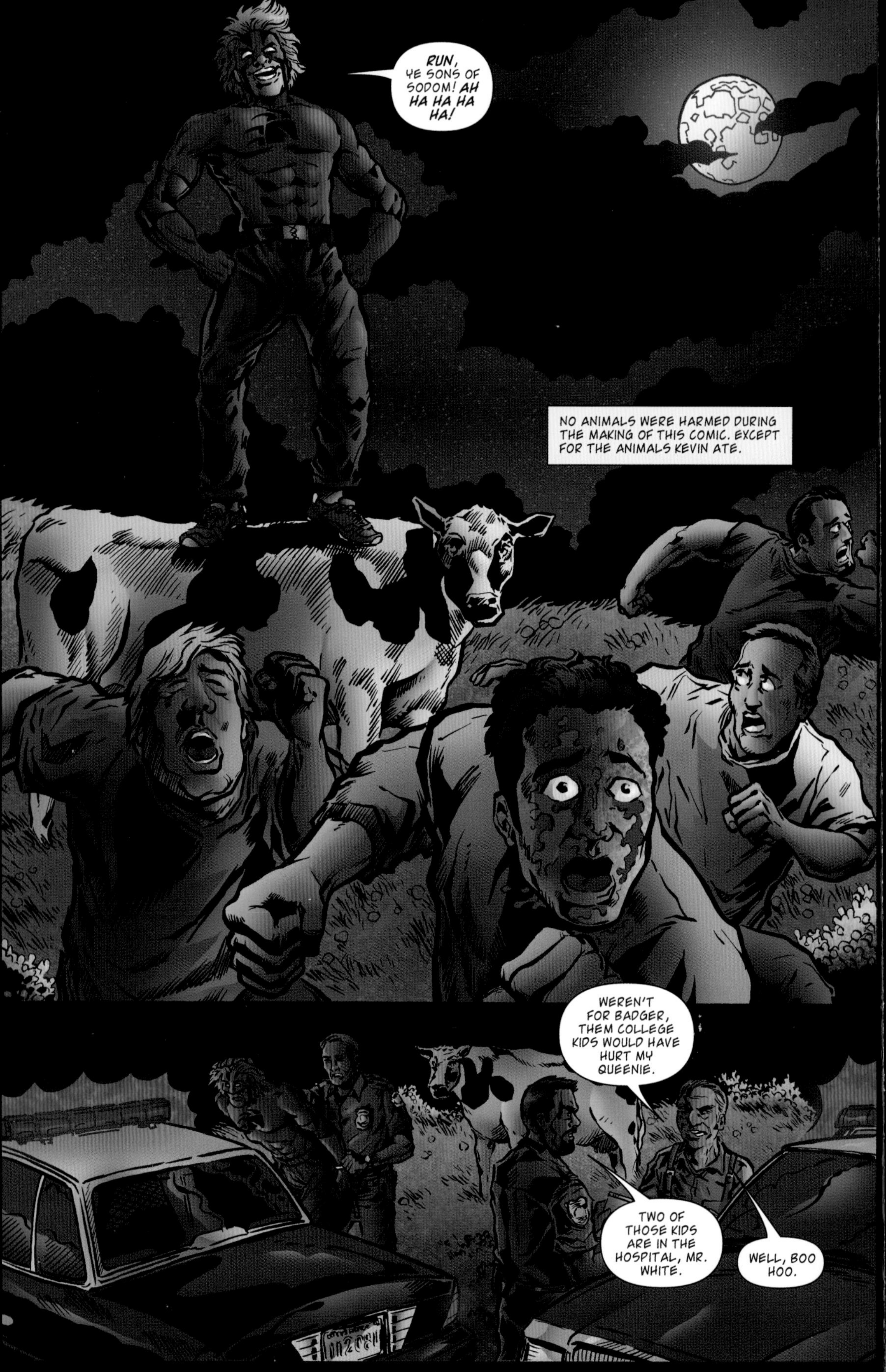
RUN, YE SONS OF SODOM! AH HA HA HA HA!
NO ANIMALS WERE HARMED DURING THE MAKING OF THIS COMIC. EXCEPT FOR THE ANIMALS KEVIN ATE.
WEREN'T FOR BADGER, THEM COLLEGE KIDS WOULD HAVE HURT MY QUEENIE.
TWO OF THOSE KIDS ARE IN THE HOSPITAL, MR. WHITE.
WELL, BOO HOO.

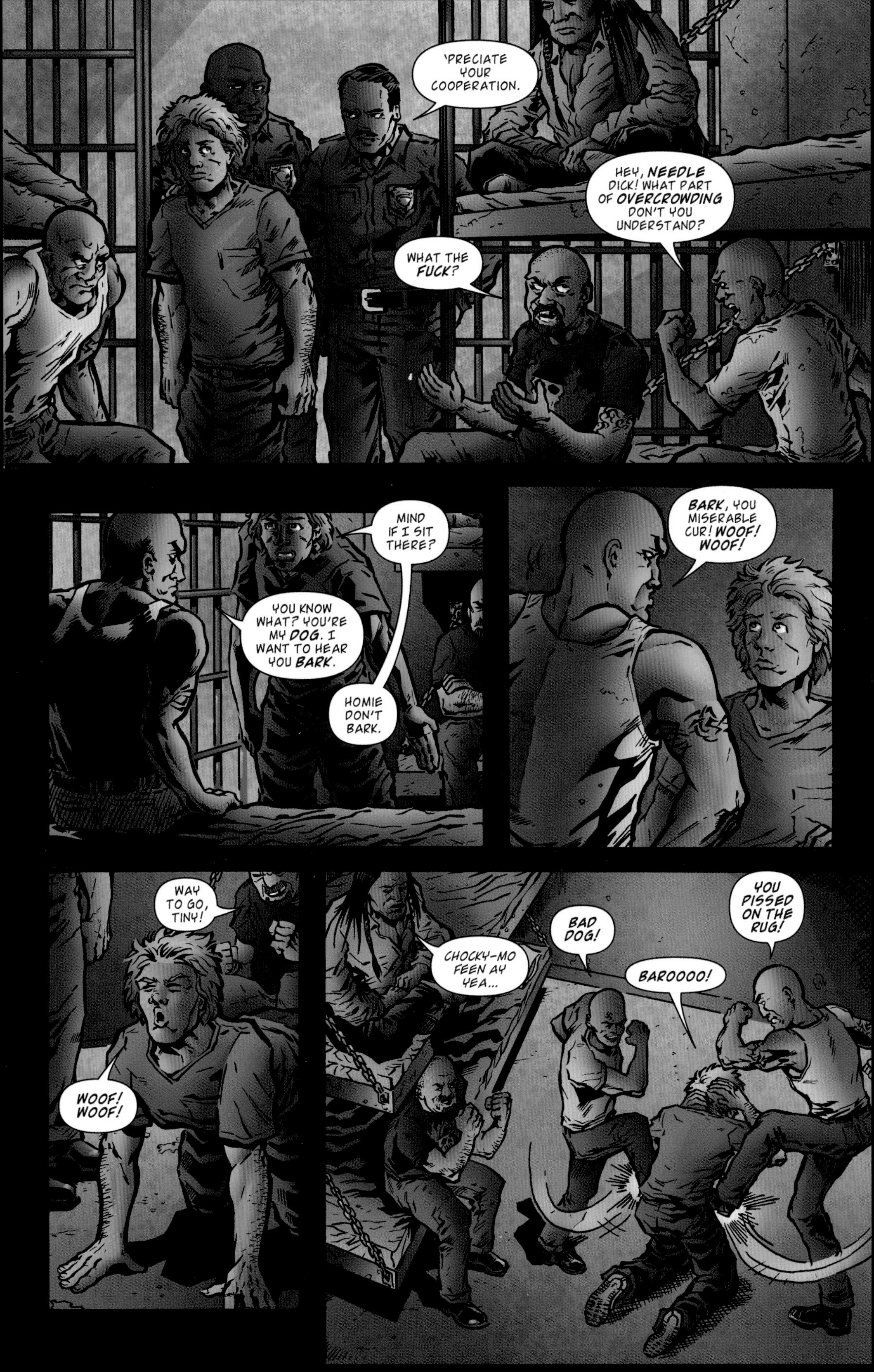
'PRECIATE YOUR COOPERATION.
HEY, NEEDLE DICK! WHAT PART OF OVERCROWDING DON'T YOU UNDERSTAND?
WHAT THE FUCK?
MIND IF I SIT THERE?
YOU KNOW WHAT? YOU'RE MY DOG. I WANT TO HEAR YOU BARK.
HOMIE DON'T BARK.
BARK, YOU MISERABLE CUR! WOOF! WOOF!
WAY TO GO, TINY!
WOOF! WOOF!
CHOCKY-MO FEEN AY YEA...
BAD DOG!
YOU PISSED ON THE RUG!
BAROOOO!

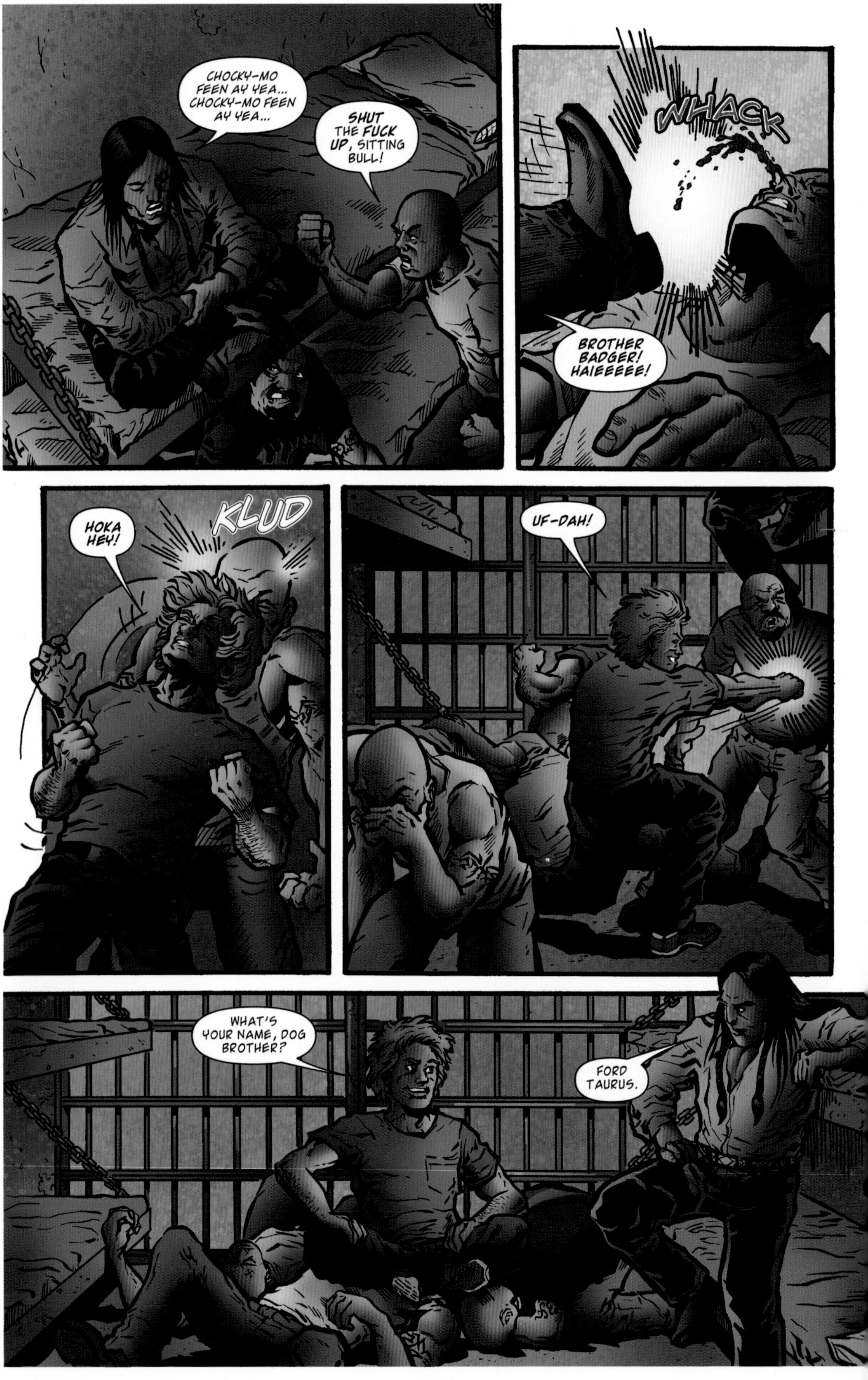
CHOCKY-MO FEEN AY YEA... CHOCKY-MO FEEN AY YEA...
SHUT THE FUCK UP, SITTING BULL!
WHACK
BROTHER BADGER! HAIEEEEE!
HOKA HEY!
KLUD
UF-DAH!
WHAT'S YOUR NAME, DOG BROTHER?
FORD TAURUS.

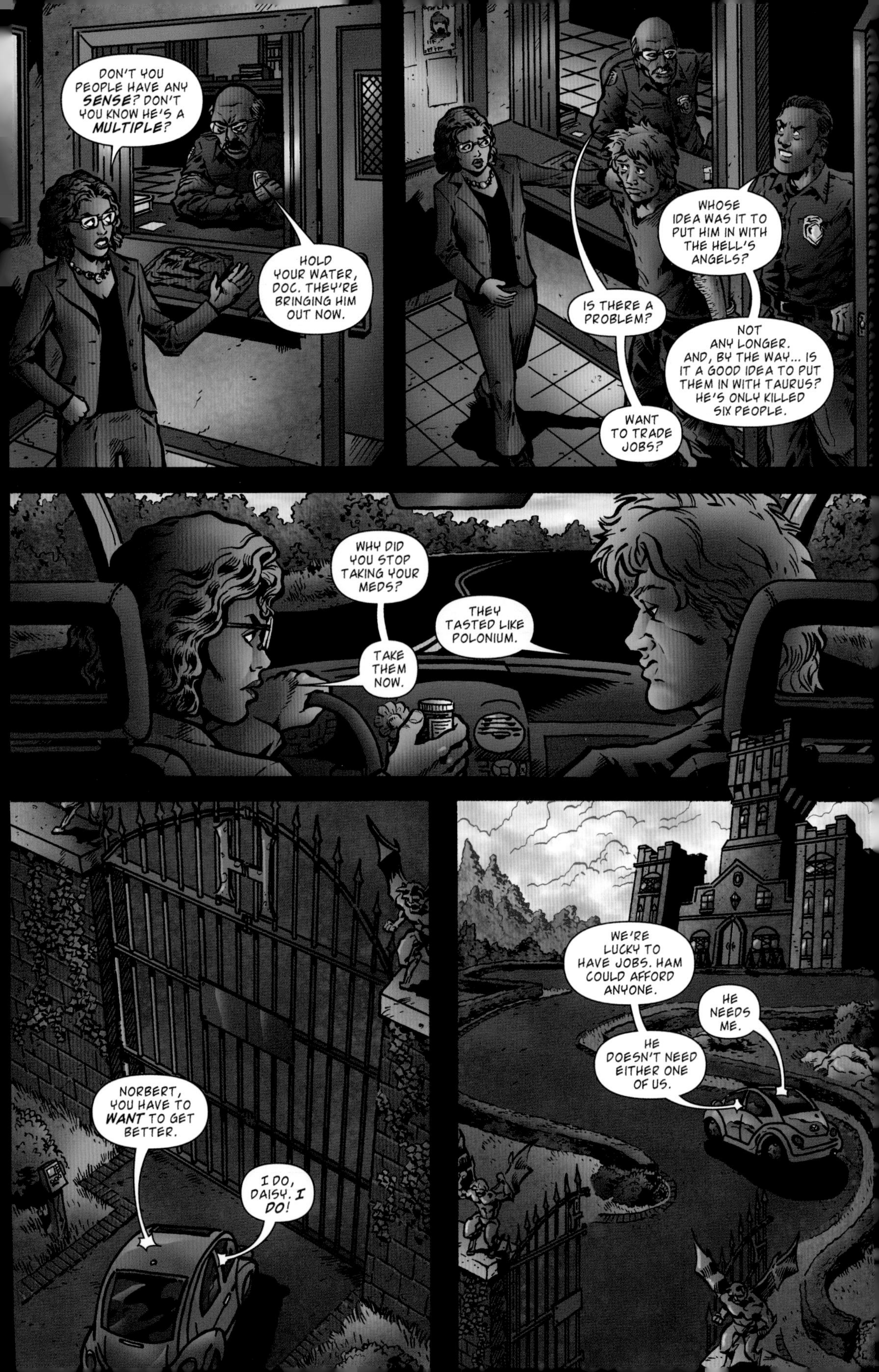
DON'T YOU PEOPLE HAVE ANY SENSE? DON'T YOU KNOW HE'S A MULTIPLE?
HOLD YOUR WATER, DOC. THEY'RE BRINGING HIM OUT NOW.
WHOSE IDEA WAS IT TO PUT HIM IN WITH THE HELL'S ANGELS?
IS THERE A PROBLEM?
NOT ANY LONGER. AND, BY THE WAY... IS IT A GOOD IDEA TO PUT THEM IN WITH TAURUS? HE'S ONLY KILLED SIX PEOPLE.
WANT TO TRADE JOBS?
WHY DID YOU STOP TAKING YOUR MEDS?
THEY TASTED LIKE POLONIUM.
TAKE THEM NOW.
NORBERT, YOU HAVE TO WANT TO GET BETTER.
I DO, DAISY. I DO!
WE'RE LUCKY TO HAVE JOBS. HAM COULD AFFORD ANYONE.
HE NEEDS ME.
HE DOESN'T NEED EITHER ONE OF US.

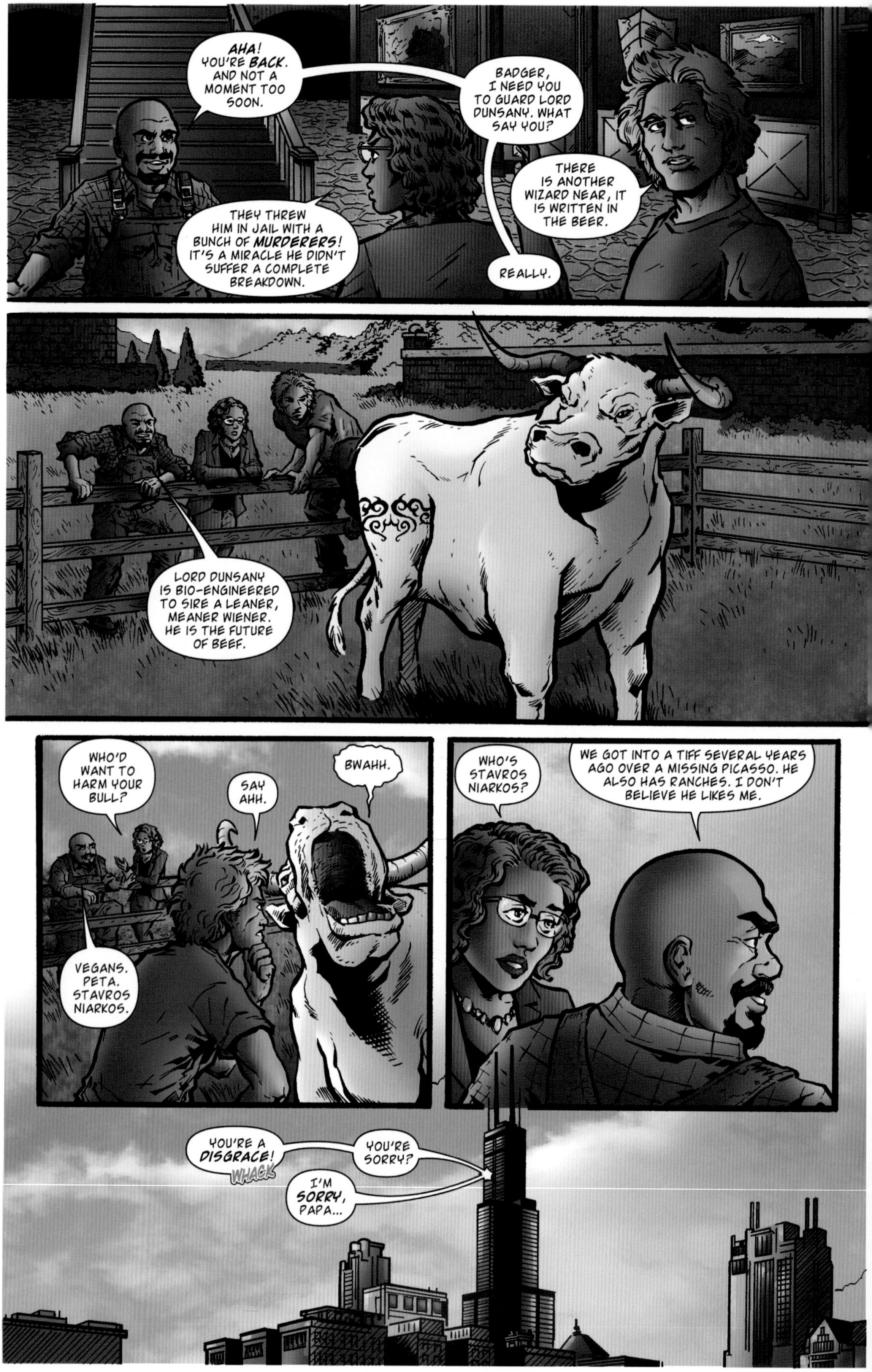
AHA! YOU'RE BACK. AND NOT A MOMENT TOO SOON.
THEY THREW HIM IN JAIL WITH A BUNCH OF MURDERERS! IT'S A MIRACLE HE DIDN'T SUFFER A COMPLETE BREAKDOWN.
BADGER, I NEED YOU TO GUARD LORD DUNSANY. WHAT SAY YOU?
REALLY.
THERE IS ANOTHER WIZARD NEAR, IT IS WRITTEN IN THE BEER.
LORD DUNSANY IS BIO-ENGINEERED TO SIRE A LEANER, MEANER WIENER. HE IS THE FUTURE OF BEEF.
WHO'D WANT TO HARM YOUR BULL?
SAY AHH.
BWAHH.
VEGANS. PETA. STAVROS NIARKOS.
WHO'S STAVROS NIARKOS?
WE GOT INTO A TIFF SEVERAL YEARS AGO OVER A MISSING PICASSO. HE ALSO HAS RANCHES. I DON'T BELIEVE HE LIKES ME.
YOU'RE A DISGRACE!
WHACK
YOU'RE SORRY?
I'M SORRY, PAPA...

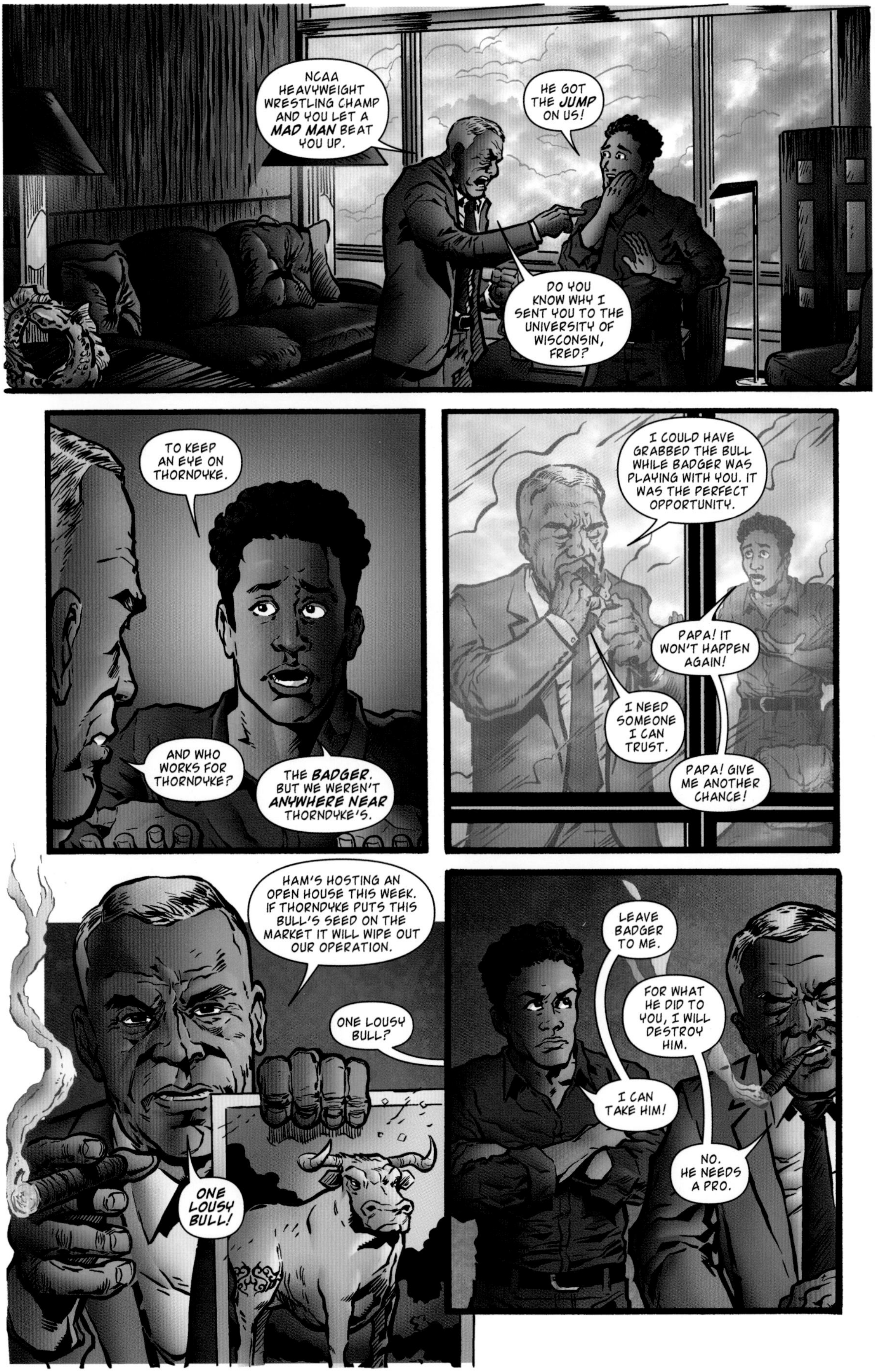

NCAA HEAVYWEIGHT WRESTLING CHAMP AND YOU LET A MAD MAN BEAT YOU UP.
HE GOT THE JUMP ON US!
DO YOU KNOW WHY I SENT YOU TO THE UNIVERSITY OF WISCONSIN, FRED?
TO KEEP AN EYE ON THORNDYKE.
AND WHO WORKS FOR THORNDYKE?
THE BADGER. BUT WE WEREN'T ANYWHERE NEAR THORNDYKE'S.
I COULD HAVE GRABBED THE BULL WHILE BADGER WAS PLAYING WITH YOU. IT WAS THE PERFECT OPPORTUNITY.
PAPA! IT WON'T HAPPEN AGAIN!
I NEED SOMEONE I CAN TRUST.
PAPA! GIVE ME ANOTHER CHANCE!
HAM'S HOSTING AN OPEN HOUSE THIS WEEK. IF THORNDYKE PUTS THIS BULL'S SEED ON THE MARKET IT WILL WIPE OUT OUR OPERATION.
ONE LOUSY BULL?
ONE LOUSY BULL!
LEAVE BADGER TO ME.
FOR WHAT HE DID TO YOU, I WILL DESTROY HIM.
I CAN TAKE HIM!
NO. HE NEEDS A PRO.

FETCH, YOUR LORDSHIP! FETCH!

GOOD BOY!

SNORT!

WHAT?

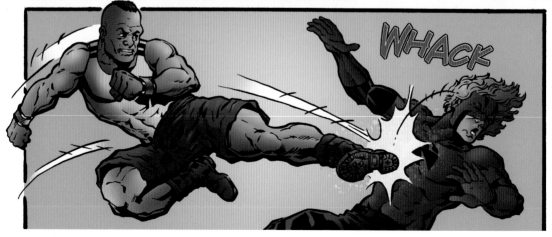

WHACK

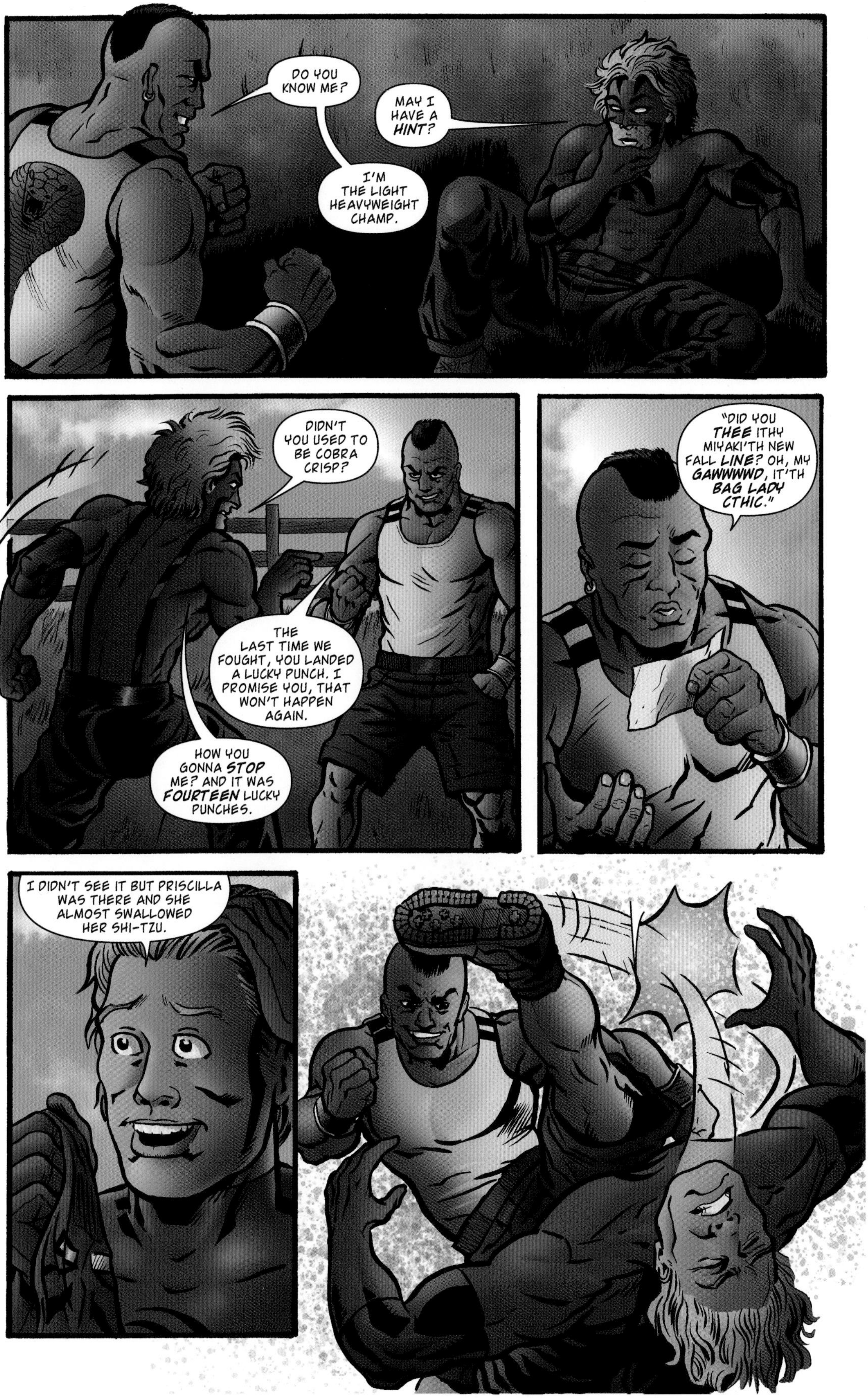
DO YOU KNOW ME?
MAY I HAVE A HINT?
I'M THE LIGHT HEAVYWEIGHT CHAMP.
DIDN'T YOU USED TO BE COBRA CRISP?
THE LAST TIME WE FOUGHT, YOU LANDED A LUCKY PUNCH. I PROMISE YOU, THAT WON'T HAPPEN AGAIN.
HOW YOU GONNA STOP ME? AND IT WAS FOURTEEN LUCKY PUNCHES.
"DID YOU THEE ITHY MIYAKI'TH NEW FALL LINE? OH, MY GAWWWWD, IT'TH BAG LADY CTHIC."
I DIDN'T SEE IT BUT PRISCILLA WAS THERE AND SHE ALMOST SWALLOWED HER SHI-TZU.

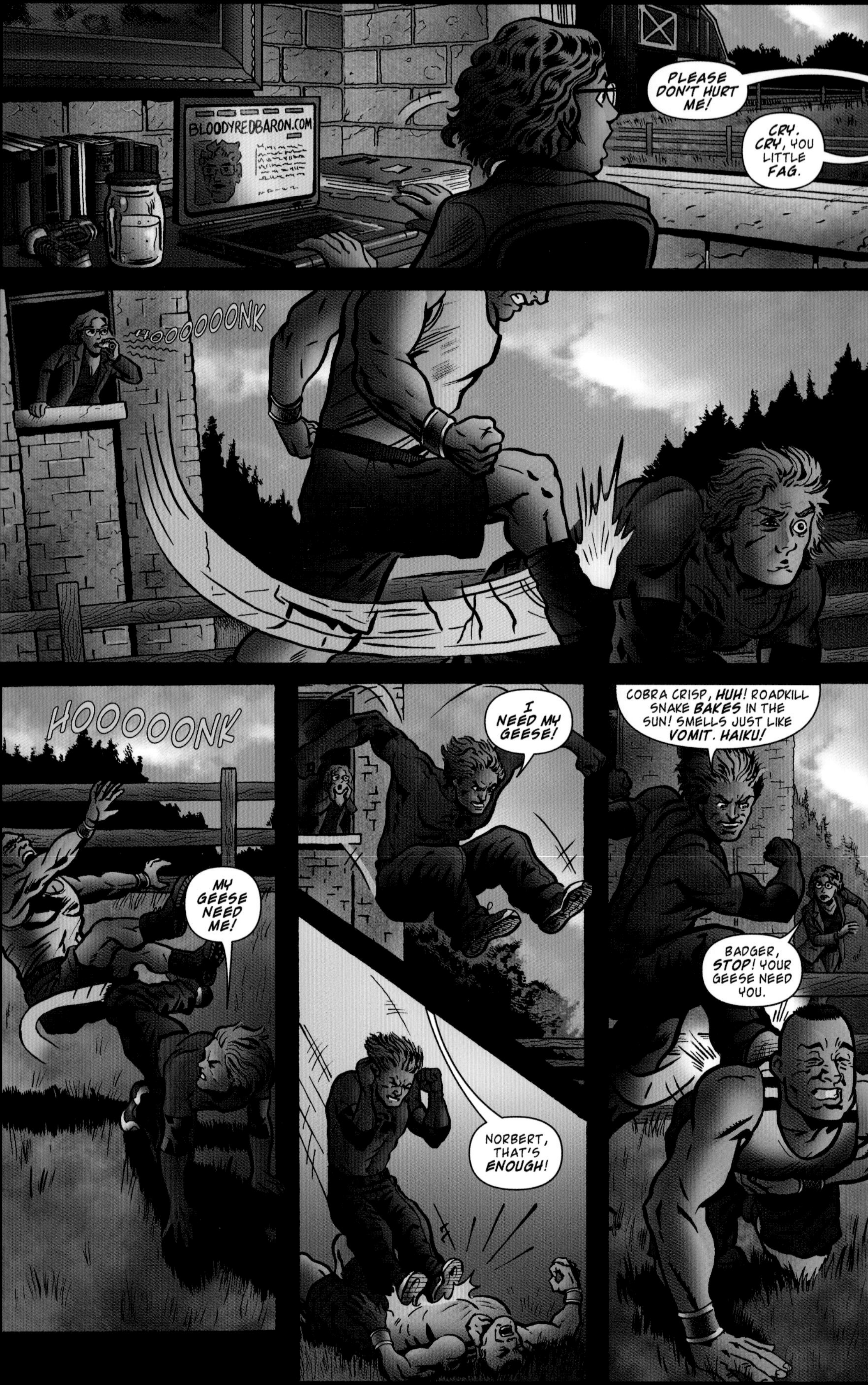
BLOODYREDBARON.COM
PLEASE DON'T HURT ME!
CRY. CRY, YOU LITTLE FAG.
HOOOOOOONK
HOOOOONK
MY GEESE NEED ME!
I NEED MY GEESE!
NORBERT, THAT'S ENOUGH!
COBRA CRISP, HUH! ROADKILL SNAKE BAKES IN THE SUN! SMELLS JUST LIKE VOMIT. HAIKU!
BADGER, STOP! YOUR GEESE NEED YOU.

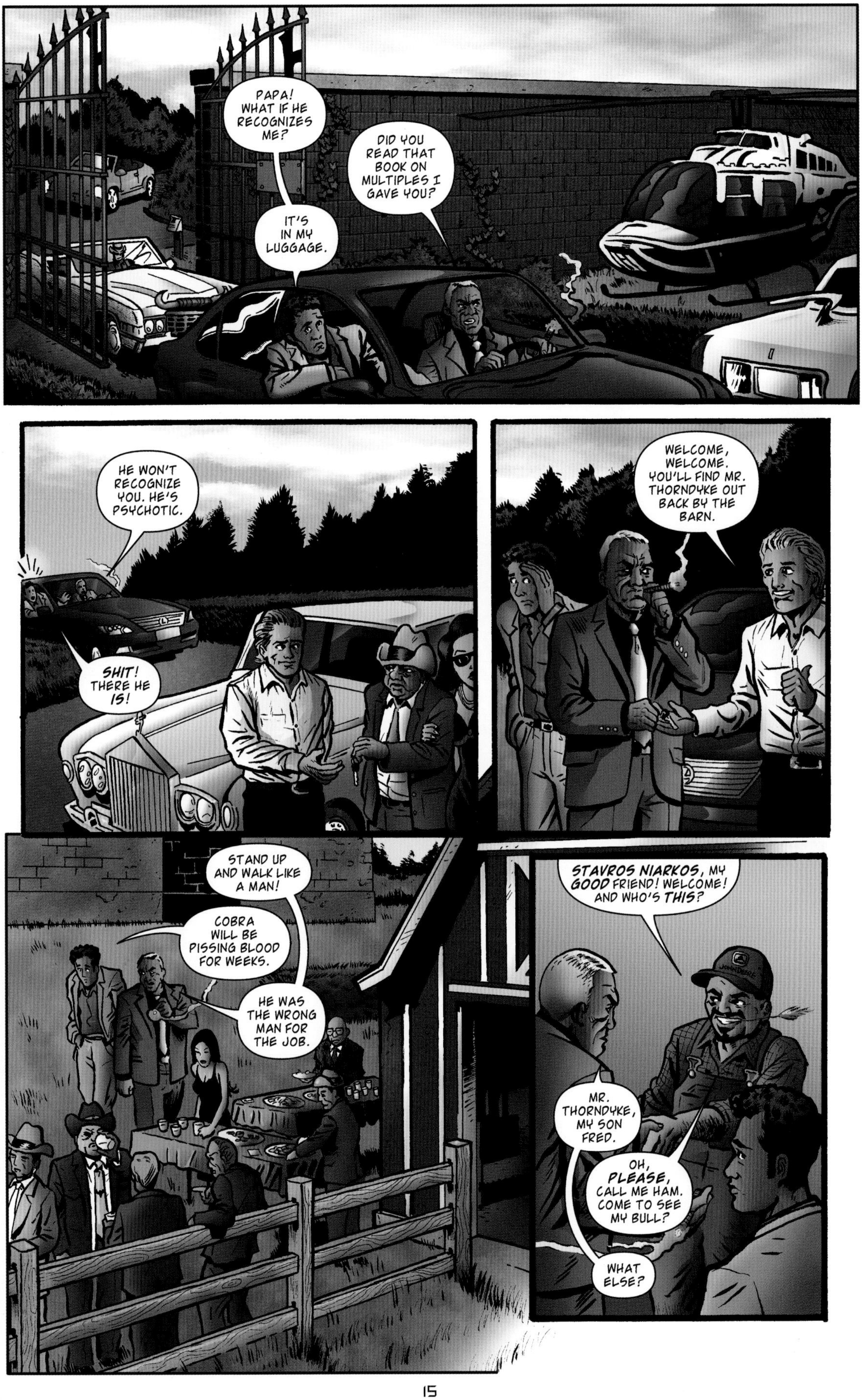
PAPA! WHAT IF HE RECOGNIZES ME?
DID YOU READ THAT BOOK ON MULTIPLES I GAVE YOU?
IT'S IN MY LUGGAGE.
HE WON'T RECOGNIZE YOU. HE'S PSYCHOTIC.
SHIT! THERE HE IS!
WELCOME, WELCOME. YOU'LL FIND MR. THORNDYKE OUT BACK BY THE BARN.
STAND UP AND WALK LIKE A MAN!
COBRA WILL BE PISSING BLOOD FOR WEEKS.
HE WAS THE WRONG MAN FOR THE JOB.
STAVROS NIARKOS, MY GOOD FRIEND! WELCOME! AND WHO'S THIS?
MR. THORNDYKE, MY SON FRED.
OH, PLEASE, CALL ME HAM. COME TO SEE MY BULL?
WHAT ELSE?

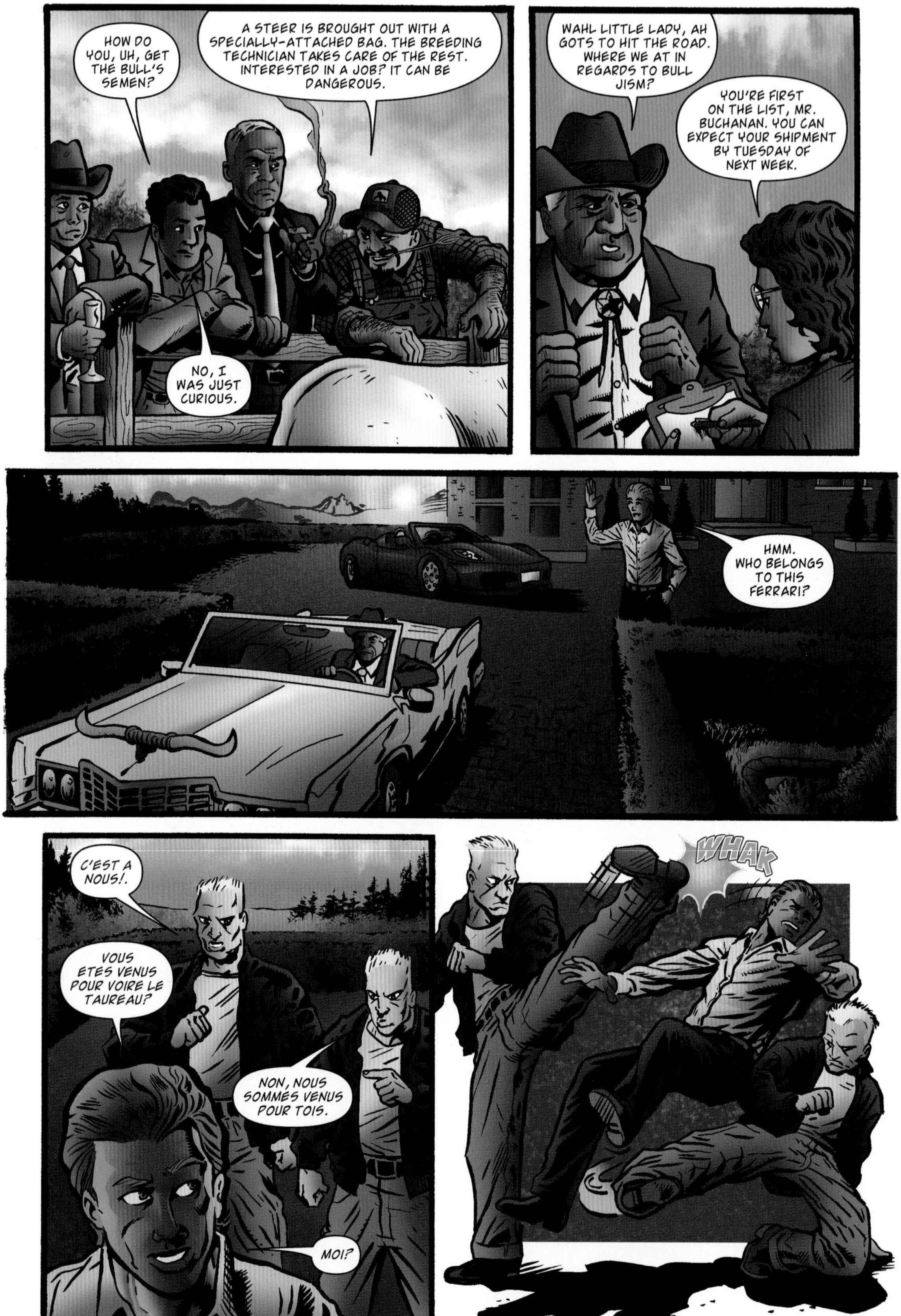
HOW DO YOU, UH, GET THE BULL'S SEMEN?
A STEER IS BROUGHT OUT WITH A SPECIALLY-ATTACHED BAG. THE BREEDING TECHNICIAN TAKES CARE OF THE REST. INTERESTED IN A JOB? IT CAN BE DANGEROUS.
NO, I WAS JUST CURIOUS.
WAHL LITTLE LADY, AH GOTS TO HIT THE ROAD. WHERE WE AT IN REGARDS TO BULL JISM?
YOU'RE FIRST ON THE LIST, MR. BUCHANAN. YOU CAN EXPECT YOUR SHIPMENT BY TUESDAY OF NEXT WEEK.
HMM. WHO BELONGS TO THIS FERRARI?
C'EST A NOUS!.
VOUS ETES VENUS POUR VOIRE LE TAUREAU?
NON, NOUS SOMMES VENUS POUR TOIS.
MOI?
WHAK

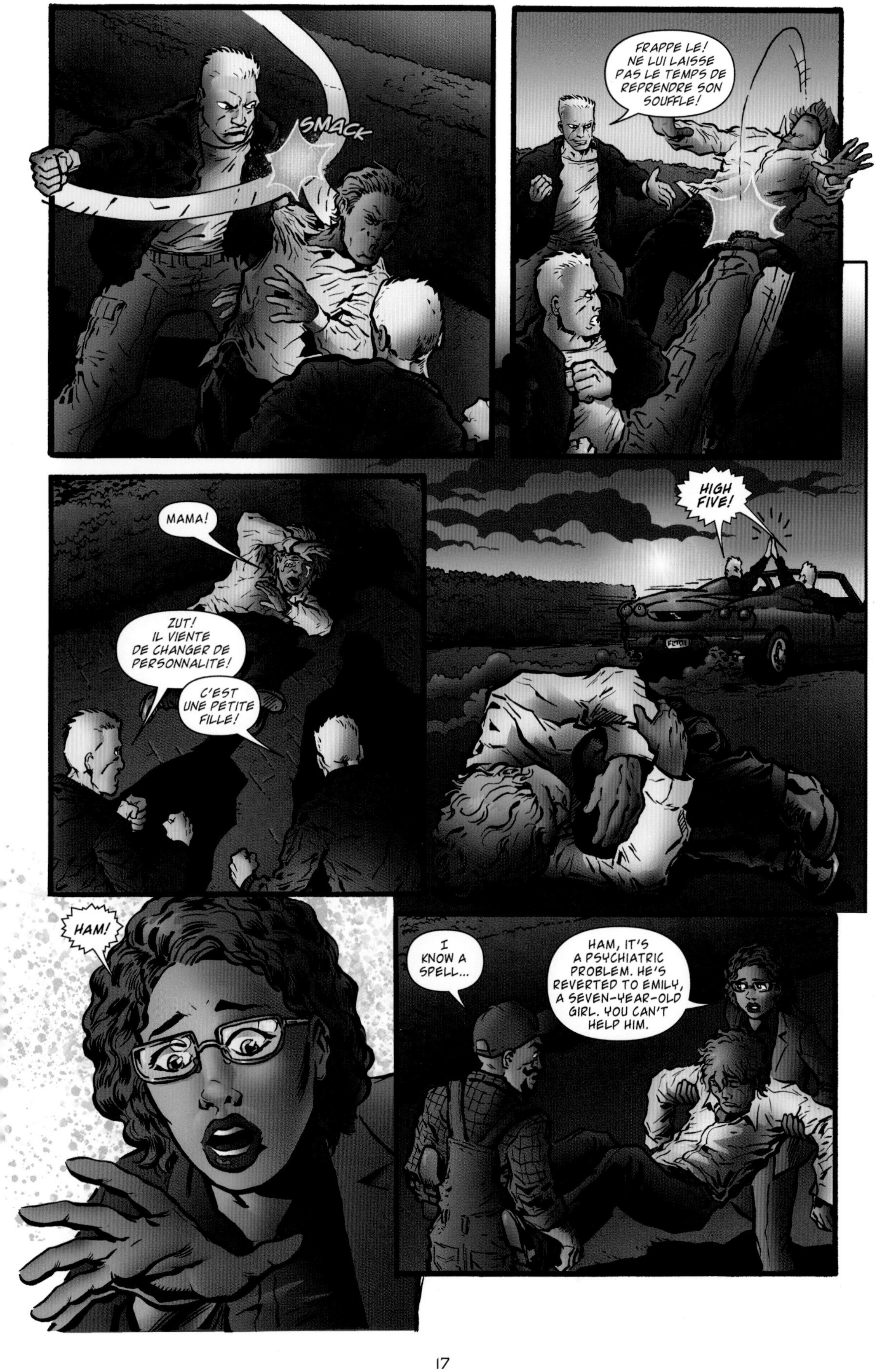
SMACK
FRAPPE LE! NE LUI LAISSE PAS LE TEMPS DE REPRENDRE SON SOUFFLE!
MAMA!
ZUT! IL VIENTE DE CHANGER DE PERSONNALITE!
C'EST UNE PETITE FILLE!
HIGH FIVE!
HAM!
I KNOW A SPELL...
HAM, IT'S A PSYCHIATRIC PROBLEM. HE'S REVERTED TO EMILY, A SEVEN-YEAR-OLD GIRL. YOU CAN'T HELP HIM.

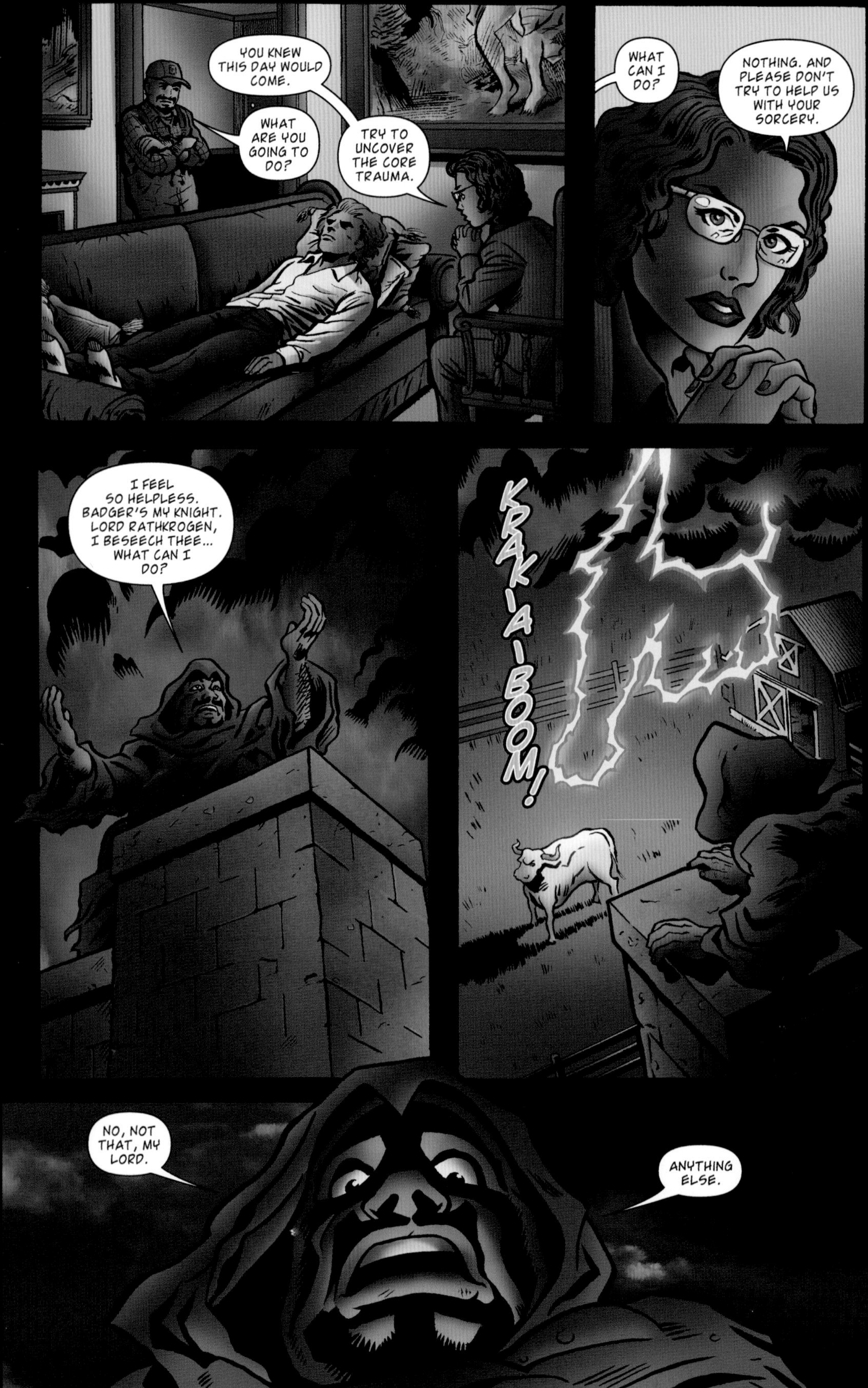

YOU KNEW THIS DAY WOULD COME.
WHAT ARE YOU GOING TO DO?
TRY TO UNCOVER THE CORE TRAUMA.
WHAT CAN I DO?
NOTHING. AND PLEASE DON'T TRY TO HELP US WITH YOUR SORCERY.
I FEEL SO HELPLESS. BADGER'S MY KNIGHT. LORD RATHKROGEN, I BESEECH THEE... WHAT CAN I DO?
KRAKAKABOOM!
NO, NOT THAT, MY LORD.
ANYTHING ELSE.

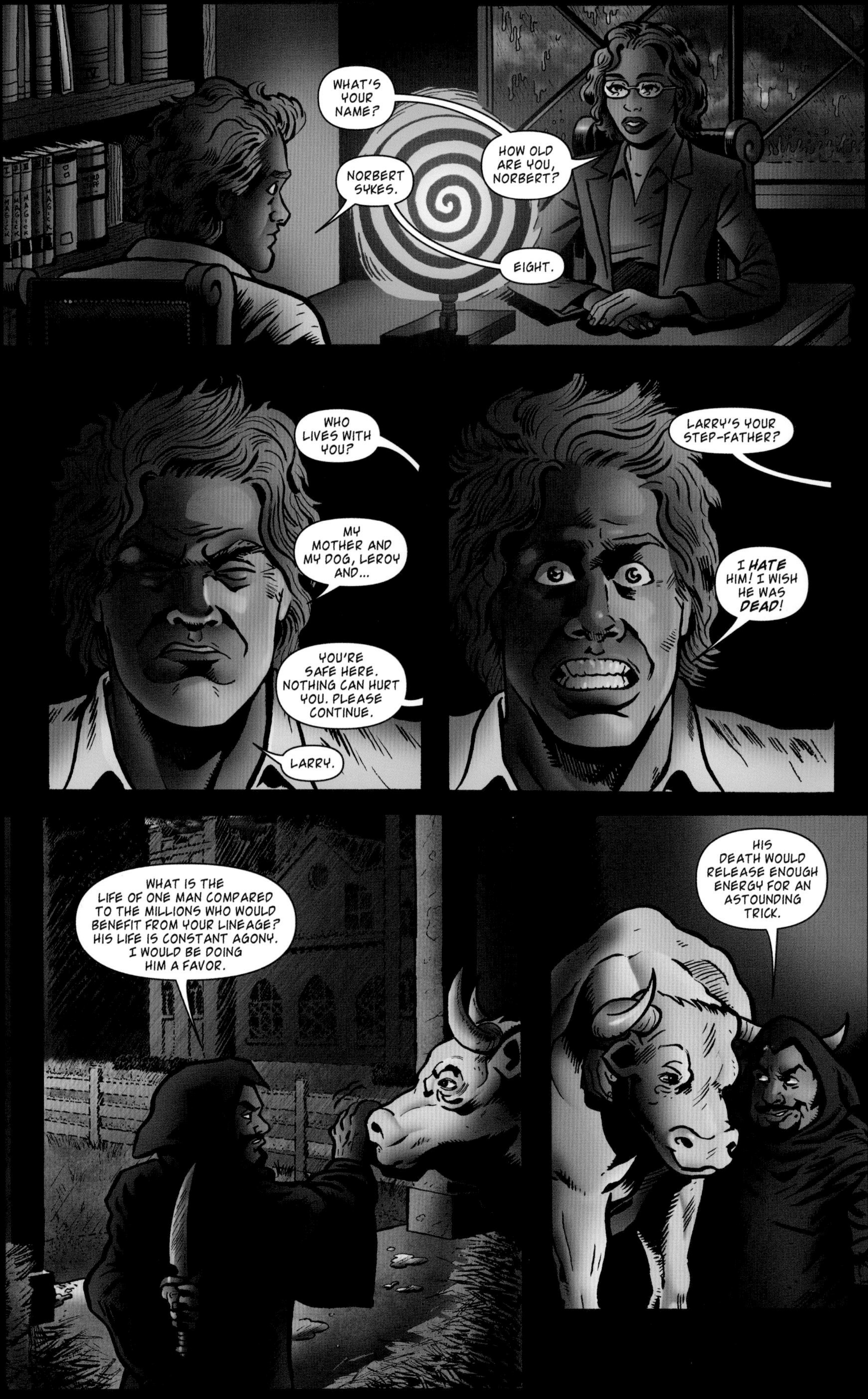
WHAT'S YOUR NAME?
NORBERT SYKES.
HOW OLD ARE YOU, NORBERT?
EIGHT.
WHO LIVES WITH YOU?
MY MOTHER AND MY DOG, LEROY AND...
YOU'RE SAFE HERE. NOTHING CAN HURT YOU. PLEASE CONTINUE.
LARRY.
LARRY'S YOUR STEP-FATHER?
I *HATE* HIM! I WISH HE WAS *DEAD*!
WHAT IS THE LIFE OF ONE MAN COMPARED TO THE MILLIONS WHO WOULD BENEFIT FROM YOUR LINEAGE? HIS LIFE IS CONSTANT AGONY. I WOULD BE DOING HIM A FAVOR.
HIS DEATH WOULD RELEASE ENOUGH ENERGY FOR AN ASTOUNDING TRICK.

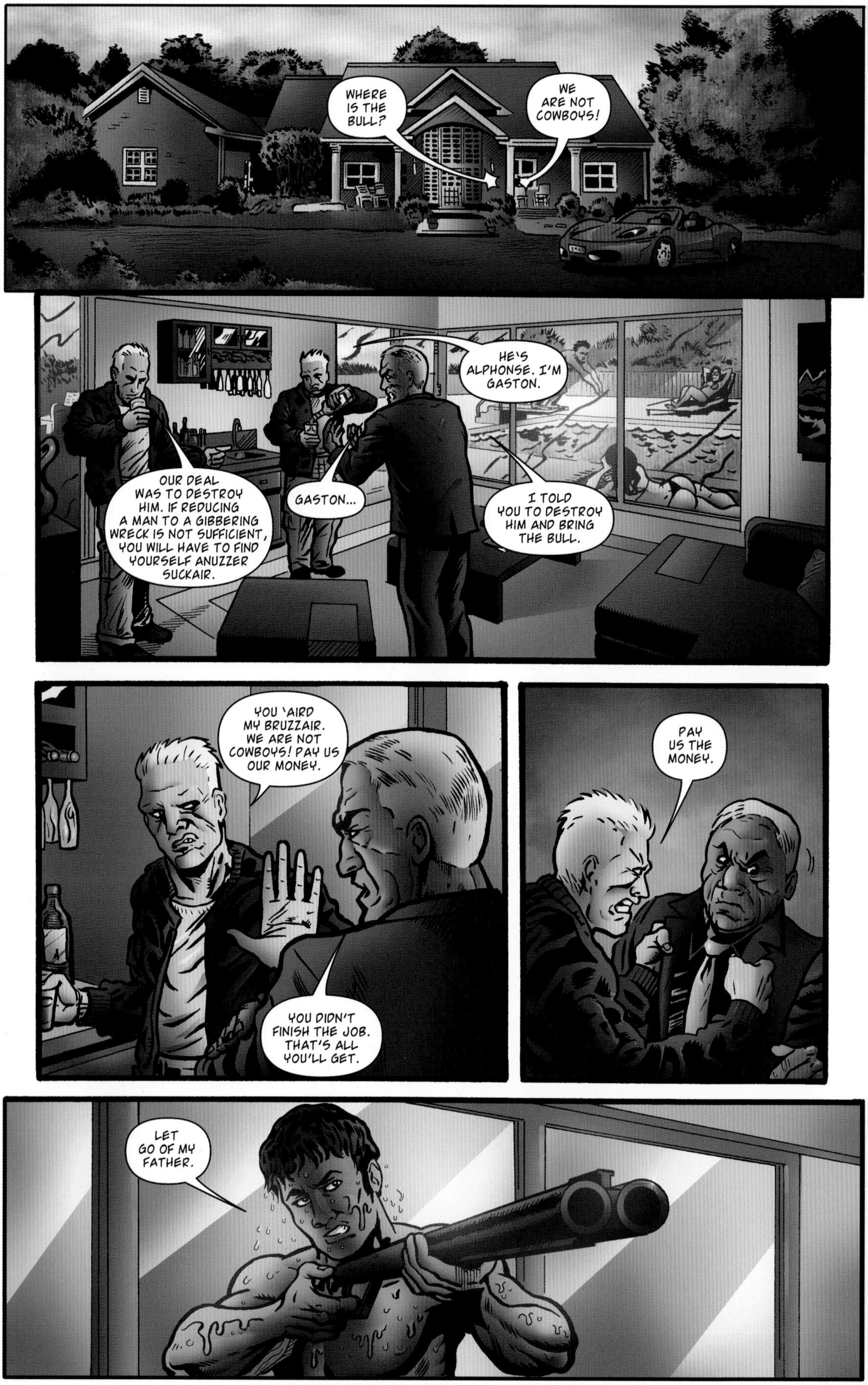
WHERE IS THE BULL?
WE ARE NOT COWBOYS!
HE'S ALPHONSE. I'M GASTON.
OUR DEAL WAS TO DESTROY HIM. IF REDUCING A MAN TO A GIBBERING WRECK IS NOT SUFFICIENT, YOU WILL HAVE TO FIND YOURSELF ANUZZER SUCKAIR.
GASTON...
I TOLD YOU TO DESTROY HIM AND BRING THE BULL.
YOU 'AIRD MY BRUZZAIR. WE ARE NOT COWBOYS! PAY US OUR MONEY.
YOU DIDN'T FINISH THE JOB. THAT'S ALL YOU'LL GET.
PAY US THE MONEY.
LET GO OF MY FATHER.

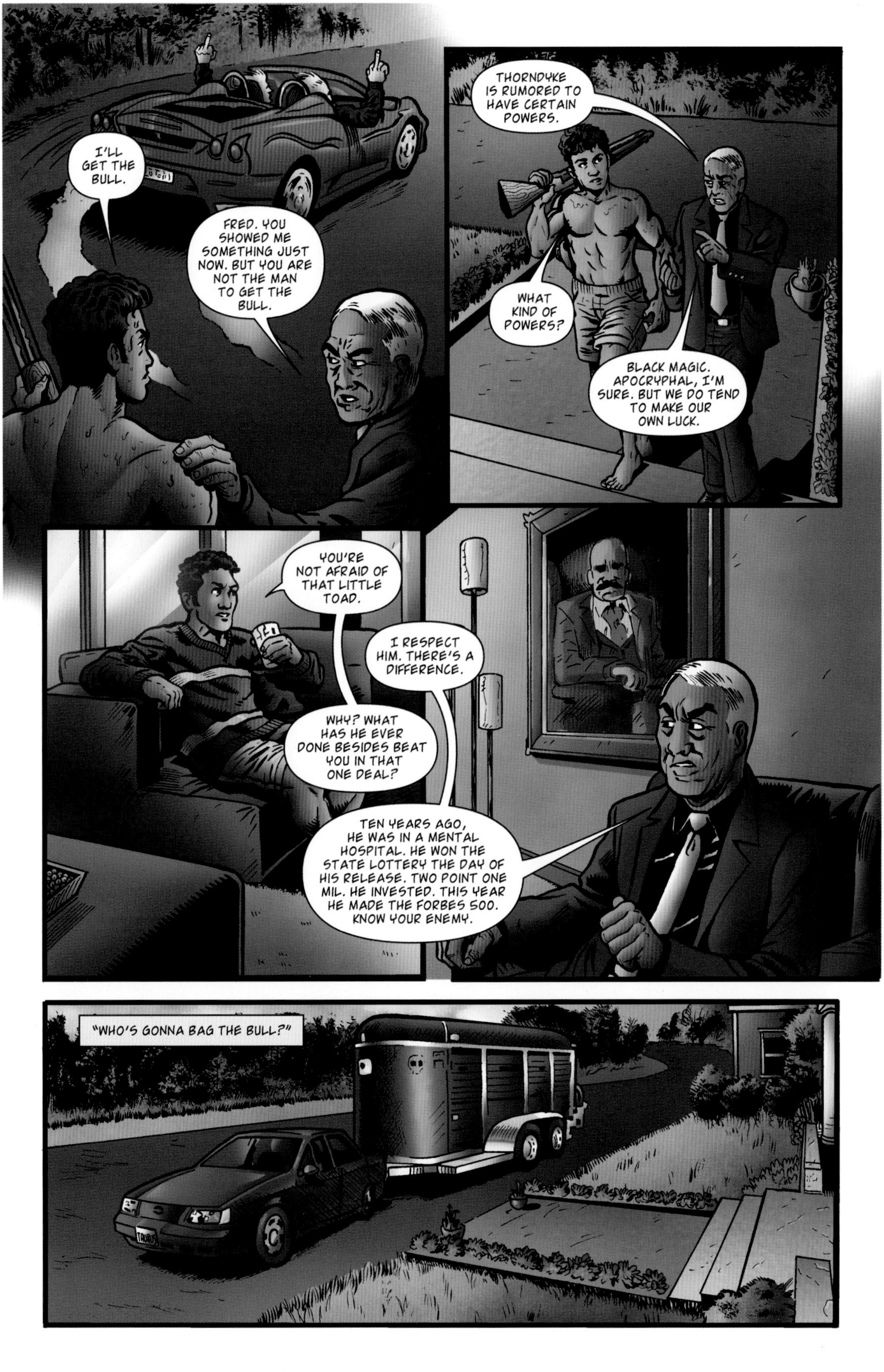

I'LL GET THE BULL.
FRED. YOU SHOWED ME SOMETHING JUST NOW. BUT YOU ARE NOT THE MAN TO GET THE BULL.
THORNDYKE IS RUMORED TO HAVE CERTAIN POWERS.
WHAT KIND OF POWERS?
BLACK MAGIC. APOCRYPHAL, I'M SURE. BUT WE DO TEND TO MAKE OUR OWN LUCK.
YOU'RE NOT AFRAID OF THAT LITTLE TOAD.
I RESPECT HIM. THERE'S A DIFFERENCE.
WHY? WHAT HAS HE EVER DONE BESIDES BEAT YOU IN THAT ONE DEAL?
TEN YEARS AGO, HE WAS IN A MENTAL HOSPITAL. HE WON THE STATE LOTTERY THE DAY OF HIS RELEASE. TWO POINT ONE MIL. HE INVESTED. THIS YEAR HE MADE THE FORBES 500. KNOW YOUR ENEMY.
"WHO'S GONNA BAG THE BULL?"

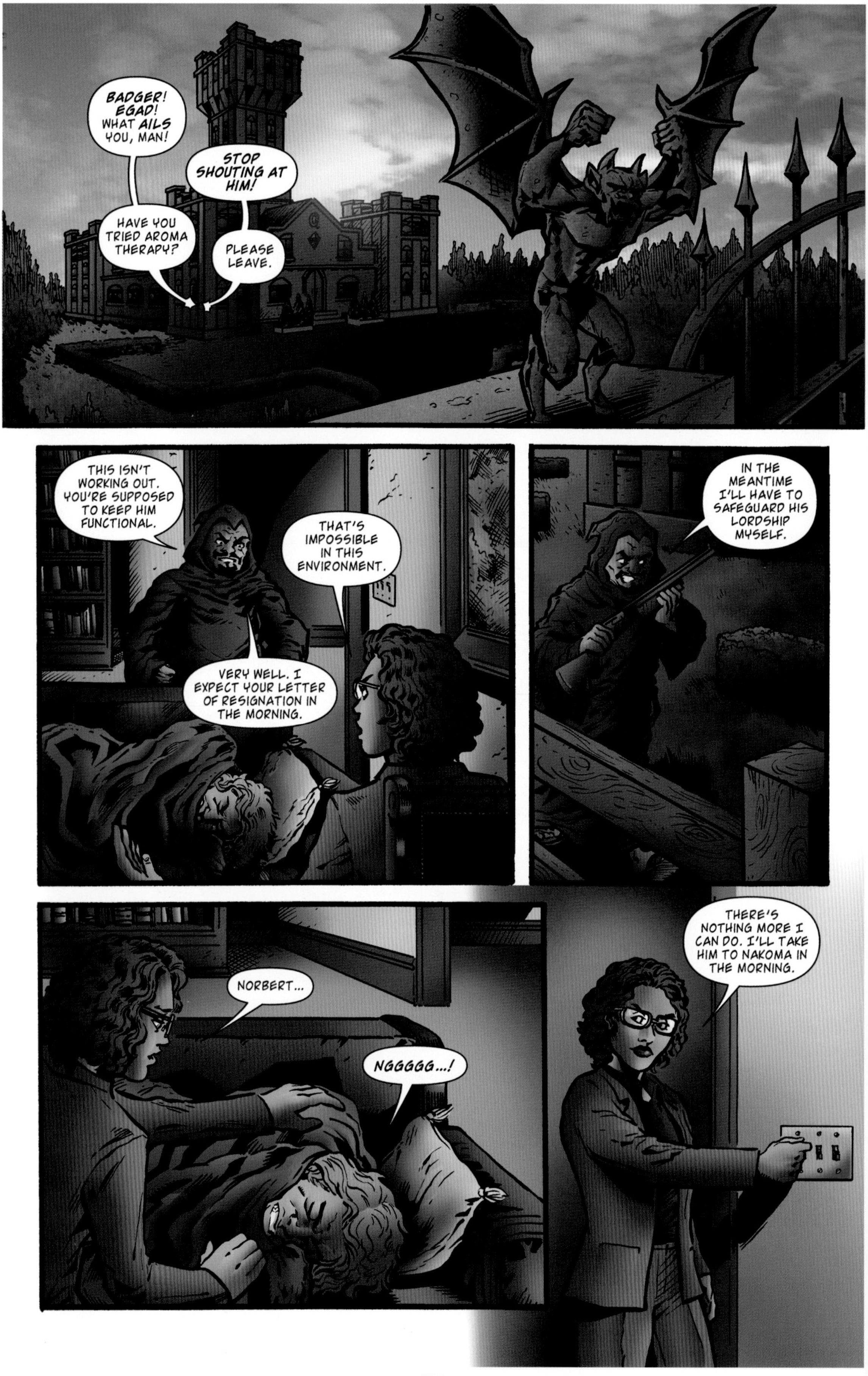
BADGER! EGAD! WHAT AILS YOU, MAN!
STOP SHOUTING AT HIM!
HAVE YOU TRIED AROMA THERAPY?
PLEASE LEAVE.
THIS ISN'T WORKING OUT. YOU'RE SUPPOSED TO KEEP HIM FUNCTIONAL.
THAT'S IMPOSSIBLE IN THIS ENVIRONMENT.
VERY WELL. I EXPECT YOUR LETTER OF RESIGNATION IN THE MORNING.
IN THE MEANTIME I'LL HAVE TO SAFEGUARD HIS LORDSHIP MYSELF.
NORBERT...
NGGGGG...!
THERE'S NOTHING MORE I CAN DO. I'LL TAKE HIM TO NAKOMA IN THE MORNING.

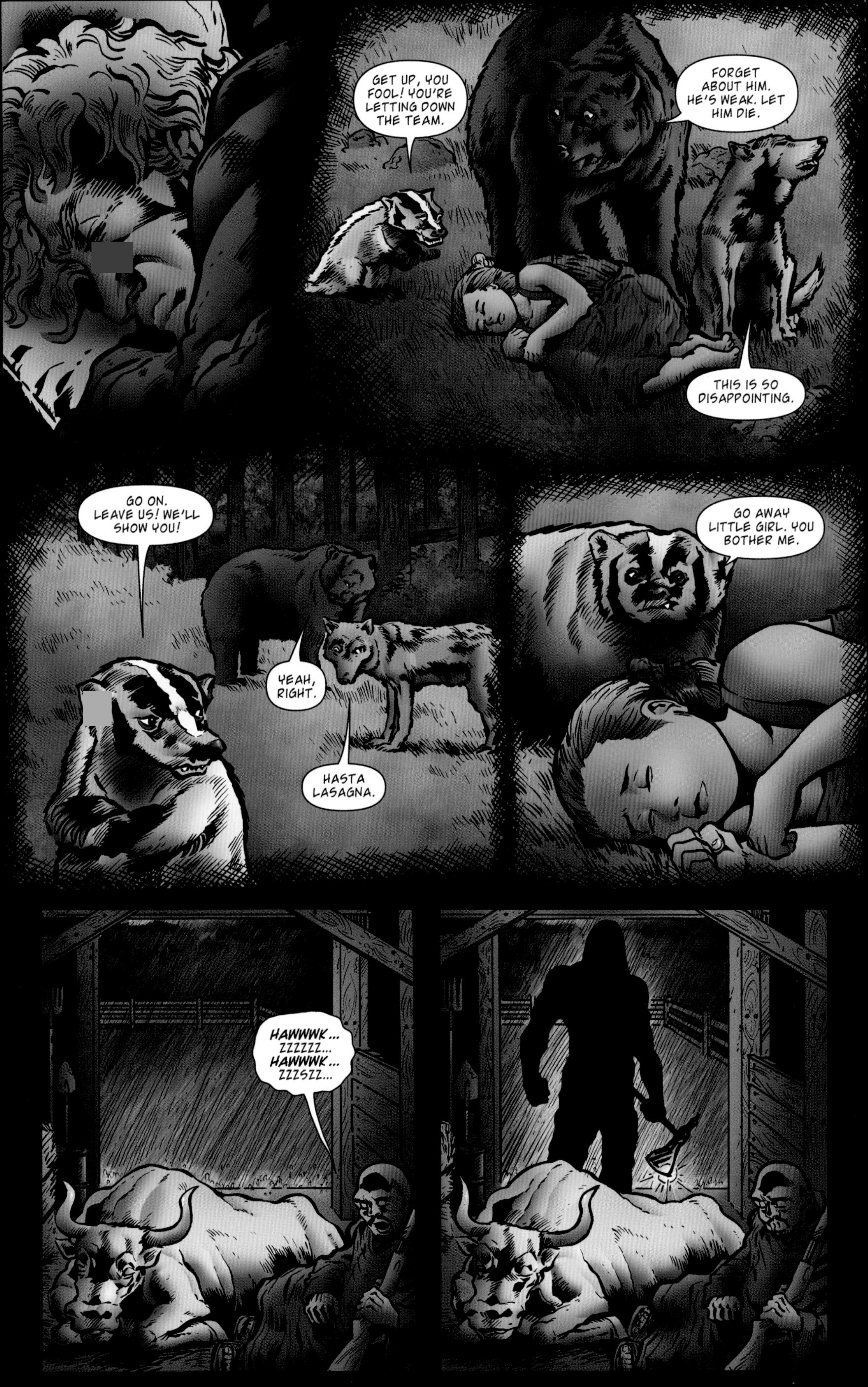
GET UP, YOU FOOL! YOU'RE LETTING DOWN THE TEAM.
FORGET ABOUT HIM. HE'S WEAK. LET HIM DIE.
THIS IS SO DISAPPOINTING.
GO ON. LEAVE US! WE'LL SHOW YOU!
YEAH, RIGHT.
HASTA LASAGNA.
GO AWAY LITTLE GIRL. YOU BOTHER ME.
HAWWWK... ZZZZZZ... HAWWWK... ZZZSZZ...

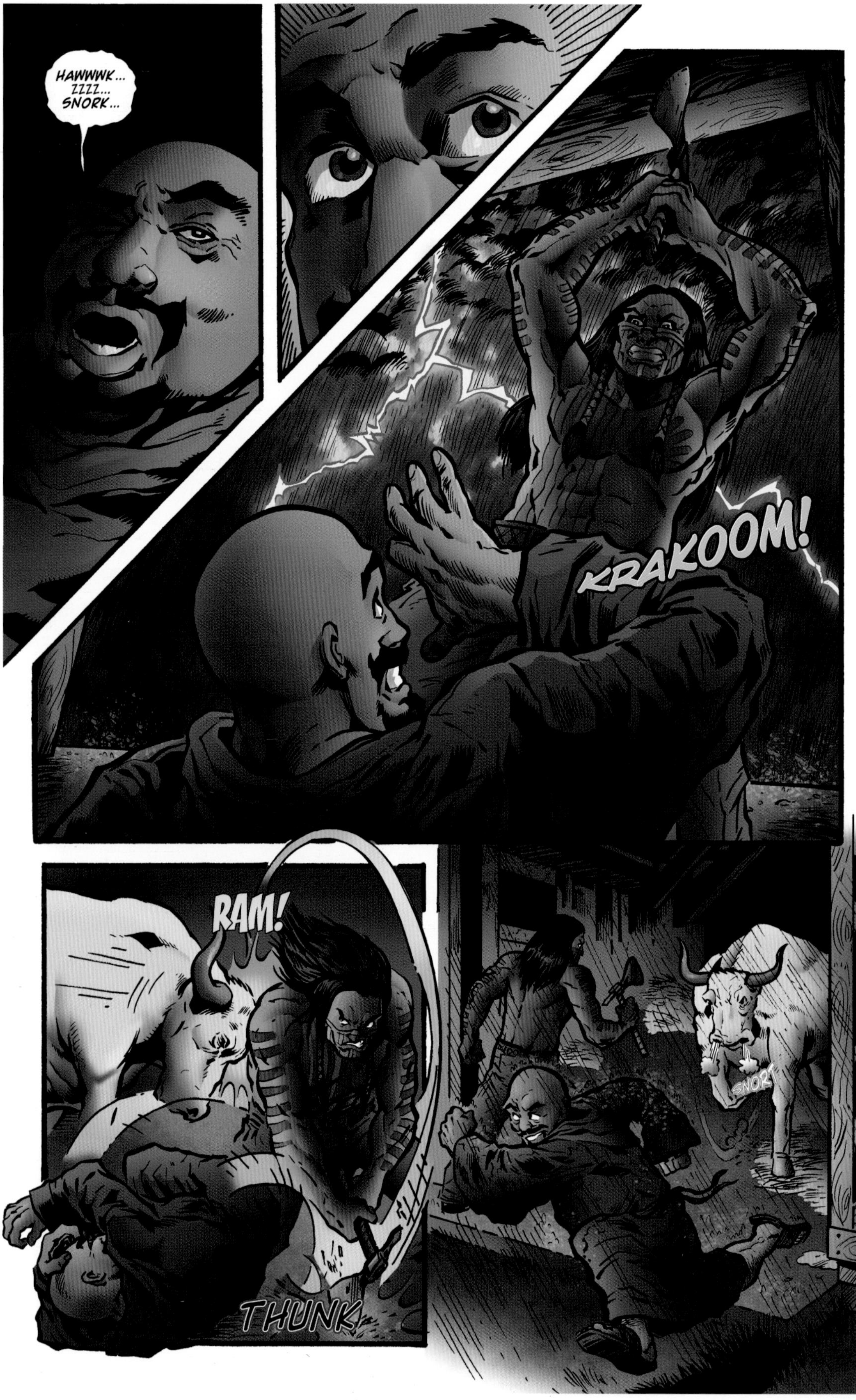
HAWWWK... ZZZZ... SNORK...
KRAKOOM!
RAM!
THUNK
SNORT

CRACK
THUD
DAISY!
HELP—!
BACK OFF! I'LL KILL HER!
YOU ARE YOUR FATHER'S SON.

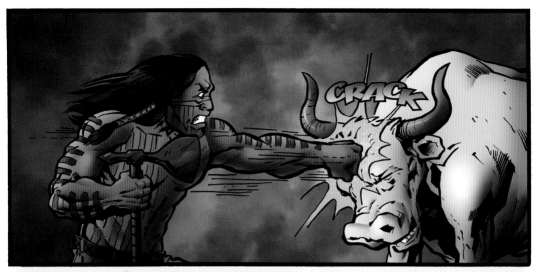

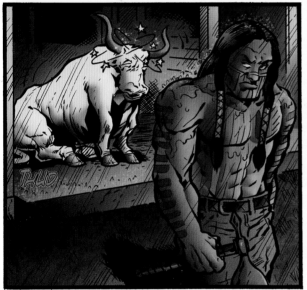

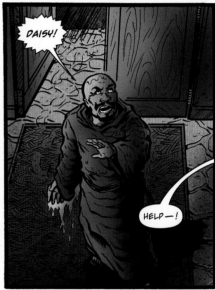

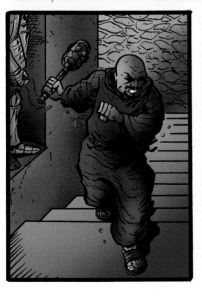

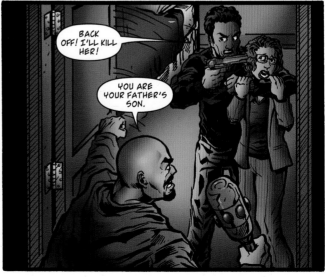

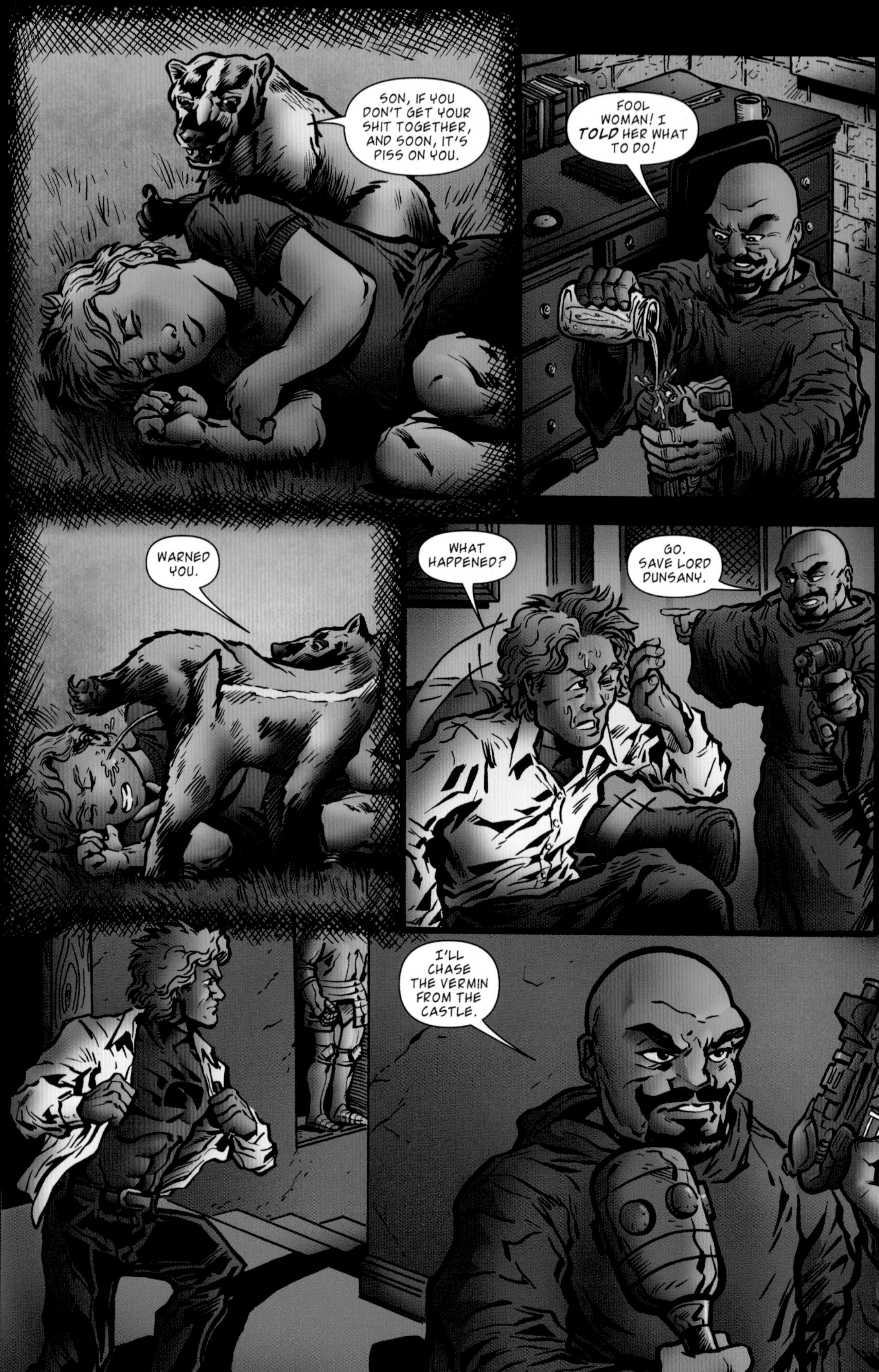
SON, IF YOU DON'T GET YOUR SHIT TOGETHER, AND SOON, IT'S PISS ON YOU.
FOOL WOMAN! I TOLD HER WHAT TO DO!
WARNED YOU.
WHAT HAPPENED?
GO. SAVE LORD DUNSANY.
I'LL CHASE THE VERMIN FROM THE CASTLE.

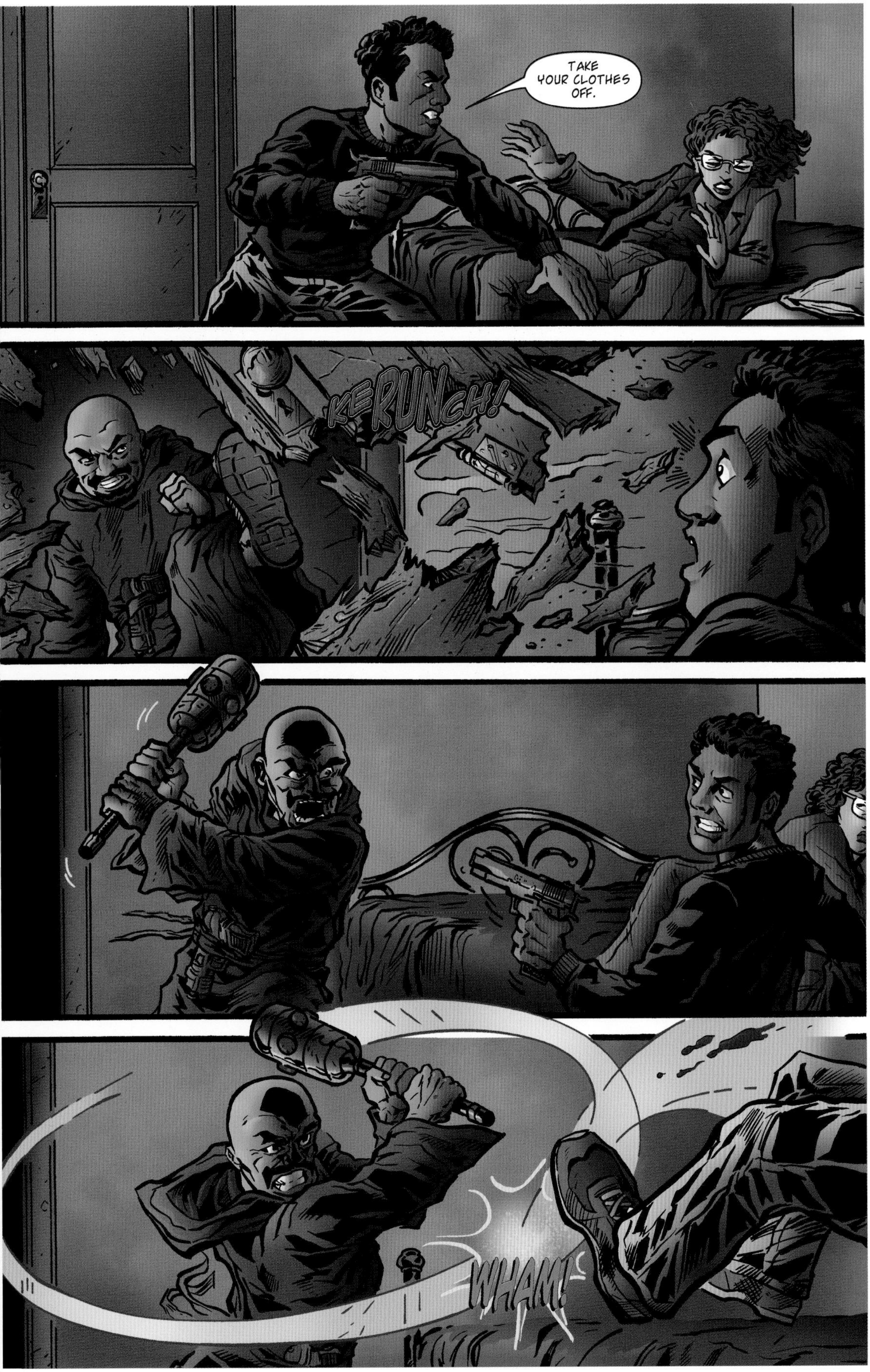
TAKE YOUR CLOTHES OFF.
KERUNCH!
WHAM!

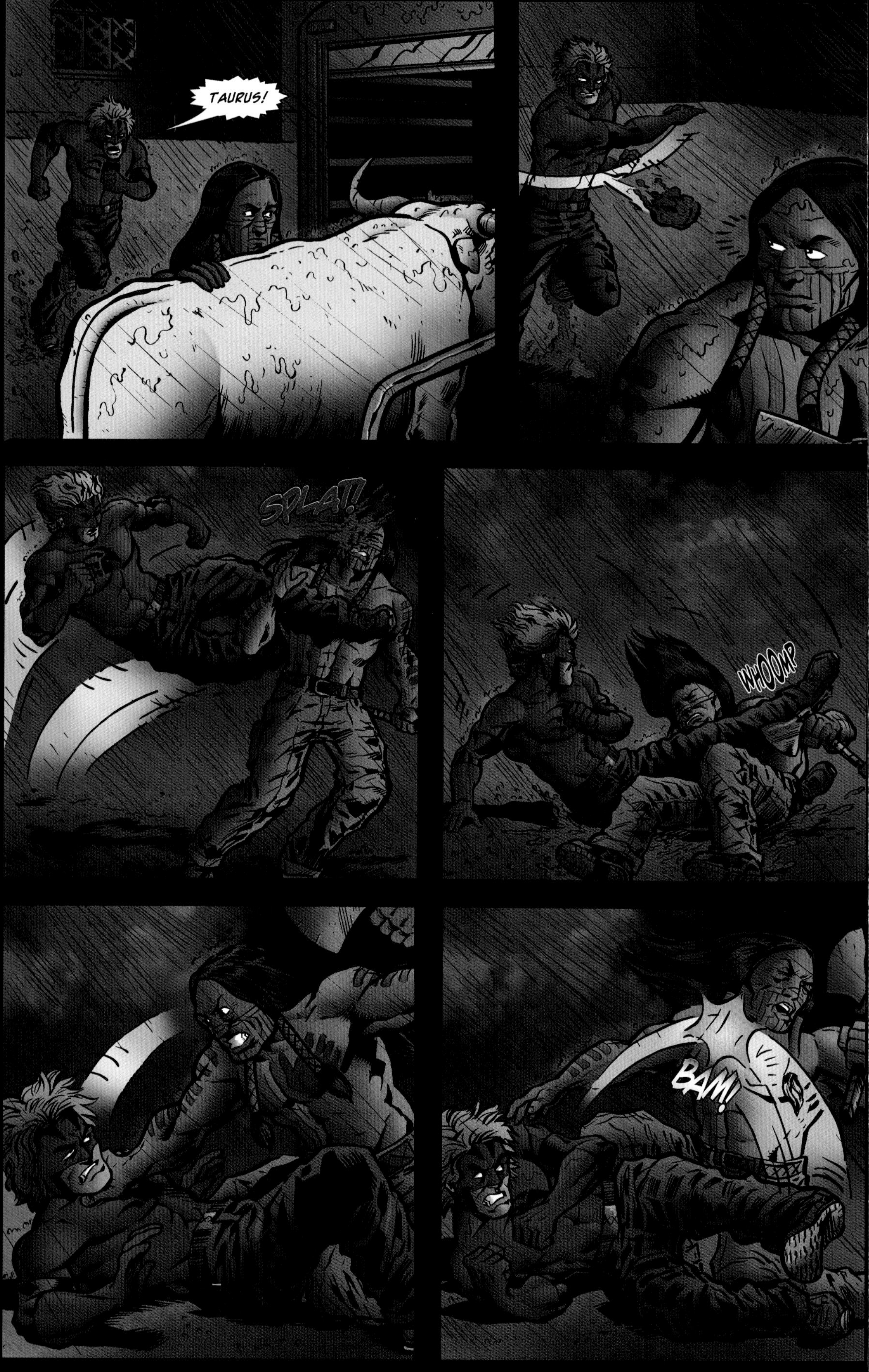
TAURUS!
SPLAT!
WHOOMP
BAM!

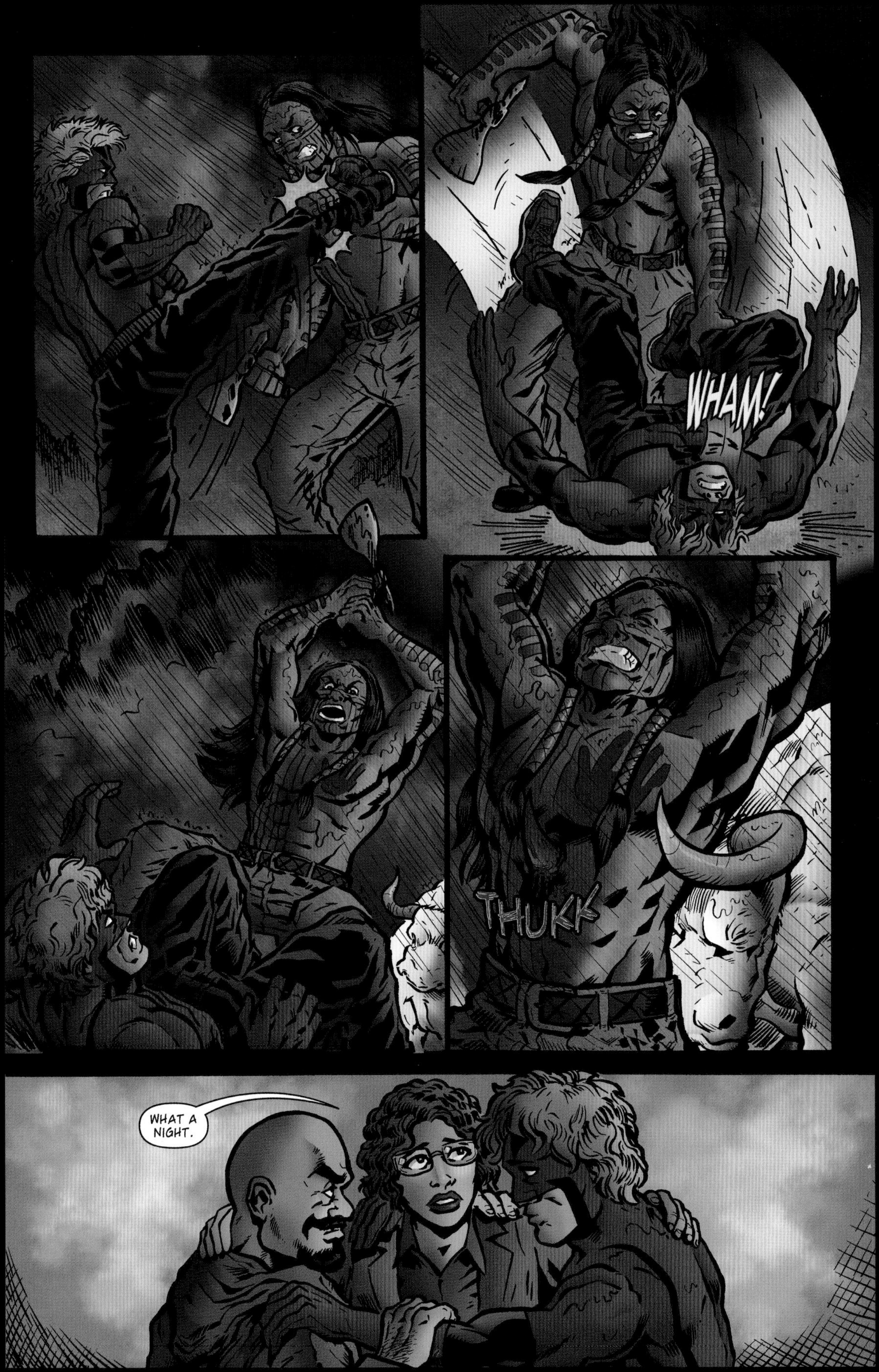
WHAM!
THUKK
WHAT A NIGHT.

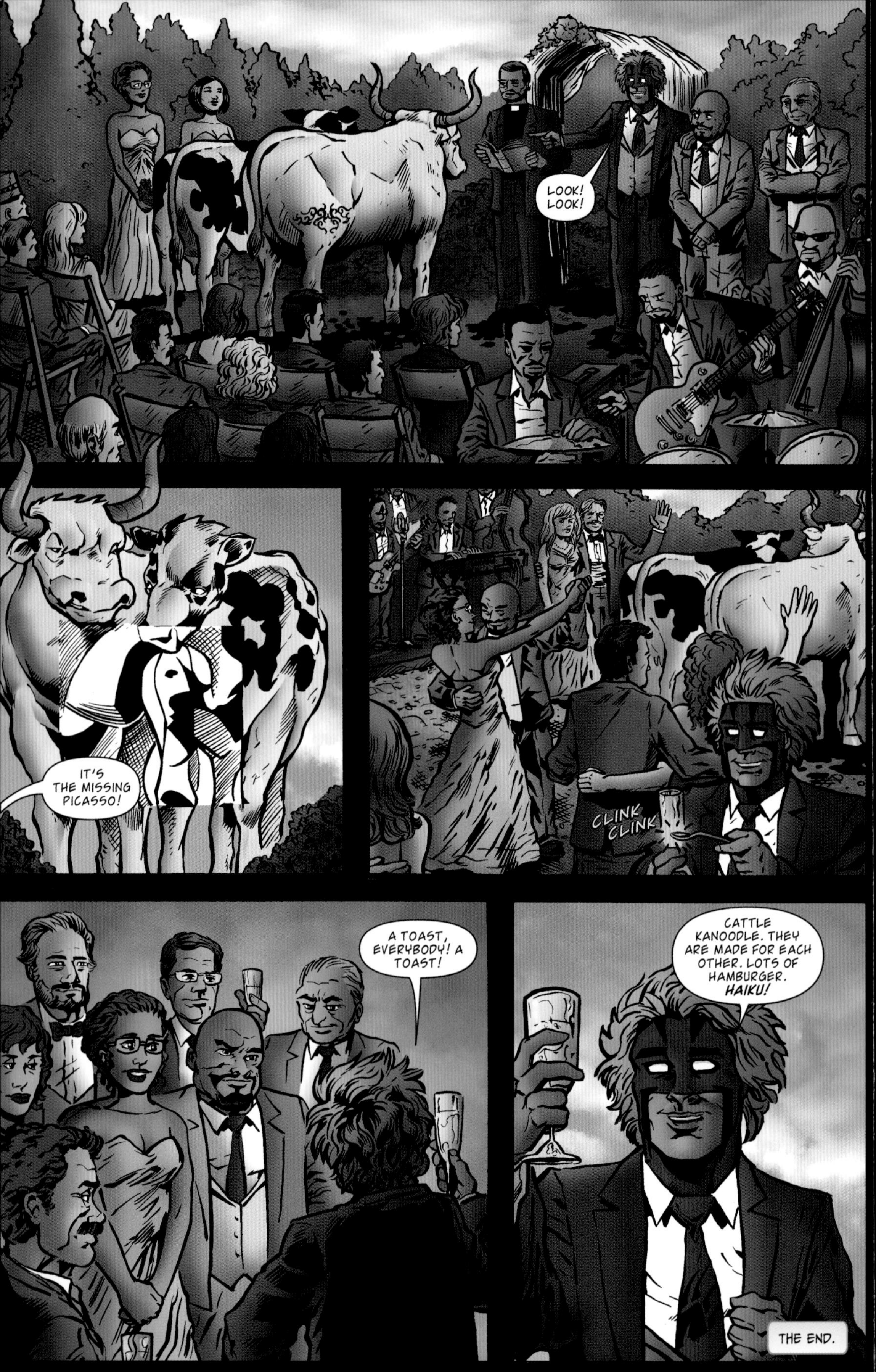
LOOK! LOOK!
IT'S THE MISSING PICASSO!
CLINK CLINK
A TOAST, EVERYBODY! A TOAST!
CATTLE KANOODLE. THEY ARE MADE FOR EACH OTHER. LOTS OF HAMBURGER. HAIKU!
THE END.

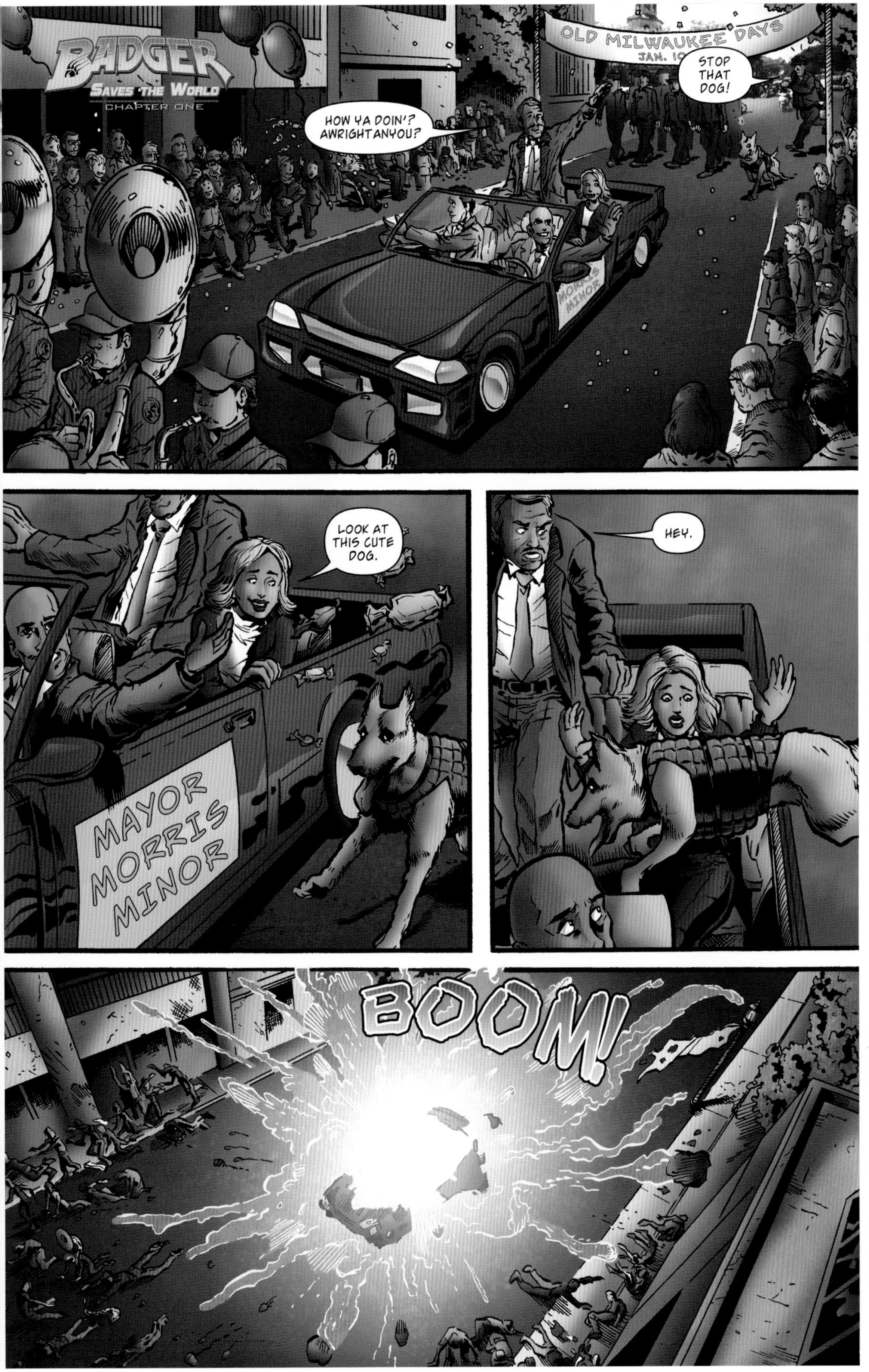
BADGER
SAVES THE WORLD
CHAPTER ONE
OLD MILWAUKEE DAYS
HOW YA DOIN'? AWRIGHTANYOU?
STOP THAT DOG!
MORRIS MINOR
LOOK AT THIS CUTE DOG.
MAYOR MORRIS MINOR
HEY.
BOOM!

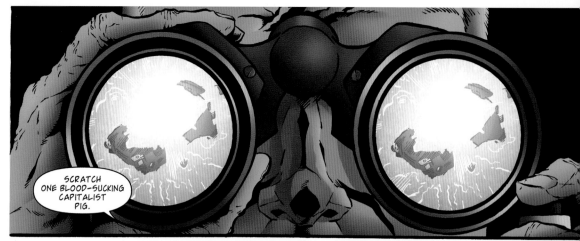

SCRATCH ONE BLOOD-SUCKING CAPITALIST PIG.

GIMME FIVE.

BEAUTY. GOOD DOG, EH?

LET'S BAIL.

THWACK

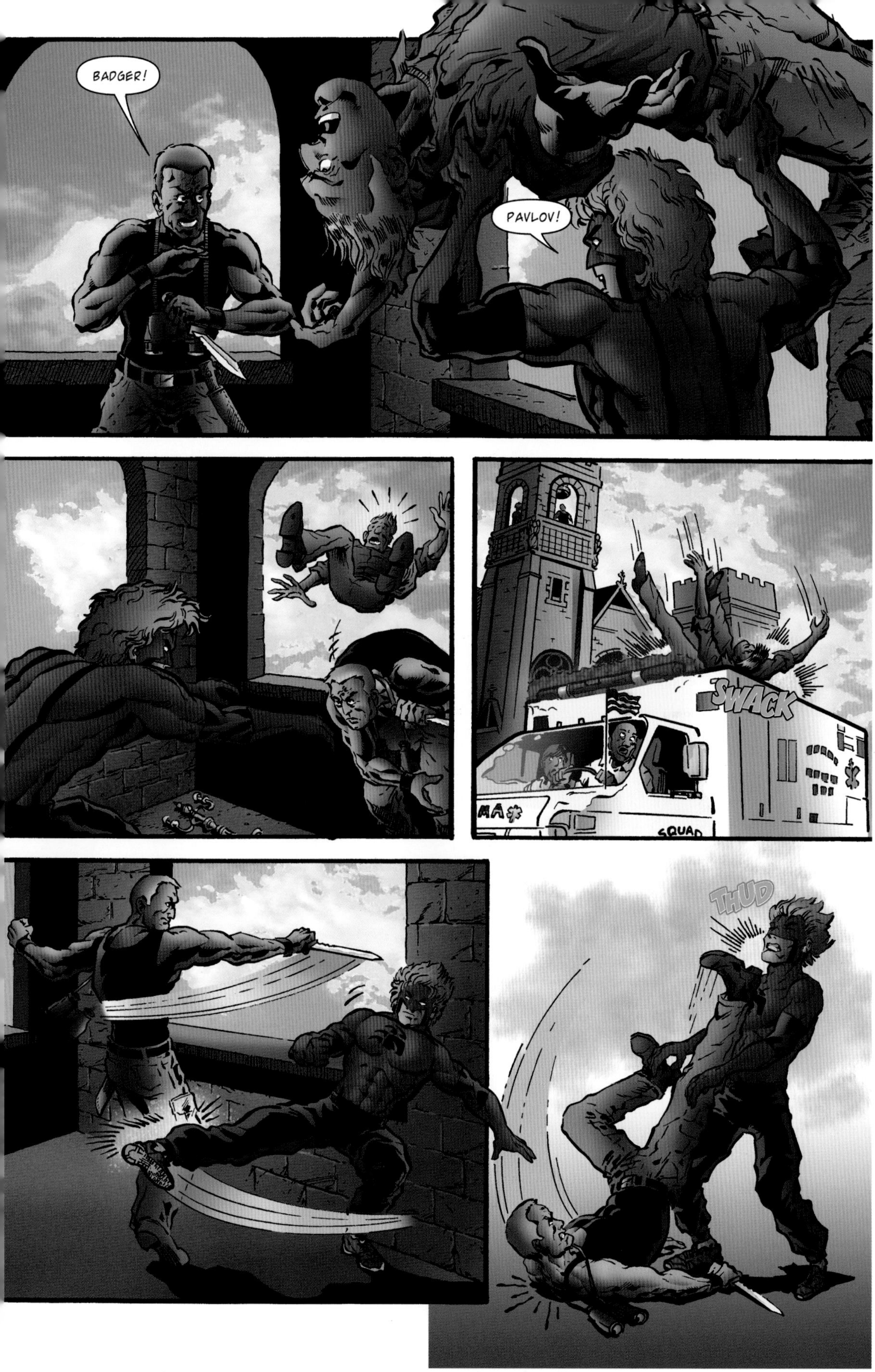
BADGER!
PAVLOV!
SWACK
MA
SQUAD
THUD

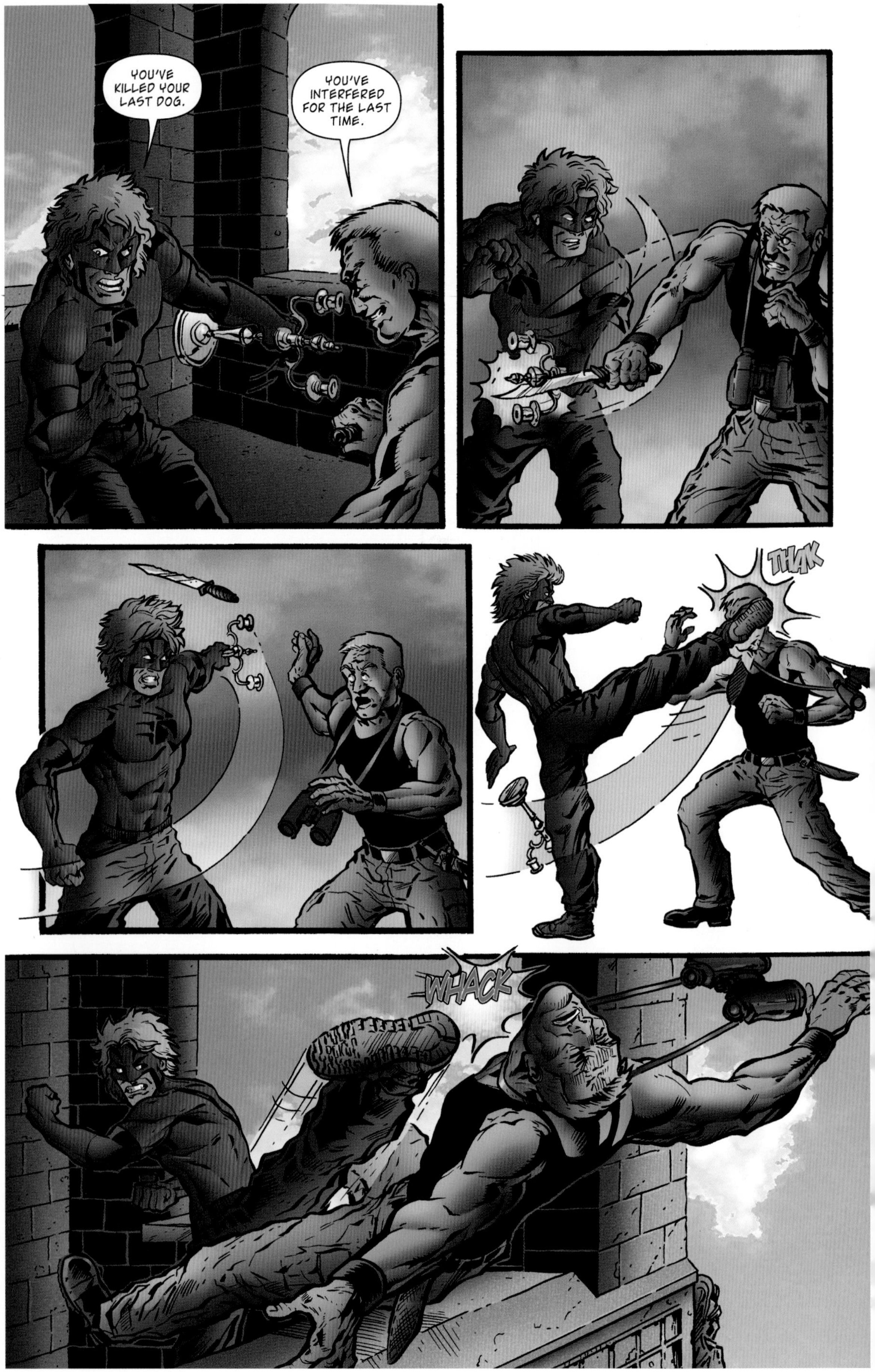
YOU'VE KILLED YOUR LAST DOG.
YOU'VE INTERFERED FOR THE LAST TIME.
THAK
WHACK

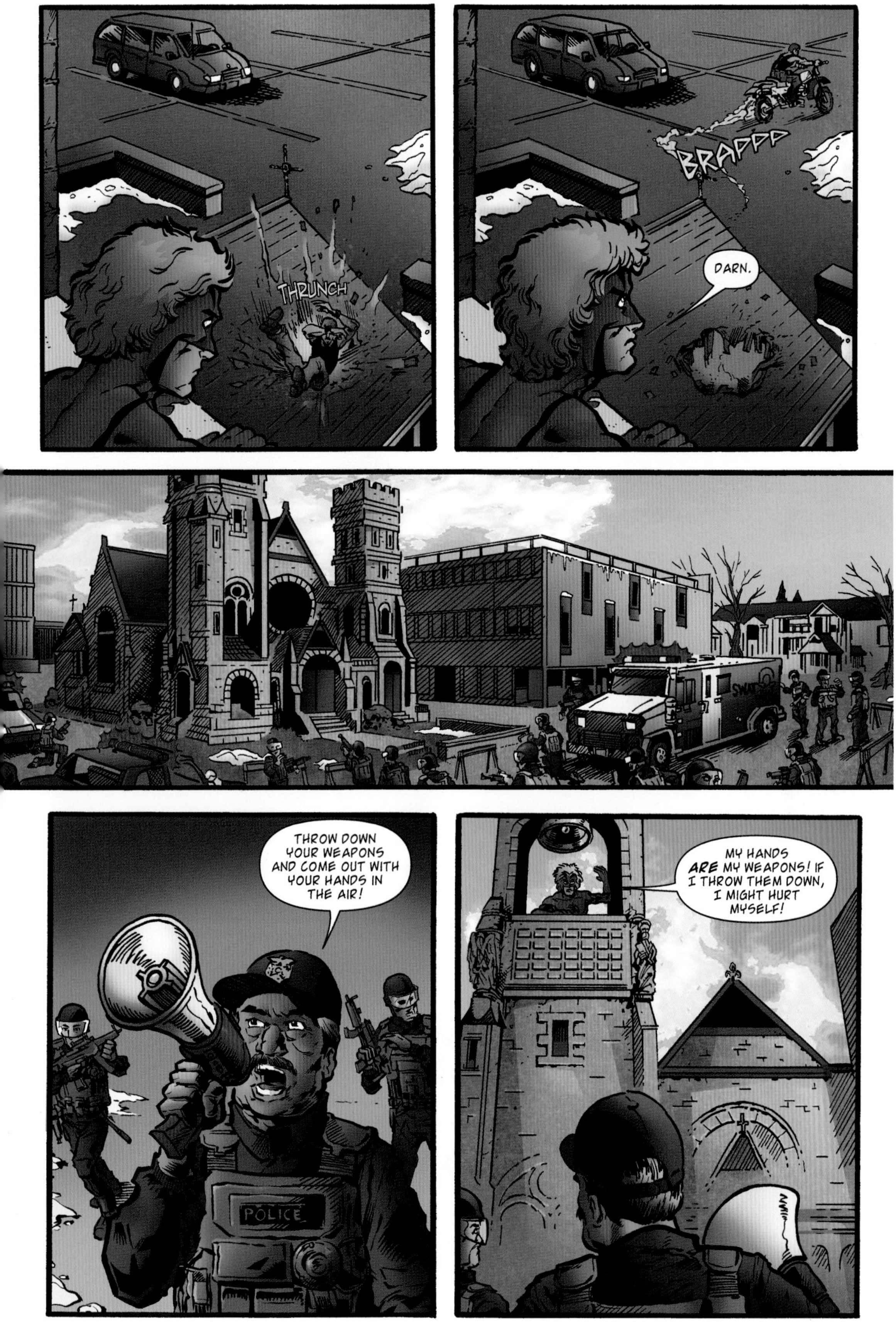
THRUNCH
BRAPPP
DARN.
THROW DOWN YOUR WEAPONS AND COME OUT WITH YOUR HANDS IN THE AIR!
POLICE
MY HANDS ARE MY WEAPONS! IF I THROW THEM DOWN, I MIGHT HURT MYSELF!

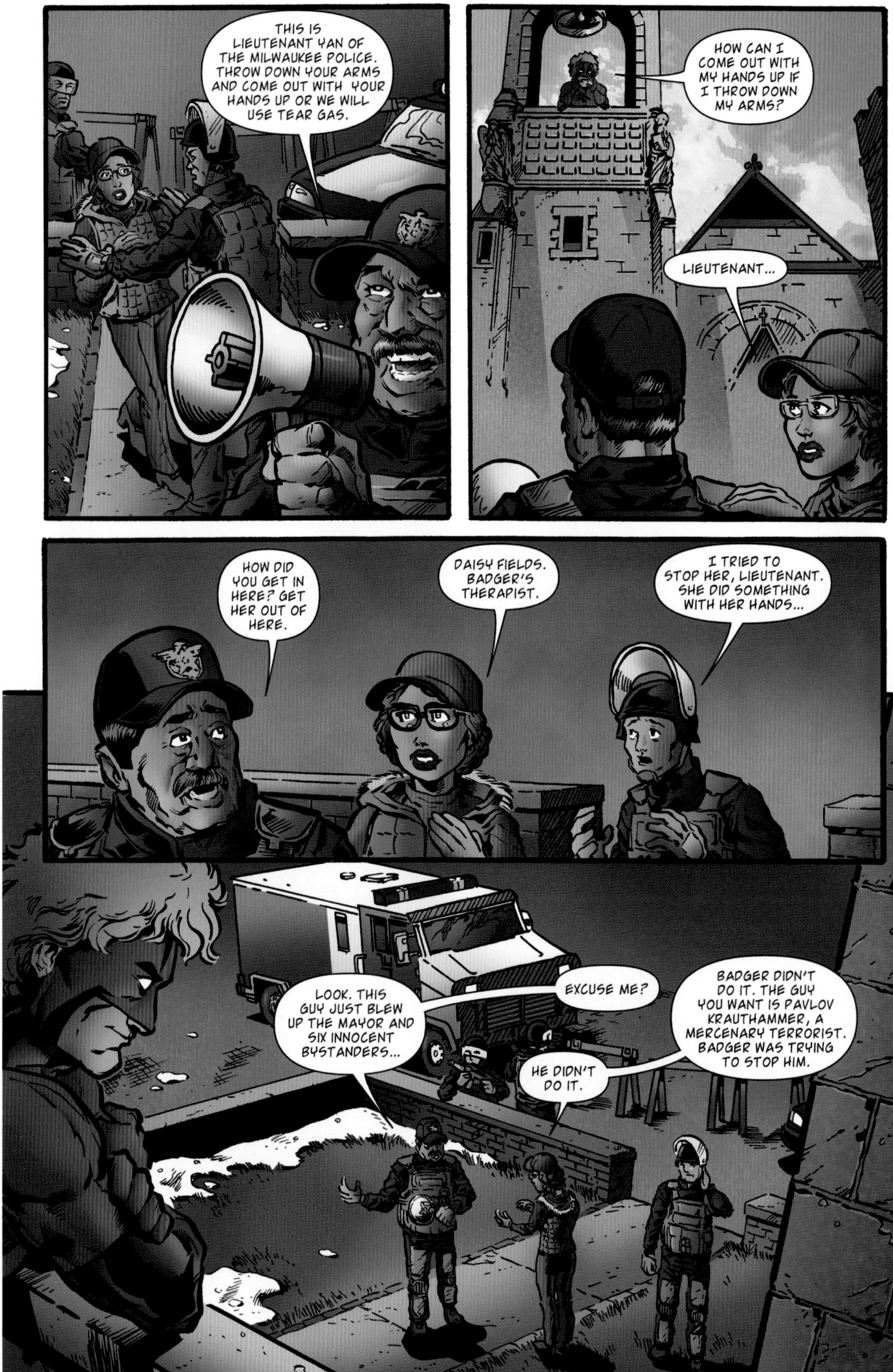
THIS IS LIEUTENANT YAN OF THE MILWAUKEE POLICE. THROW DOWN YOUR ARMS AND COME OUT WITH YOUR HANDS UP OR WE WILL USE TEAR GAS.
HOW CAN I COME OUT WITH MY HANDS UP IF I THROW DOWN MY ARMS?
LIEUTENANT...
HOW DID YOU GET IN HERE? GET HER OUT OF HERE.
DAISY FIELDS. BADGER'S THERAPIST.
I TRIED TO STOP HER, LIEUTENANT. SHE DID SOMETHING WITH HER HANDS...
LOOK. THIS GUY JUST BLEW UP THE MAYOR AND SIX INNOCENT BYSTANDERS...
EXCUSE ME?
HE DIDN'T DO IT.
BADGER DIDN'T DO IT. THE GUY YOU WANT IS PAVLOV KRAUTHAMMER, A MERCENARY TERRORIST. BADGER WAS TRYING TO STOP HIM.

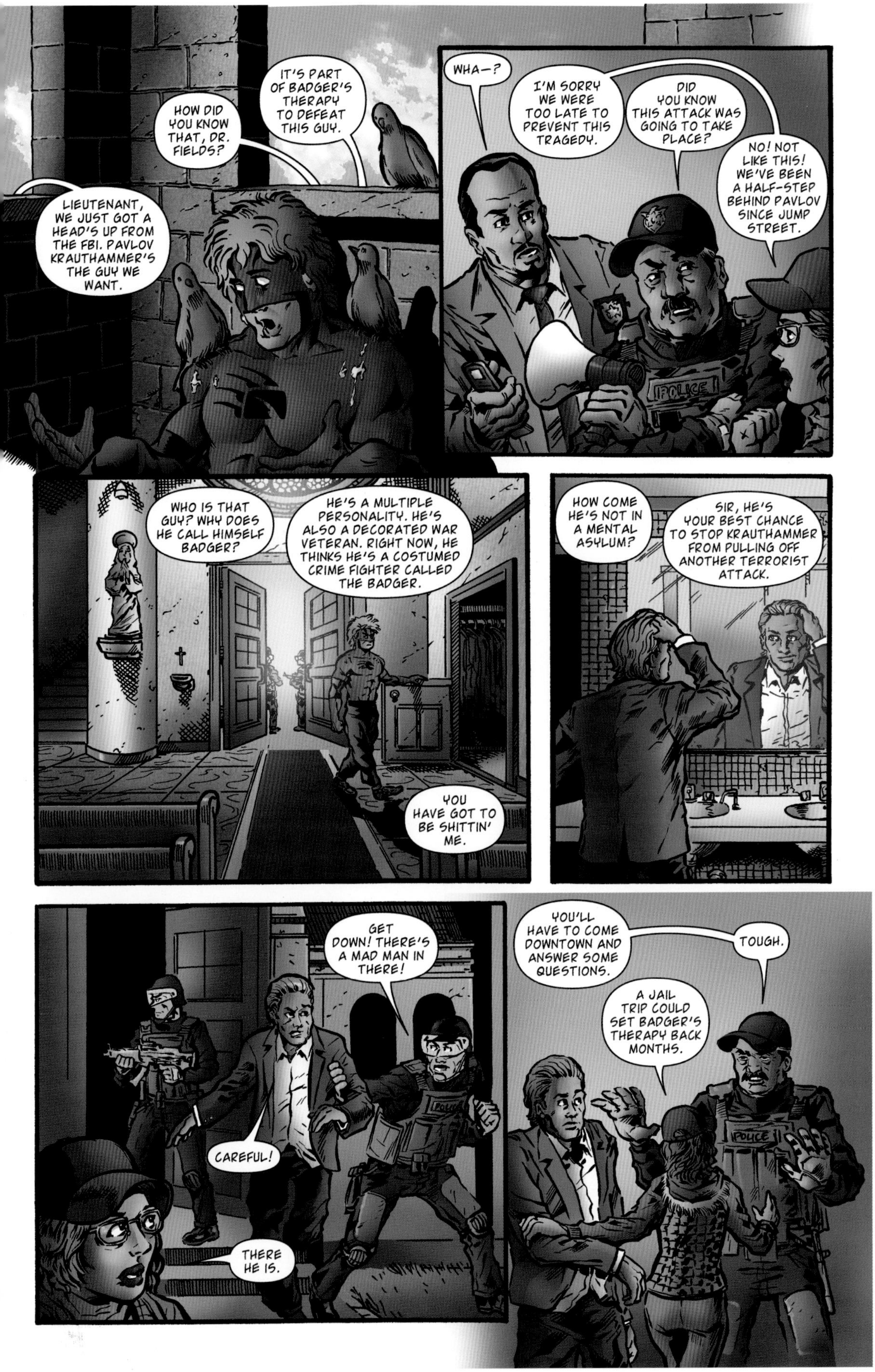
LIEUTENANT, WE JUST GOT A HEAD'S UP FROM THE FBI. PAVLOV KRAUTHAMMER'S THE GUY WE WANT.
HOW DID YOU KNOW THAT, DR. FIELDS?
IT'S PART OF BADGER'S THERAPY TO DEFEAT THIS GUY.
WHA—?
I'M SORRY WE WERE TOO LATE TO PREVENT THIS TRAGEDY.
DID YOU KNOW THIS ATTACK WAS GOING TO TAKE PLACE?
NO! NOT LIKE THIS! WE'VE BEEN A HALF-STEP BEHIND PAVLOV SINCE JUMP STREET.
POLICE
WHO IS THAT GUY? WHY DOES HE CALL HIMSELF BADGER?
HE'S A MULTIPLE PERSONALITY. HE'S ALSO A DECORATED WAR VETERAN. RIGHT NOW, HE THINKS HE'S A COSTUMED CRIME FIGHTER CALLED THE BADGER.
YOU HAVE GOT TO BE SHITTIN' ME.
HOW COME HE'S NOT IN A MENTAL ASYLUM?
SIR, HE'S YOUR BEST CHANCE TO STOP KRAUTHAMMER FROM PULLING OFF ANOTHER TERRORIST ATTACK.
GET DOWN! THERE'S A MAD MAN IN THERE!
CAREFUL!
THERE HE IS.
POLICE
YOU'LL HAVE TO COME DOWNTOWN AND ANSWER SOME QUESTIONS.
TOUGH.
A JAIL TRIP COULD SET BADGER'S THERAPY BACK MONTHS.
POLICE

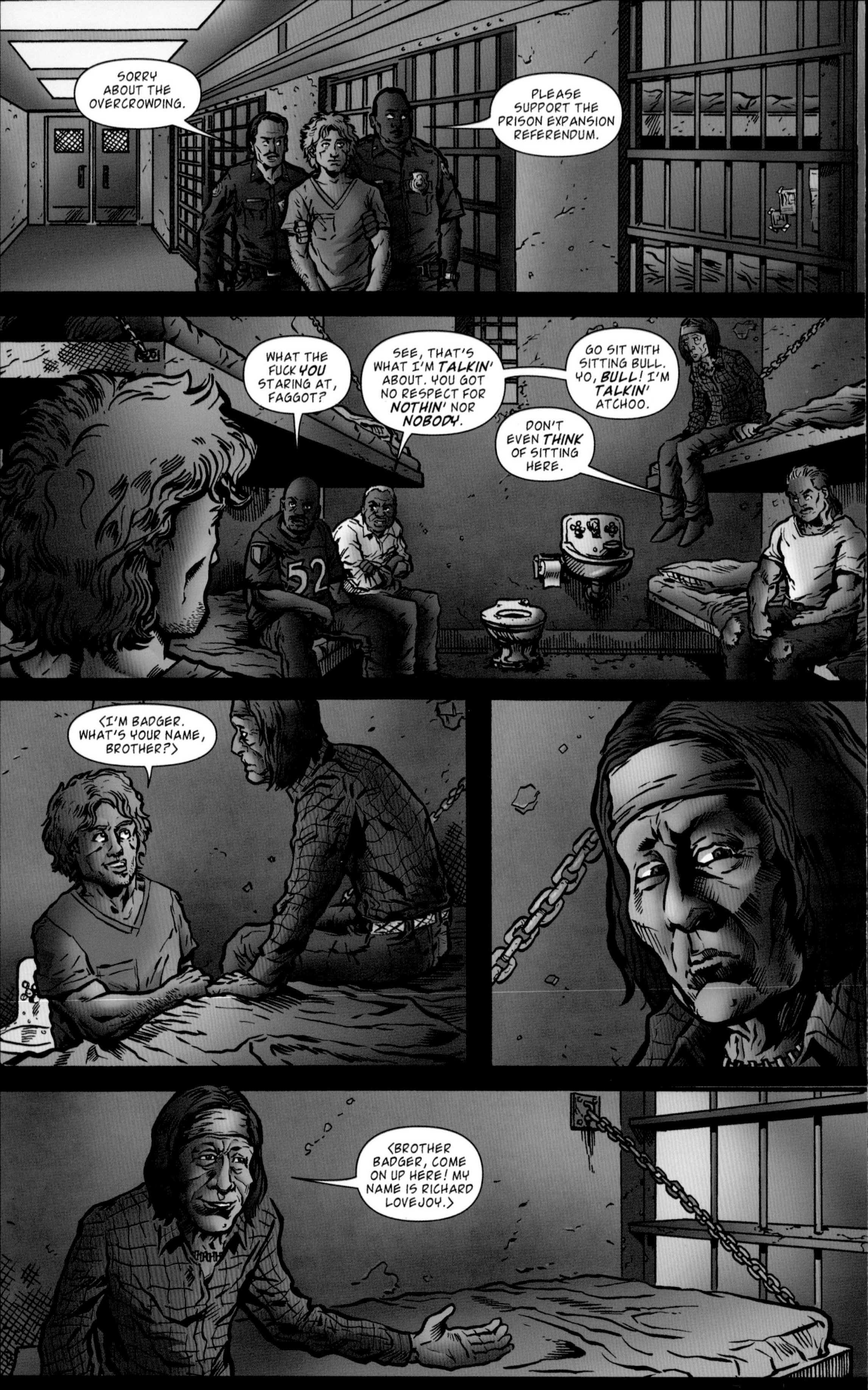
SORRY ABOUT THE OVERCROWDING.
PLEASE SUPPORT THE PRISON EXPANSION REFERENDUM.
WHAT THE FUCK YOU STARING AT, FAGGOT?
SEE, THAT'S WHAT I'M TALKIN' ABOUT. YOU GOT NO RESPECT FOR NOTHIN' NOR NOBODY.
GO SIT WITH SITTING BULL. YO, BULL! I'M TALKIN' ATCHOO.
DON'T EVEN THINK OF SITTING HERE.
<I'M BADGER. WHAT'S YOUR NAME, BROTHER?>
<BROTHER BADGER, COME ON UP HERE! MY NAME IS RICHARD LOVEJOY.>

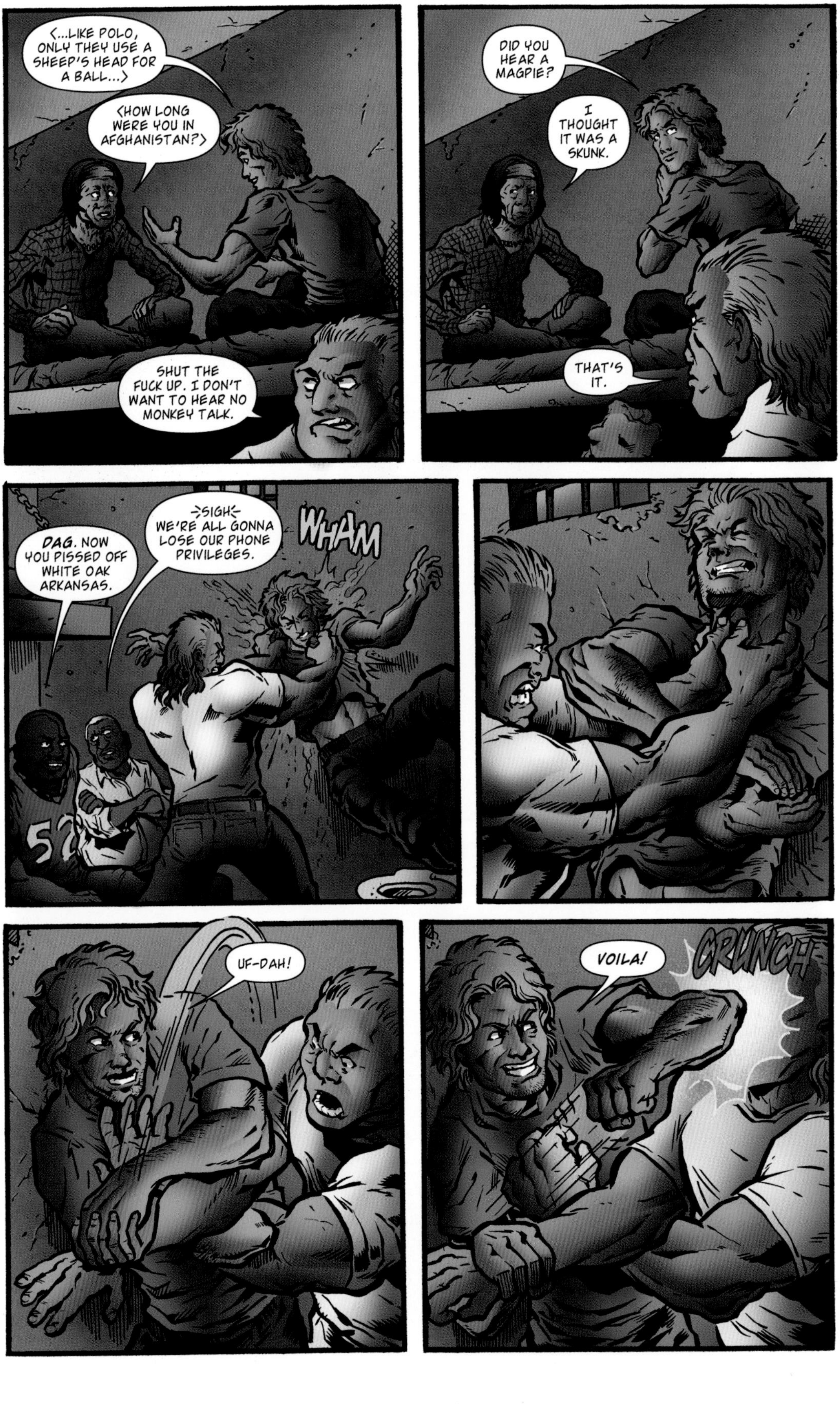
<...LIKE POLO, ONLY THEY USE A SHEEP'S HEAD FOR A BALL...>
<HOW LONG WERE YOU IN AFGHANISTAN?>
SHUT THE FUCK UP. I DON'T WANT TO HEAR NO MONKEY TALK.
DID YOU HEAR A MAGPIE?
I THOUGHT IT WAS A SKUNK.
THAT'S IT.
DAG. NOW YOU PISSED OFF WHITE OAK ARKANSAS.
-SIGH- WE'RE ALL GONNA LOSE OUR PHONE PRIVILEGES.
WHAM
UF-DAH!
VOILA!
CRUNCH

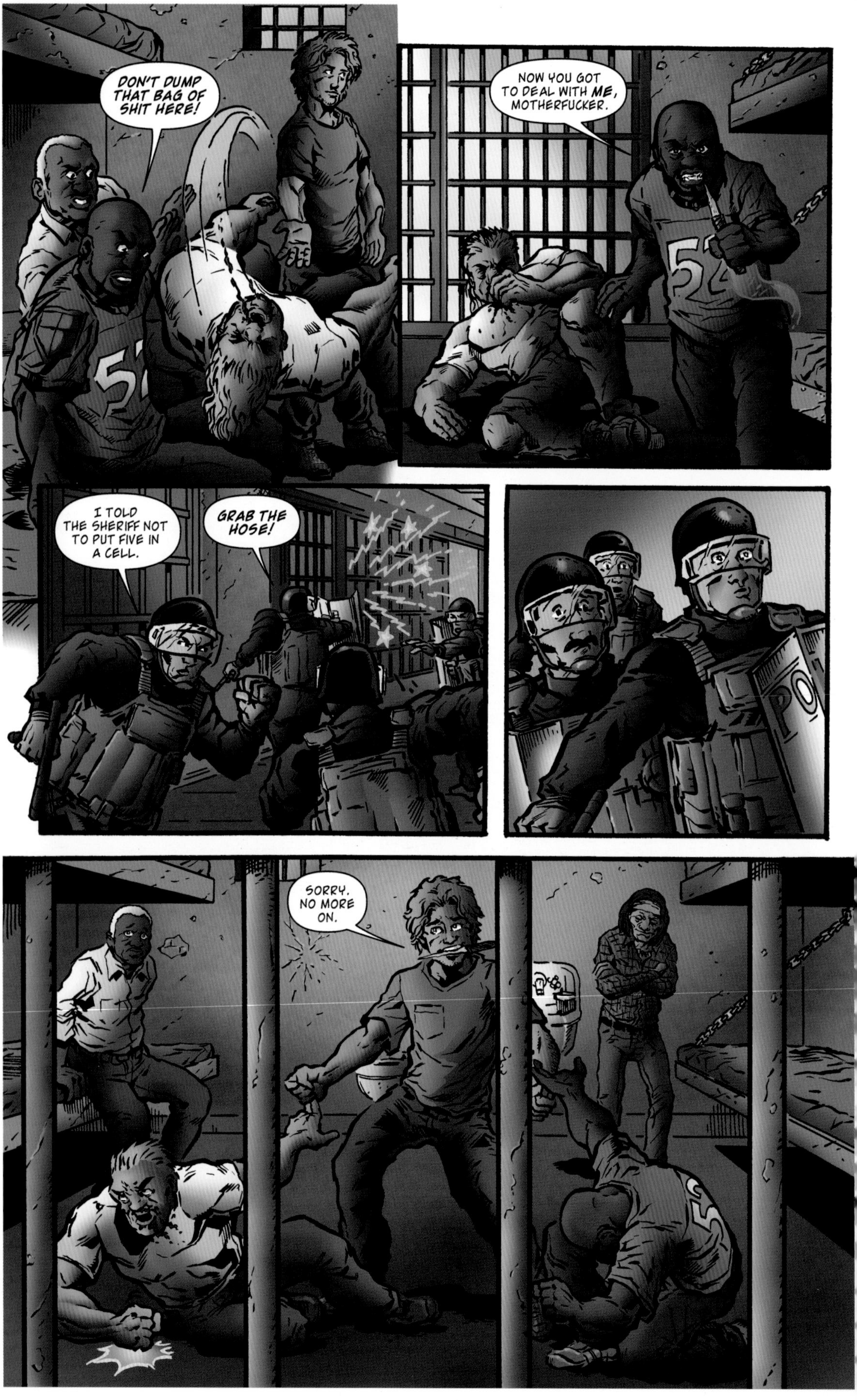
DON'T DUMP THAT BAG OF SHIT HERE!
NOW YOU GOT TO DEAL WITH ME, MOTHERFUCKER.
I TOLD THE SHERIFF NOT TO PUT FIVE IN A CELL.
GRAB THE HOSE!
SORRY. NO MORE ON.

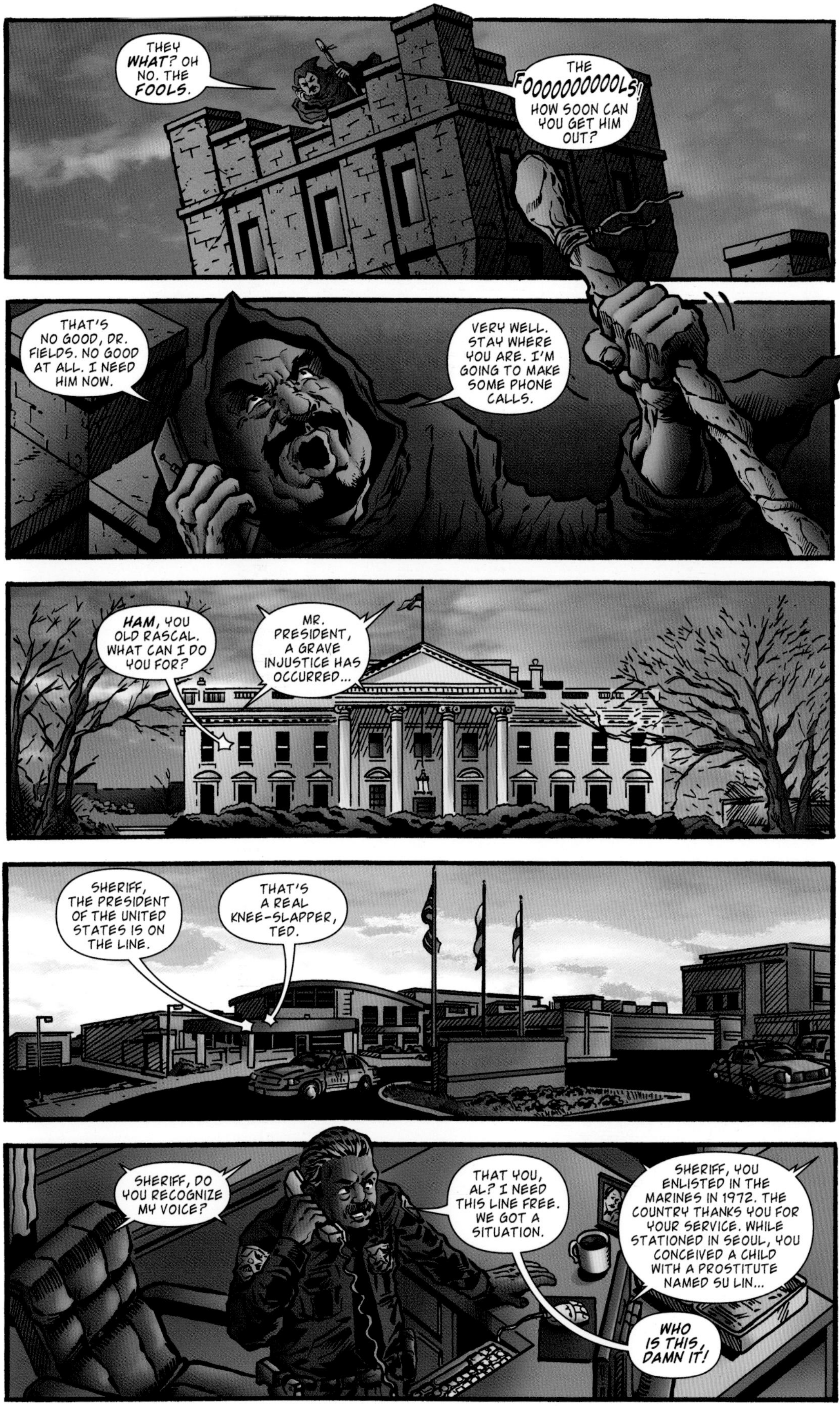
THEY WHAT? OH NO. THE FOOLS.
THE FOOOOOOOOOOLS! HOW SOON CAN YOU GET HIM OUT?
THAT'S NO GOOD, DR. FIELDS. NO GOOD AT ALL. I NEED HIM NOW.
VERY WELL. STAY WHERE YOU ARE. I'M GOING TO MAKE SOME PHONE CALLS.
HAM, YOU OLD RASCAL. WHAT CAN I DO YOU FOR?
MR. PRESIDENT, A GRAVE INJUSTICE HAS OCCURRED...
SHERIFF, THE PRESIDENT OF THE UNITED STATES IS ON THE LINE.
THAT'S A REAL KNEE-SLAPPER, TED.
SHERIFF, DO YOU RECOGNIZE MY VOICE?
THAT YOU, AL? I NEED THIS LINE FREE. WE GOT A SITUATION.
SHERIFF, YOU ENLISTED IN THE MARINES IN 1972. THE COUNTRY THANKS YOU FOR YOUR SERVICE. WHILE STATIONED IN SEOUL, YOU CONCEIVED A CHILD WITH A PROSTITUTE NAMED SU LIN...
WHO IS THIS, DAMN IT!

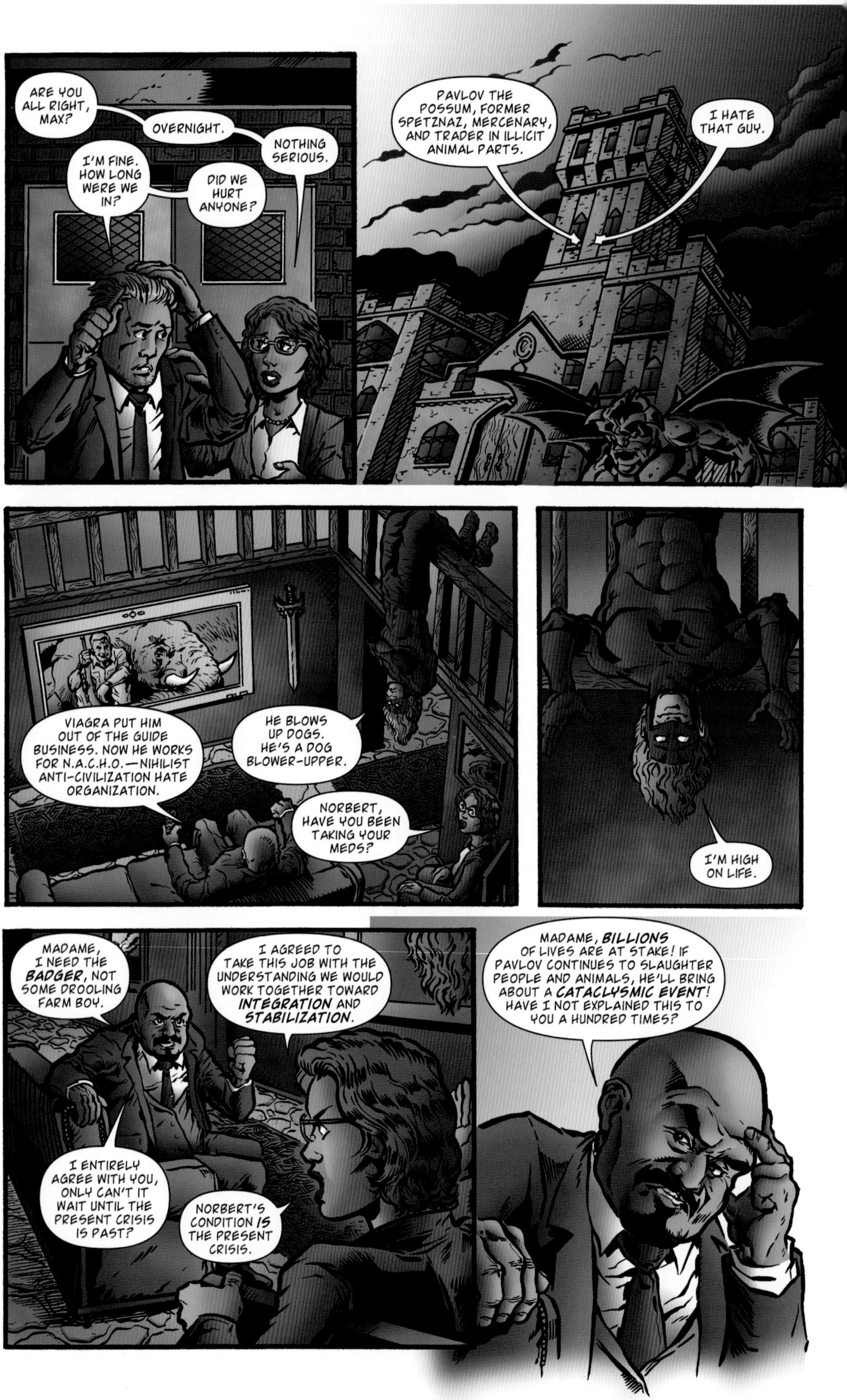
ARE YOU ALL RIGHT, MAX?
I'M FINE. HOW LONG WERE WE IN?
OVERNIGHT.
DID WE HURT ANYONE?
NOTHING SERIOUS.
PAVLOV THE POSSUM, FORMER SPETZNAZ, MERCENARY, AND TRADER IN ILLICIT ANIMAL PARTS.
I HATE THAT GUY.
VIAGRA PUT HIM OUT OF THE GUIDE BUSINESS. NOW HE WORKS FOR N.A.C.H.O.—NIHILIST ANTI-CIVILIZATION HATE ORGANIZATION.
HE BLOWS UP DOGS. HE'S A DOG BLOWER-UPPER.
NORBERT, HAVE YOU BEEN TAKING YOUR MEDS?
I'M HIGH ON LIFE.
MADAME, I NEED THE **BADGER**, NOT SOME DROOLING FARM BOY.
I AGREED TO TAKE THIS JOB WITH THE UNDERSTANDING WE WOULD WORK TOGETHER TOWARD **INTEGRATION** AND **STABILIZATION**.
MADAME, **BILLIONS** OF LIVES ARE AT STAKE! IF PAVLOV CONTINUES TO SLAUGHTER PEOPLE AND ANIMALS, HE'LL BRING ABOUT A **CATACLYSMIC EVENT**! HAVE I NOT EXPLAINED THIS TO YOU A HUNDRED TIMES?
I ENTIRELY AGREE WITH YOU, ONLY CAN'T IT WAIT UNTIL THE PRESENT CRISIS IS PAST?
NORBERT'S CONDITION **IS** THE PRESENT CRISIS.

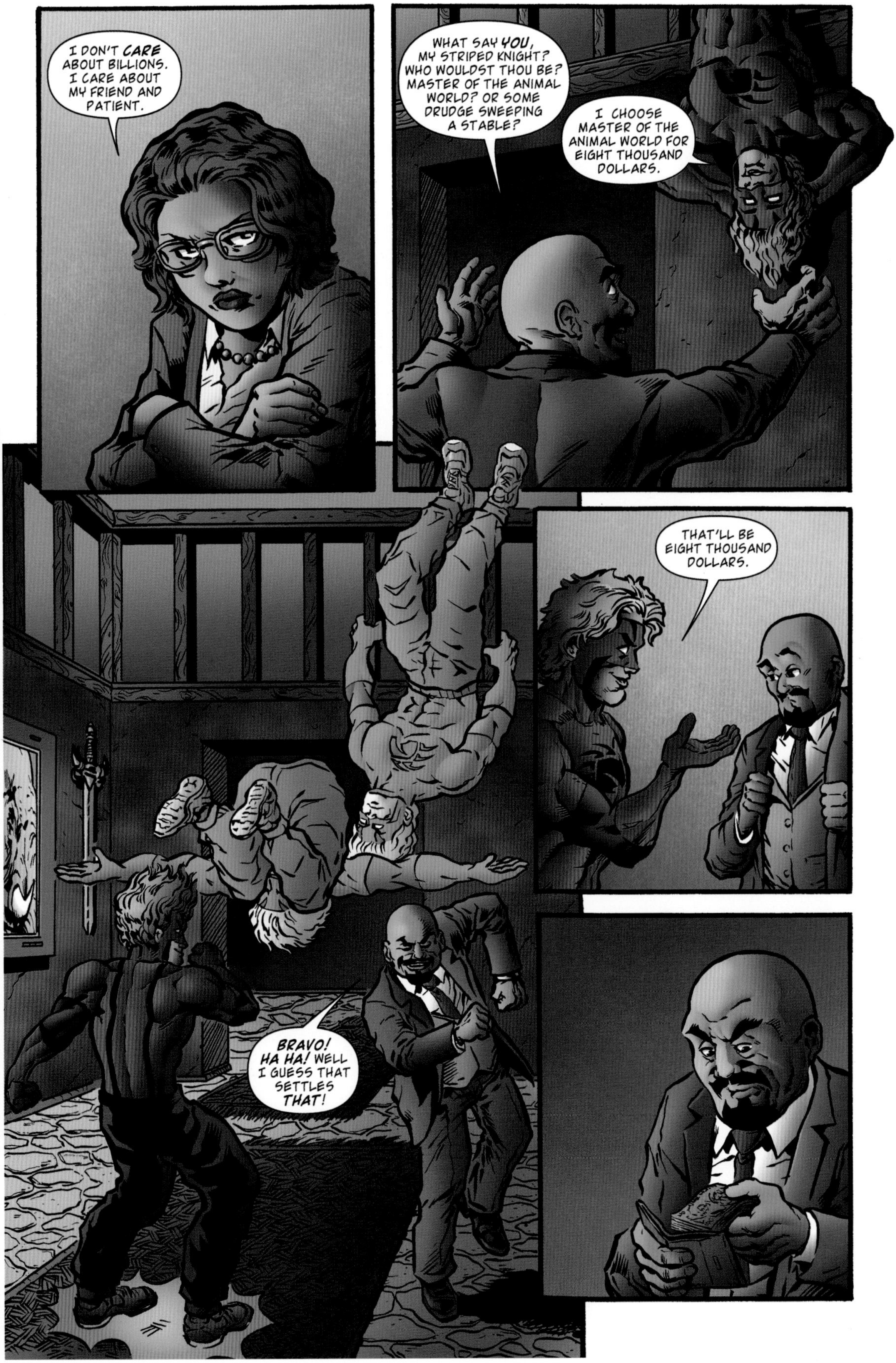
I DON'T CARE ABOUT BILLIONS. I CARE ABOUT MY FRIEND AND PATIENT.
WHAT SAY YOU, MY STRIPED KNIGHT? WHO WOULDST THOU BE? MASTER OF THE ANIMAL WORLD? OR SOME DRUDGE SWEEPING A STABLE?
I CHOOSE MASTER OF THE ANIMAL WORLD FOR EIGHT THOUSAND DOLLARS.
THAT'LL BE EIGHT THOUSAND DOLLARS.
BRAVO! HA HA! WELL I GUESS THAT SETTLES THAT!

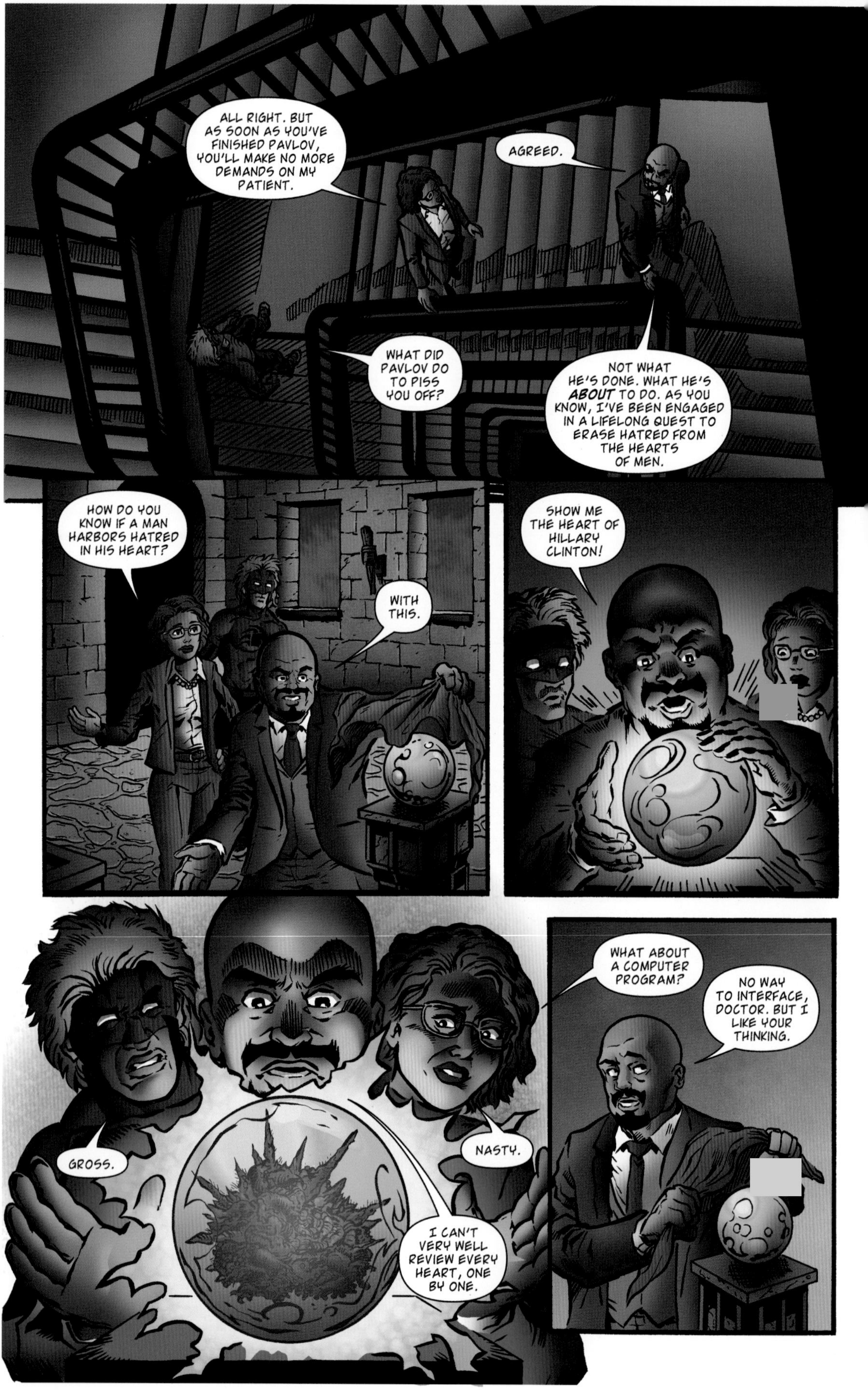
ALL RIGHT. BUT AS SOON AS YOU'VE FINISHED PAVLOV, YOU'LL MAKE NO MORE DEMANDS ON MY PATIENT.
AGREED.
WHAT DID PAVLOV DO TO PISS YOU OFF?
NOT WHAT HE'S DONE. WHAT HE'S *ABOUT* TO DO. AS YOU KNOW, I'VE BEEN ENGAGED IN A LIFELONG QUEST TO ERASE HATRED FROM THE HEARTS OF MEN.
HOW DO YOU KNOW IF A MAN HARBORS HATRED IN HIS HEART?
WITH THIS.
SHOW ME THE HEART OF HILLARY CLINTON!
GROSS.
NASTY.
I CAN'T VERY WELL REVIEW EVERY HEART, ONE BY ONE.
WHAT ABOUT A COMPUTER PROGRAM?
NO WAY TO INTERFACE, DOCTOR. BUT I LIKE YOUR THINKING.

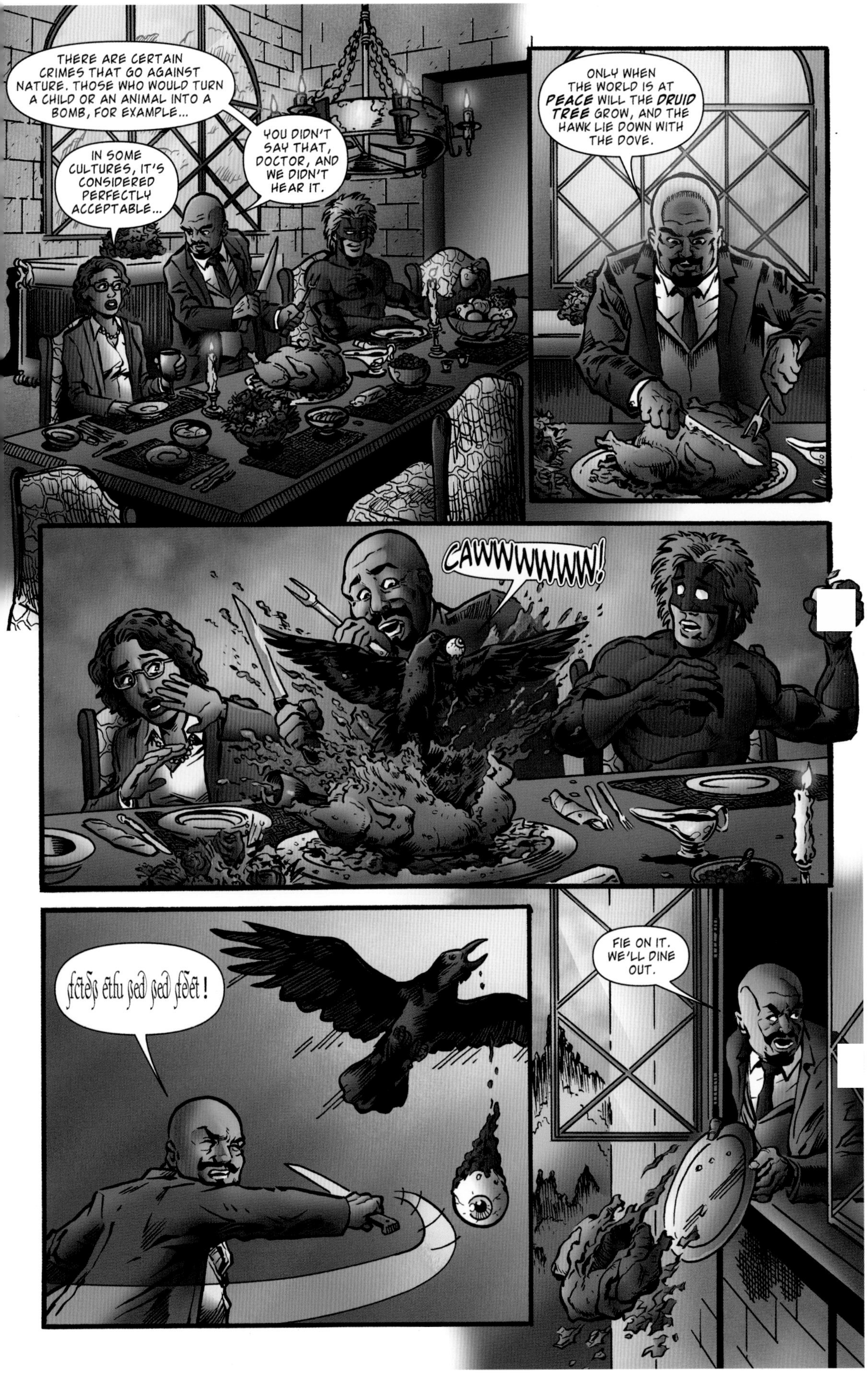
THERE ARE CERTAIN CRIMES THAT GO AGAINST NATURE. THOSE WHO WOULD TURN A CHILD OR AN ANIMAL INTO A BOMB, FOR EXAMPLE...
IN SOME CULTURES, IT'S CONSIDERED PERFECTLY ACCEPTABLE...
YOU DIDN'T SAY THAT, DOCTOR, AND WE DIDN'T HEAR IT.
ONLY WHEN THE WORLD IS AT PEACE WILL THE DRUID TREE GROW, AND THE HAWK LIE DOWN WITH THE DOVE.
CAWWWWWW!
FIE ON IT. WE'LL DINE OUT.

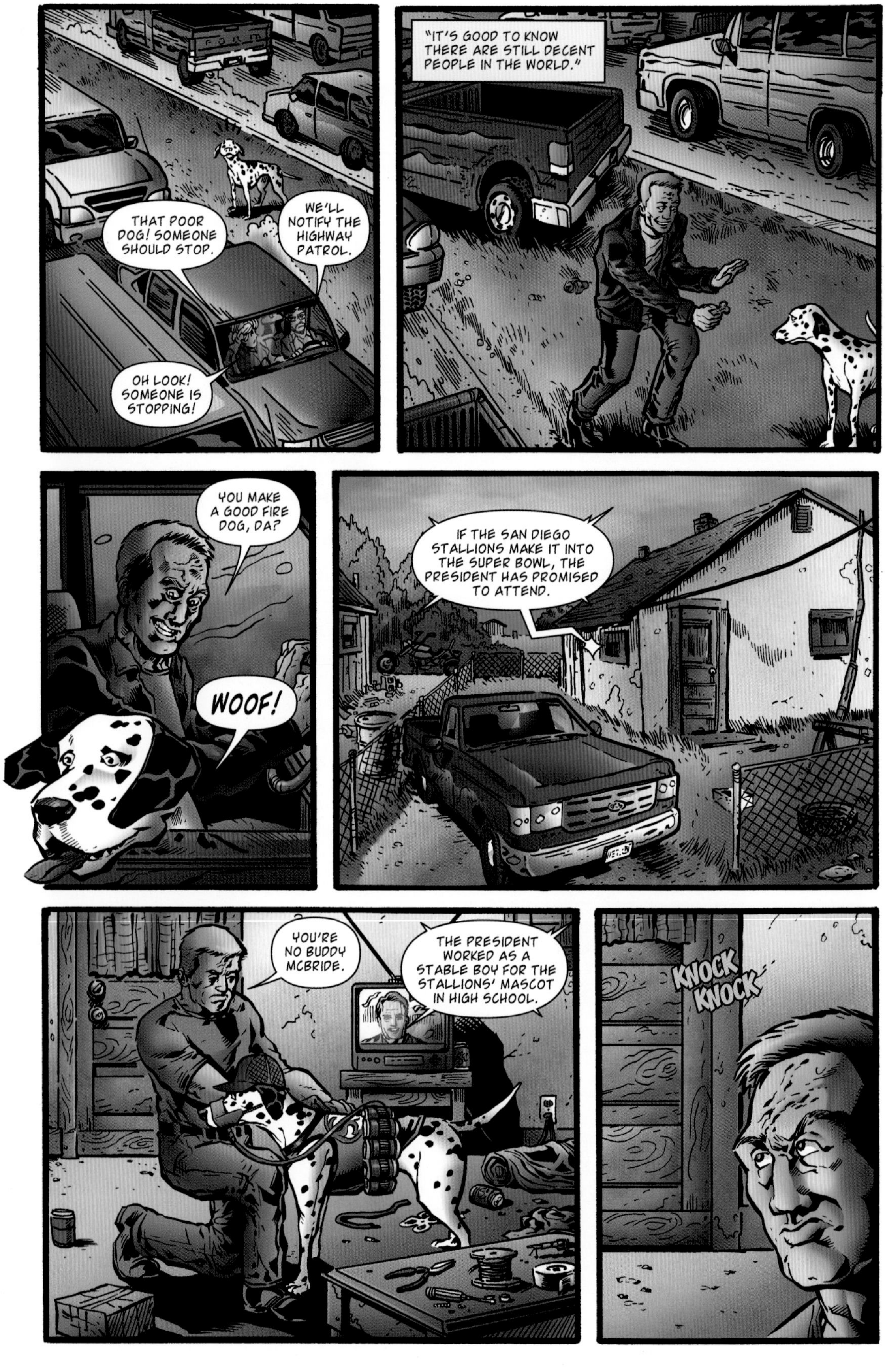
THAT POOR DOG! SOMEONE SHOULD STOP.
WE'LL NOTIFY THE HIGHWAY PATROL.
OH LOOK! SOMEONE IS STOPPING!
"IT'S GOOD TO KNOW THERE ARE STILL DECENT PEOPLE IN THE WORLD."
YOU MAKE A GOOD FIRE DOG, DA?
WOOF!
IF THE SAN DIEGO STALLIONS MAKE IT INTO THE SUPER BOWL, THE PRESIDENT HAS PROMISED TO ATTEND.
YOU'RE NO BUDDY MCBRIDE.
THE PRESIDENT WORKED AS A STABLE BOY FOR THE STALLIONS' MASCOT IN HIGH SCHOOL.
KNOCK KNOCK

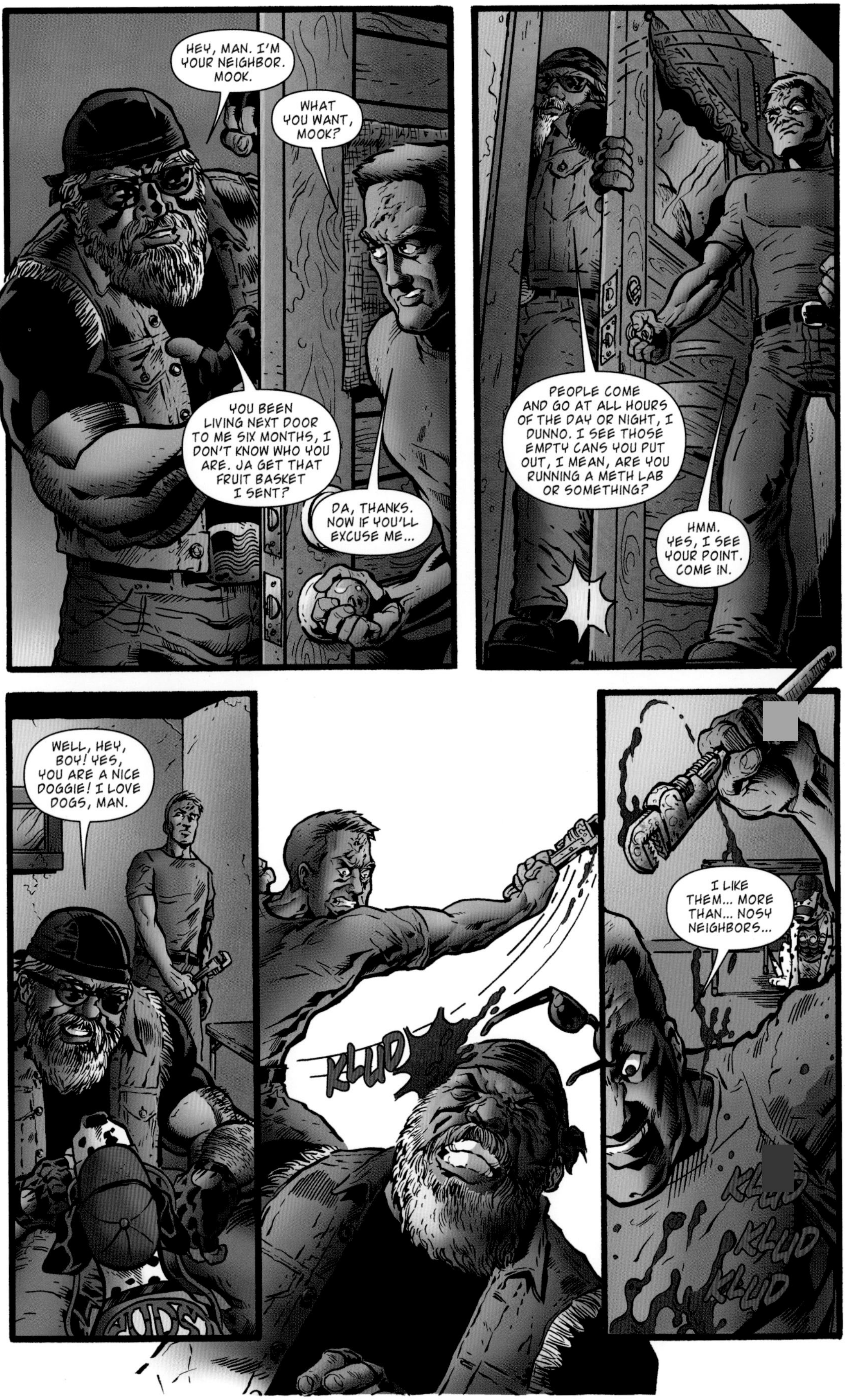
HEY, MAN. I'M YOUR NEIGHBOR. MOOK.
WHAT YOU WANT, MOOK?
YOU BEEN LIVING NEXT DOOR TO ME SIX MONTHS, I DON'T KNOW WHO YOU ARE. JA GET THAT FRUIT BASKET I SENT?
DA, THANKS. NOW IF YOU'LL EXCUSE ME...
PEOPLE COME AND GO AT ALL HOURS OF THE DAY OR NIGHT, I DUNNO. I SEE THOSE EMPTY CANS YOU PUT OUT, I MEAN, ARE YOU RUNNING A METH LAB OR SOMETHING?
HMM. YES, I SEE YOUR POINT. COME IN.
WELL, HEY, BOY! YES, YOU ARE A NICE DOGGIE! I LOVE DOGS, MAN.
KLUD
I LIKE THEM... MORE THAN... NOSY NEIGHBORS...
KLUD
KLUD
KLUD

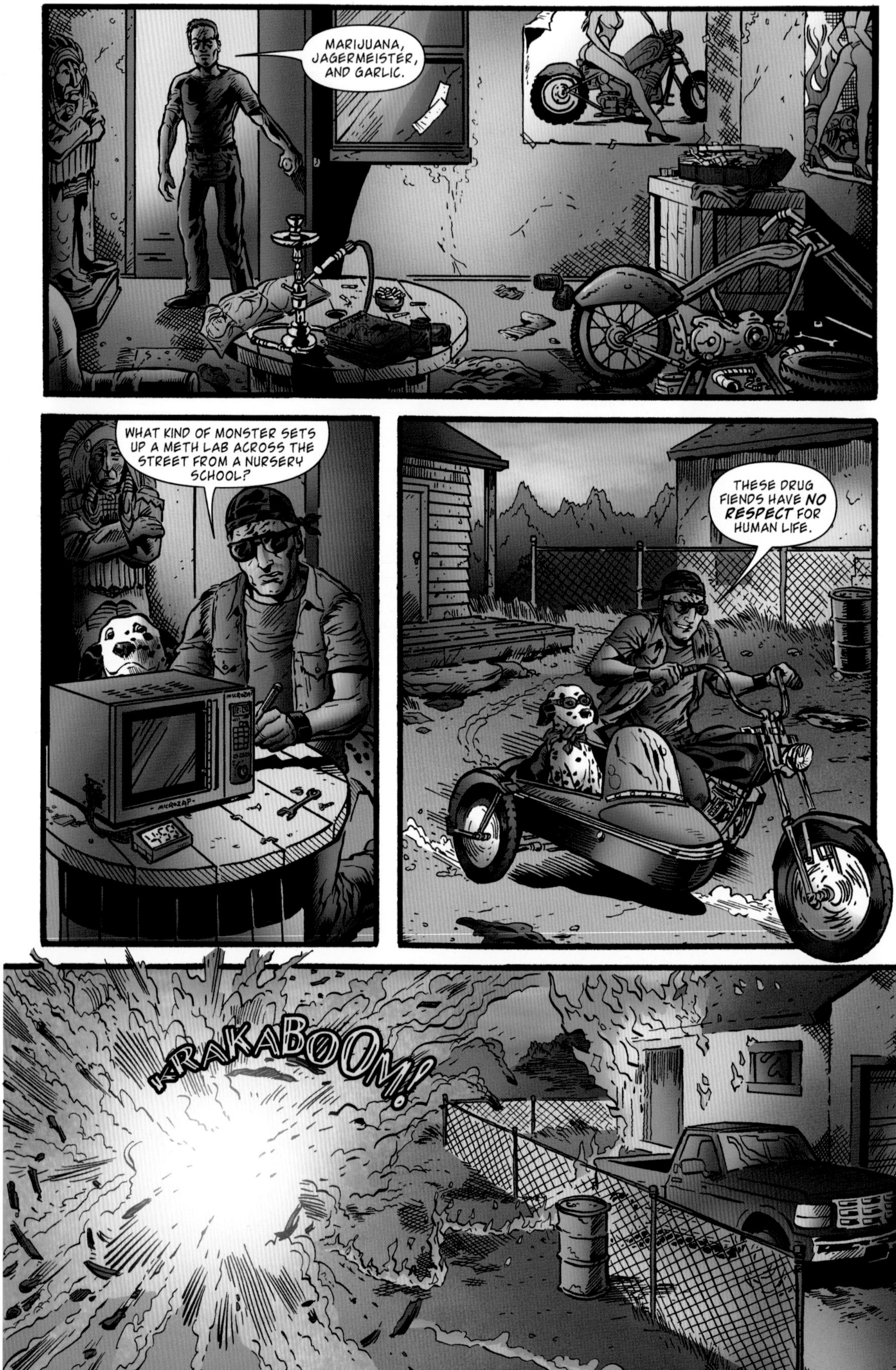
MARIJUANA, JAGERMEISTER, AND GARLIC.
WHAT KIND OF MONSTER SETS UP A METH LAB ACROSS THE STREET FROM A NURSERY SCHOOL?
MICROZAP
THESE DRUG FIENDS HAVE **NO RESPECT** FOR HUMAN LIFE.
KRAKABOOM!

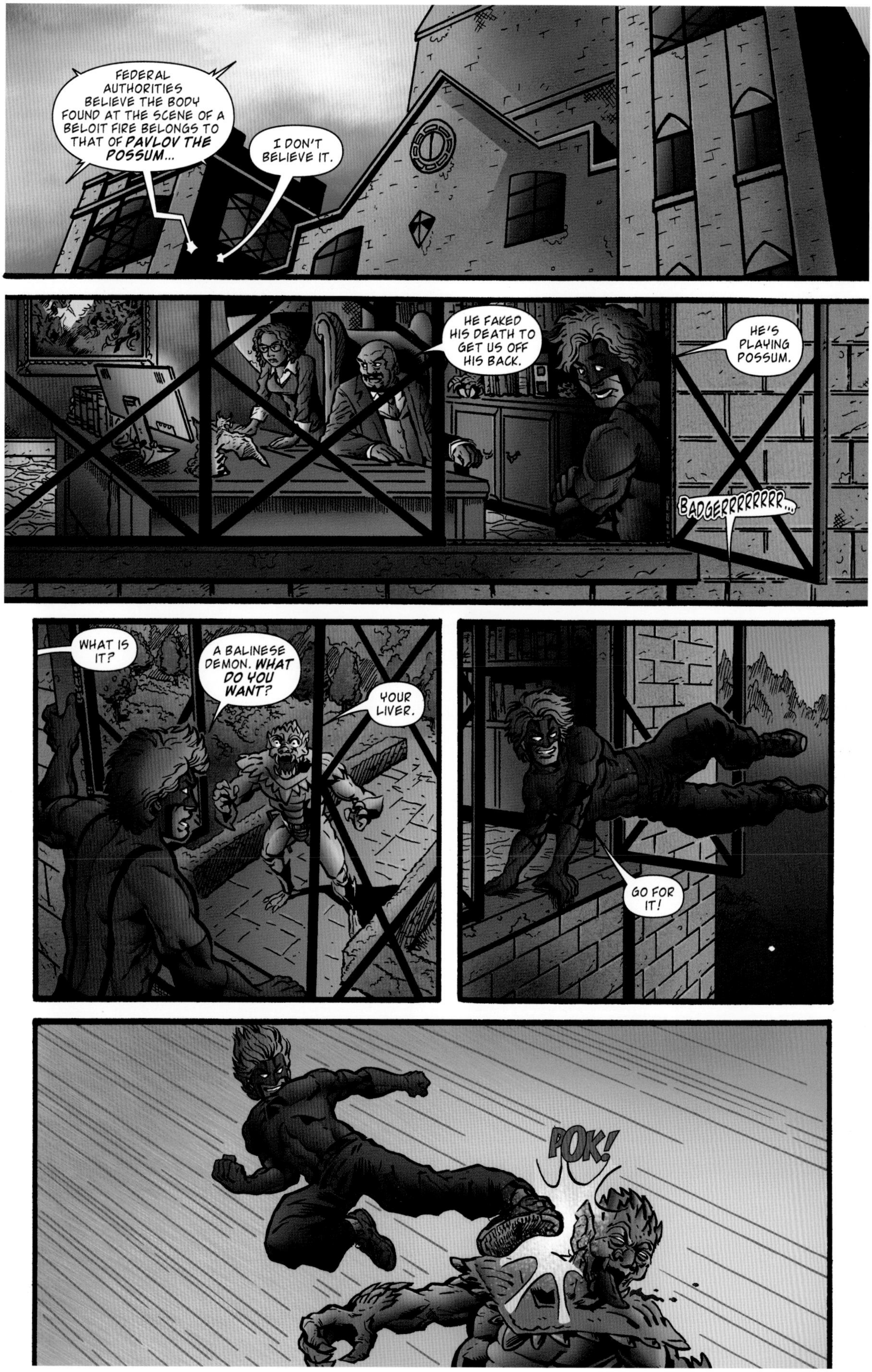
FEDERAL AUTHORITIES BELIEVE THE BODY FOUND AT THE SCENE OF A BELOIT FIRE BELONGS TO THAT OF **PAVLOV THE POSSUM**...
I DON'T BELIEVE IT.
HE FAKED HIS DEATH TO GET US OFF HIS BACK.
HE'S PLAYING POSSUM.
BADGERRRRRRR...
WHAT IS IT?
A BALINESE DEMON. **WHAT DO YOU WANT?**
YOUR LIVER.
GO FOR IT!
POK!

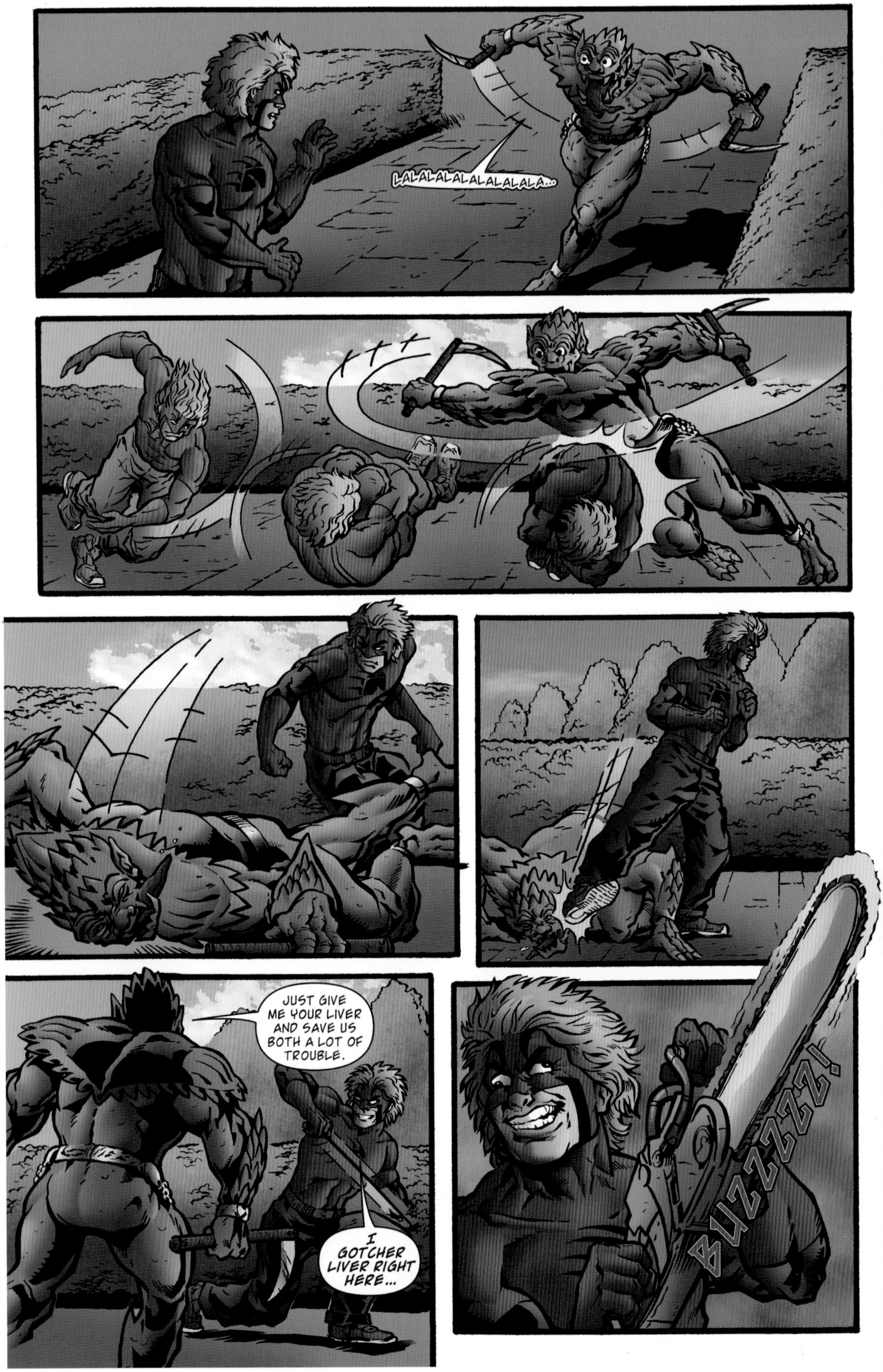
LALALALALALALALALA...
JUST GIVE ME YOUR LIVER AND SAVE US BOTH A LOT OF TROUBLE.
I GOTCHER LIVER RIGHT HERE...
BUZZZZZZ!

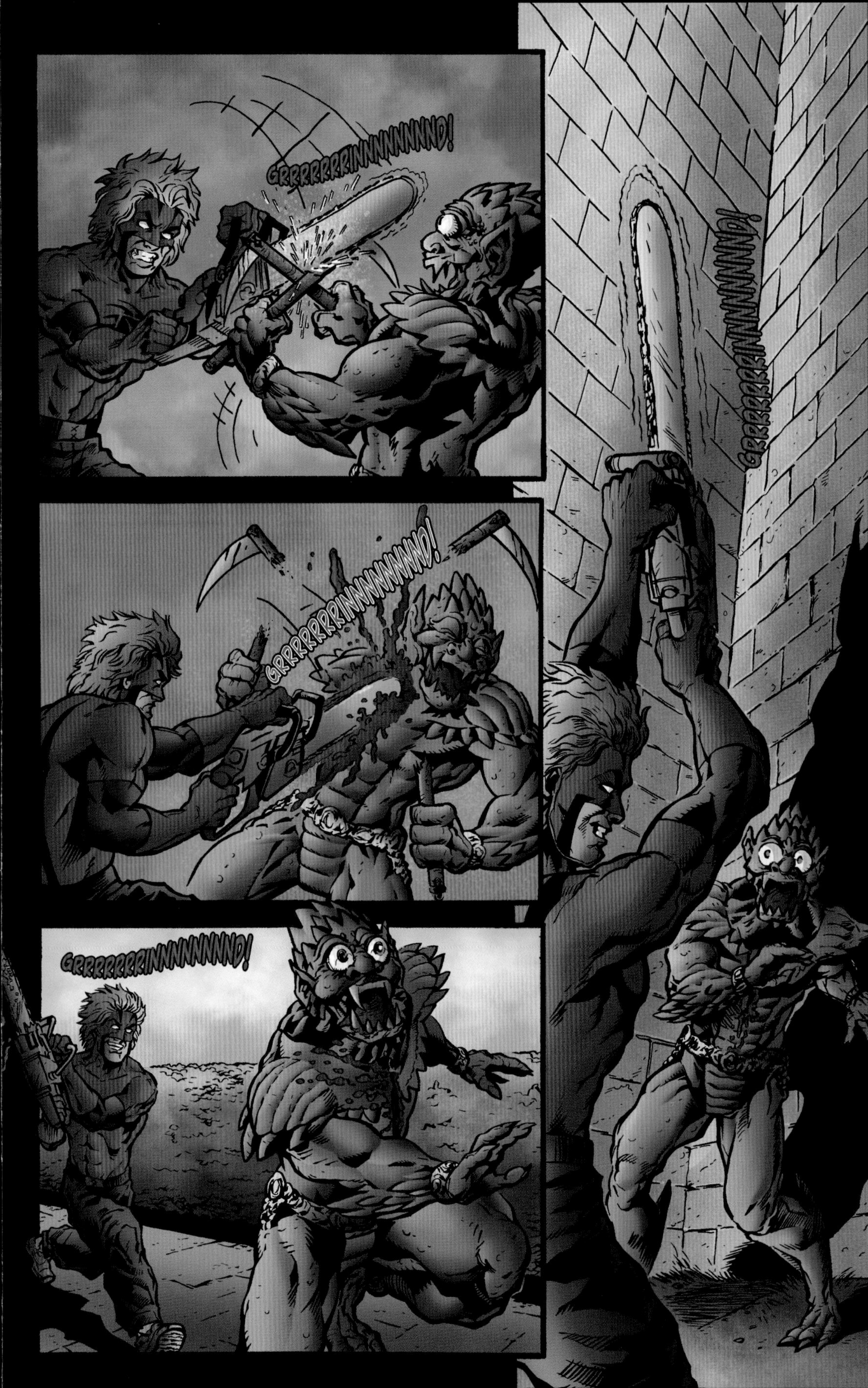
GRRRRRRRINNNNNNNND!
GRRRRRRRINNNNNNNND!
GRRRRRRRINNNNNNNND!
GRRRRRRRINNNNNNNND!

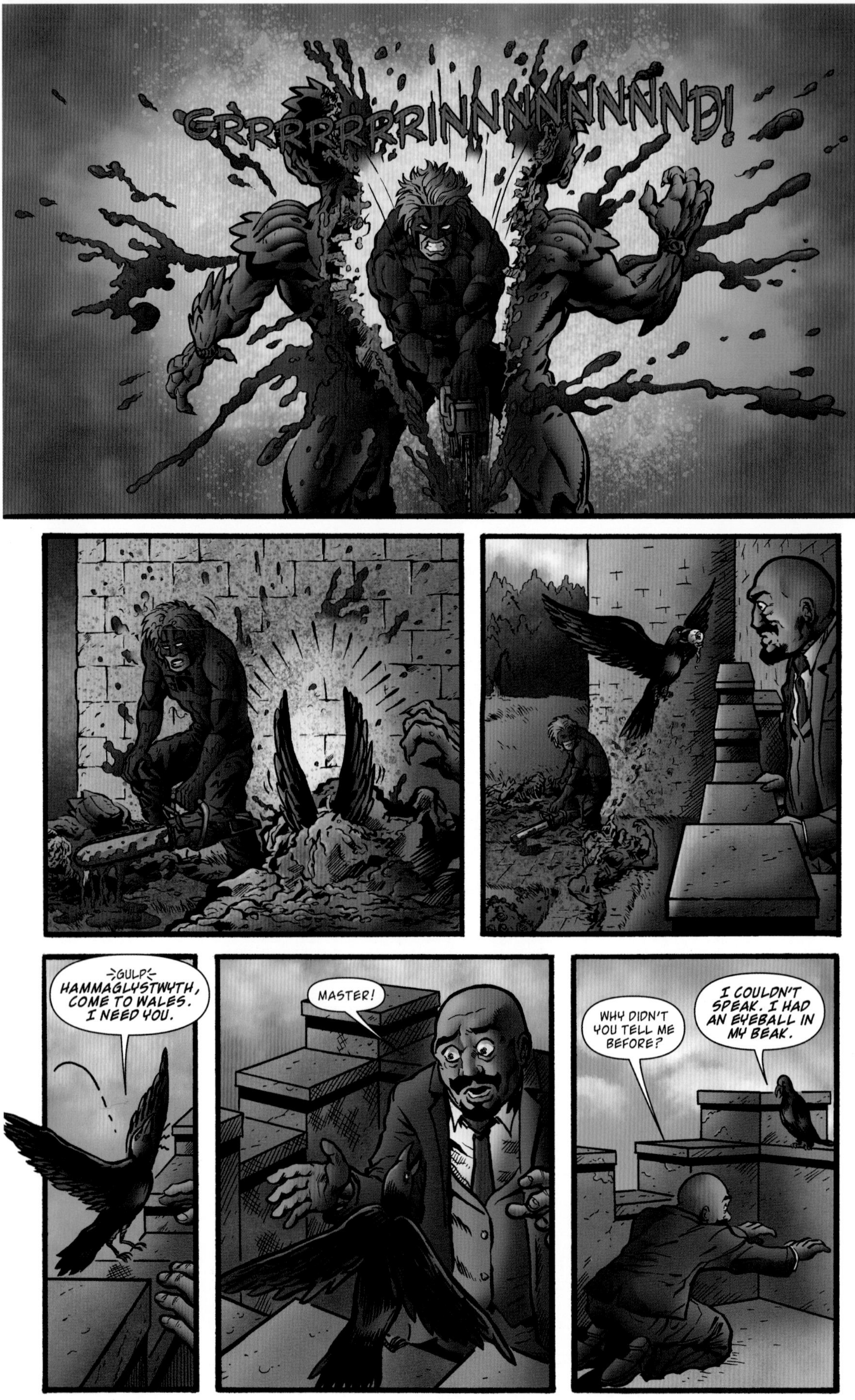
GRRRRRRRINNNNNNNND!
GULP
HAMMAGLYSTWYTH, COME TO WALES. I NEED YOU.
MASTER!
WHY DIDN'T YOU TELL ME BEFORE?
I COULDN'T SPEAK. I HAD AN EYEBALL IN MY BEAK.

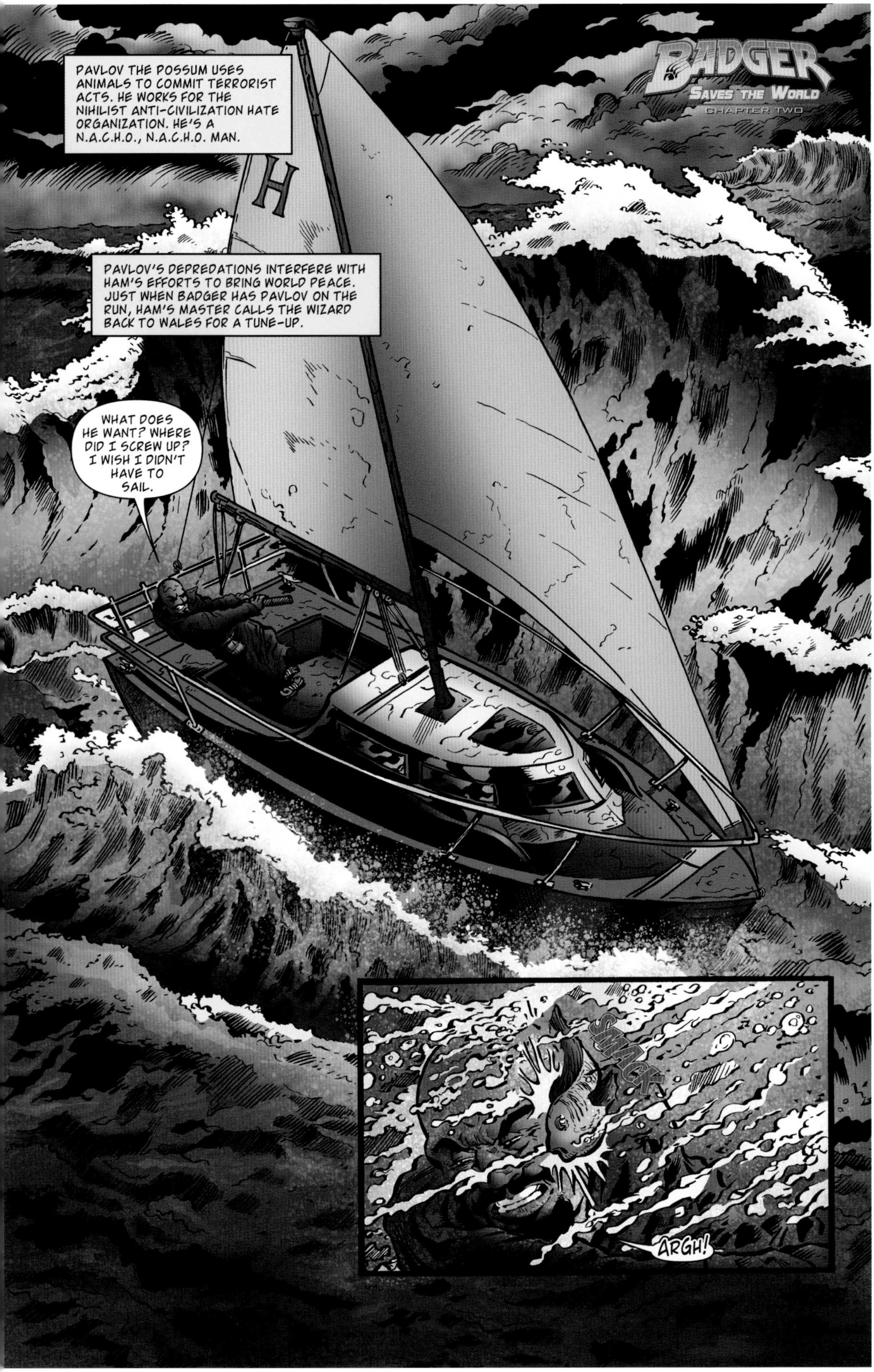
BADGER
SAVES THE WORLD
CHAPTER TWO
PAVLOV THE POSSUM USES ANIMALS TO COMMIT TERRORIST ACTS. HE WORKS FOR THE NIHILIST ANTI-CIVILIZATION HATE ORGANIZATION. HE'S A N.A.C.H.O., N.A.C.H.O. MAN.
PAVLOV'S DEPREDATIONS INTERFERE WITH HAM'S EFFORTS TO BRING WORLD PEACE. JUST WHEN BADGER HAS PAVLOV ON THE RUN, HAM'S MASTER CALLS THE WIZARD BACK TO WALES FOR A TUNE-UP.
WHAT DOES HE WANT? WHERE DID I SCREW UP? I WISH I DIDN'T HAVE TO SAIL.
SMACK
ARGH!

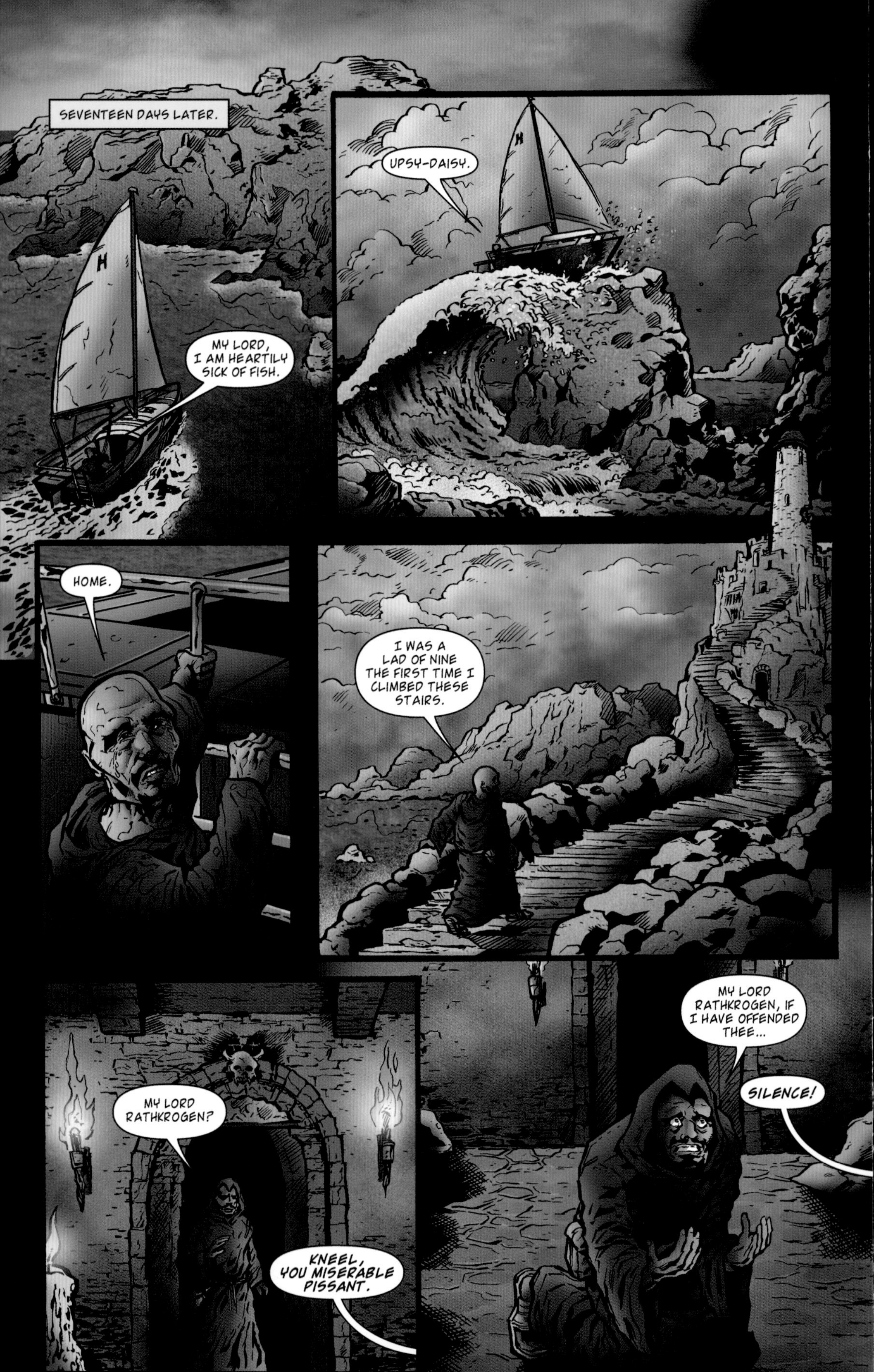
SEVENTEEN DAYS LATER.
MY LORD, I AM HEARTILY SICK OF FISH.
UPSY-DAISY.
HOME.
I WAS A LAD OF NINE THE FIRST TIME I CLIMBED THESE STAIRS.
MY LORD RATHKROGEN?
KNEEL, YOU MISERABLE PISSANT.
MY LORD RATHKROGEN, IF I HAVE OFFENDED THEE...
SILENCE!

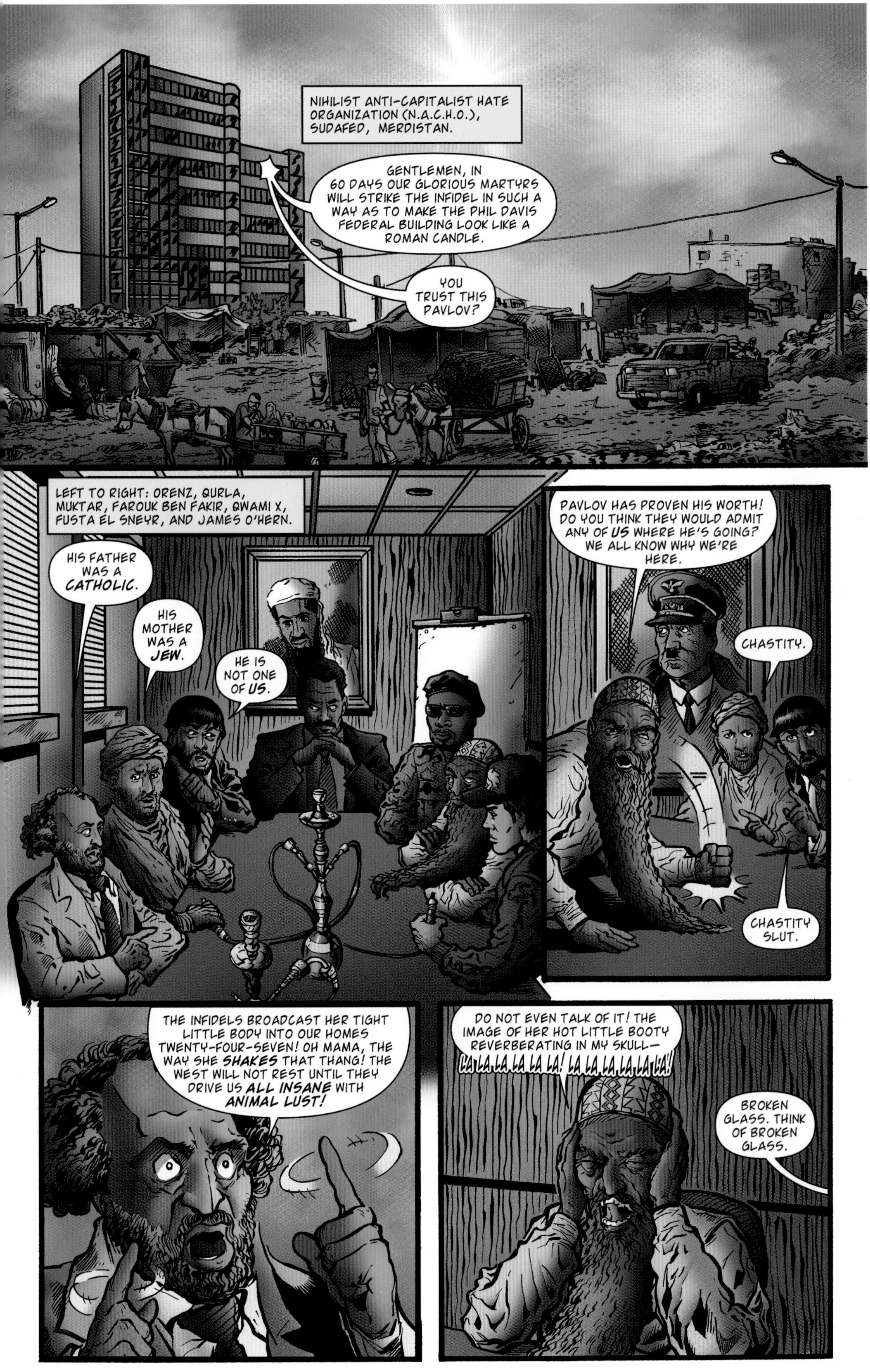
NIHILIST ANTI-CAPITALIST HATE ORGANIZATION (N.A.C.H.O.), SUDAFED, MERDISTAN.
GENTLEMEN, IN 60 DAYS OUR GLORIOUS MARTYRS WILL STRIKE THE INFIDEL IN SUCH A WAY AS TO MAKE THE PHIL DAVIS FEDERAL BUILDING LOOK LIKE A ROMAN CANDLE.
YOU TRUST THIS PAVLOV?
LEFT TO RIGHT: ORENZ, QURLA, MUKTAR, FAROUK BEN FAKIR, QWAMI X, FUSTA EL SNEYR, AND JAMES O'HERN.
HIS FATHER WAS A CATHOLIC.
HIS MOTHER WAS A JEW.
HE IS NOT ONE OF US.
PAVLOV HAS PROVEN HIS WORTH! DO YOU THINK THEY WOULD ADMIT ANY OF US WHERE HE'S GOING? WE ALL KNOW WHY WE'RE HERE.
CHASTITY.
CHASTITY SLUT.
THE INFIDELS BROADCAST HER TIGHT LITTLE BODY INTO OUR HOMES TWENTY-FOUR-SEVEN! OH MAMA, THE WAY SHE SHAKES THAT THANG! THE WEST WILL NOT REST UNTIL THEY DRIVE US ALL INSANE WITH ANIMAL LUST!
DO NOT EVEN TALK OF IT! THE IMAGE OF HER HOT LITTLE BOOTY REVERBERATING IN MY SKULL— LA LA LA LA LA LA! LA LA LA LA LA LA!
BROKEN GLASS. THINK OF BROKEN GLASS.

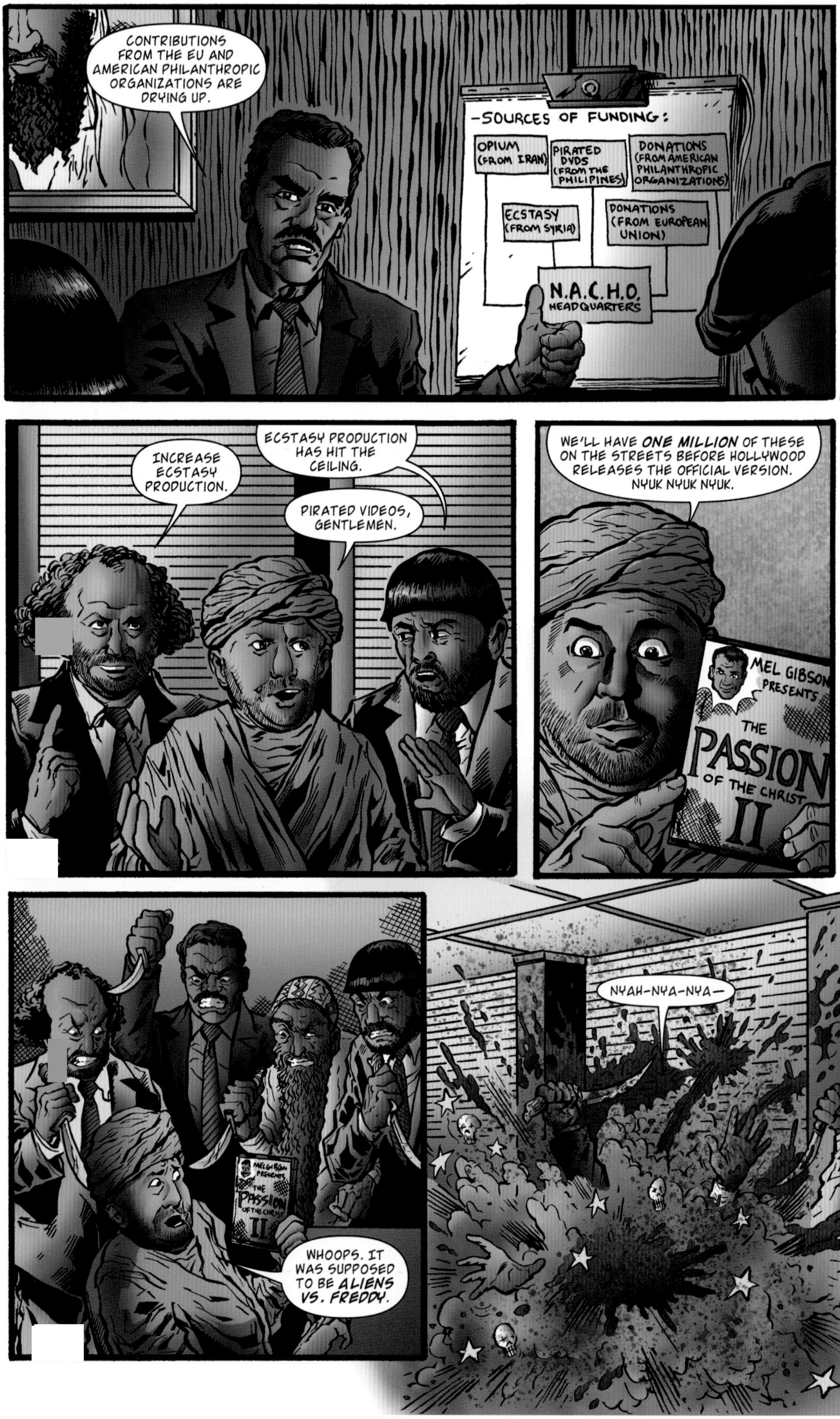
CONTRIBUTIONS FROM THE EU AND AMERICAN PHILANTHROPIC ORGANIZATIONS ARE DRYING UP.
-SOURCES OF FUNDING:
OPIUM (FROM IRAN)
PIRATED DVDS (FROM THE PHILIPINES)
DONATIONS (FROM AMERICAN PHILANTHROPIC ORGANIZATIONS)
ECSTASY (FROM SYRIA)
DONATIONS (FROM EUROPEAN UNION)
N.A.C.H.O. HEADQUARTERS
INCREASE ECSTASY PRODUCTION.
ECSTASY PRODUCTION HAS HIT THE CEILING.
PIRATED VIDEOS, GENTLEMEN.
WE'LL HAVE ONE MILLION OF THESE ON THE STREETS BEFORE HOLLYWOOD RELEASES THE OFFICIAL VERSION. NYUK NYUK NYUK.
MEL GIBSON PRESENTS THE PASSION OF THE CHRIST II
WHOOPS. IT WAS SUPPOSED TO BE ALIENS VS. FREDDY.
NYAH-NYA-NYA—

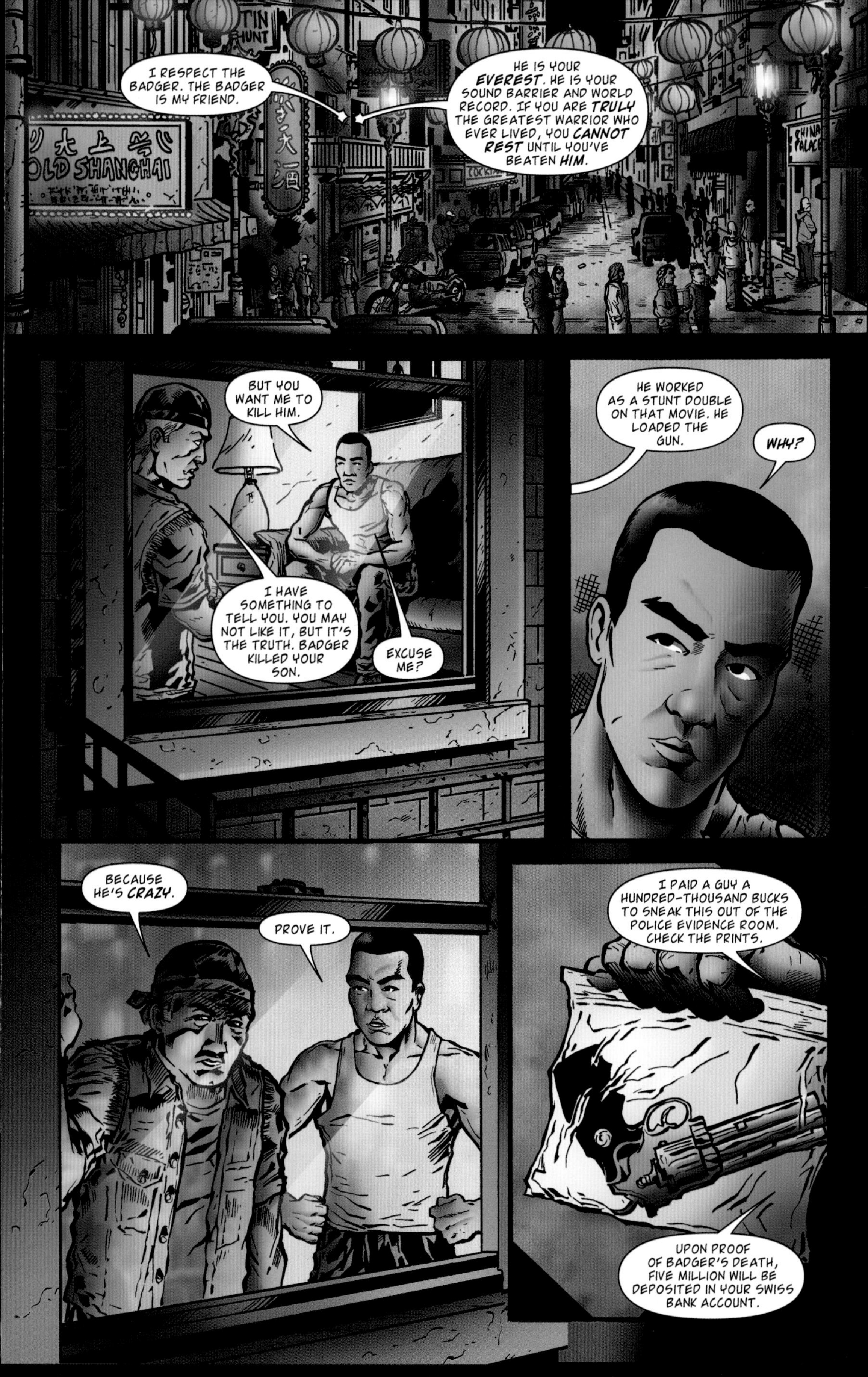
OLD SHANGHAI
CHINA PALACE
I RESPECT THE BADGER. THE BADGER IS MY FRIEND.
HE IS YOUR EVEREST. HE IS YOUR SOUND BARRIER AND WORLD RECORD. IF YOU ARE TRULY THE GREATEST WARRIOR WHO EVER LIVED, YOU CANNOT REST UNTIL YOU'VE BEATEN HIM.
BUT YOU WANT ME TO KILL HIM.
I HAVE SOMETHING TO TELL YOU. YOU MAY NOT LIKE IT, BUT IT'S THE TRUTH. BADGER KILLED YOUR SON.
EXCUSE ME?
HE WORKED AS A STUNT DOUBLE ON THAT MOVIE. HE LOADED THE GUN.
WHY?
BECAUSE HE'S CRAZY.
PROVE IT.
I PAID A GUY A HUNDRED-THOUSAND BUCKS TO SNEAK THIS OUT OF THE POLICE EVIDENCE ROOM. CHECK THE PRINTS.
UPON PROOF OF BADGER'S DEATH, FIVE MILLION WILL BE DEPOSITED IN YOUR SWISS BANK ACCOUNT.

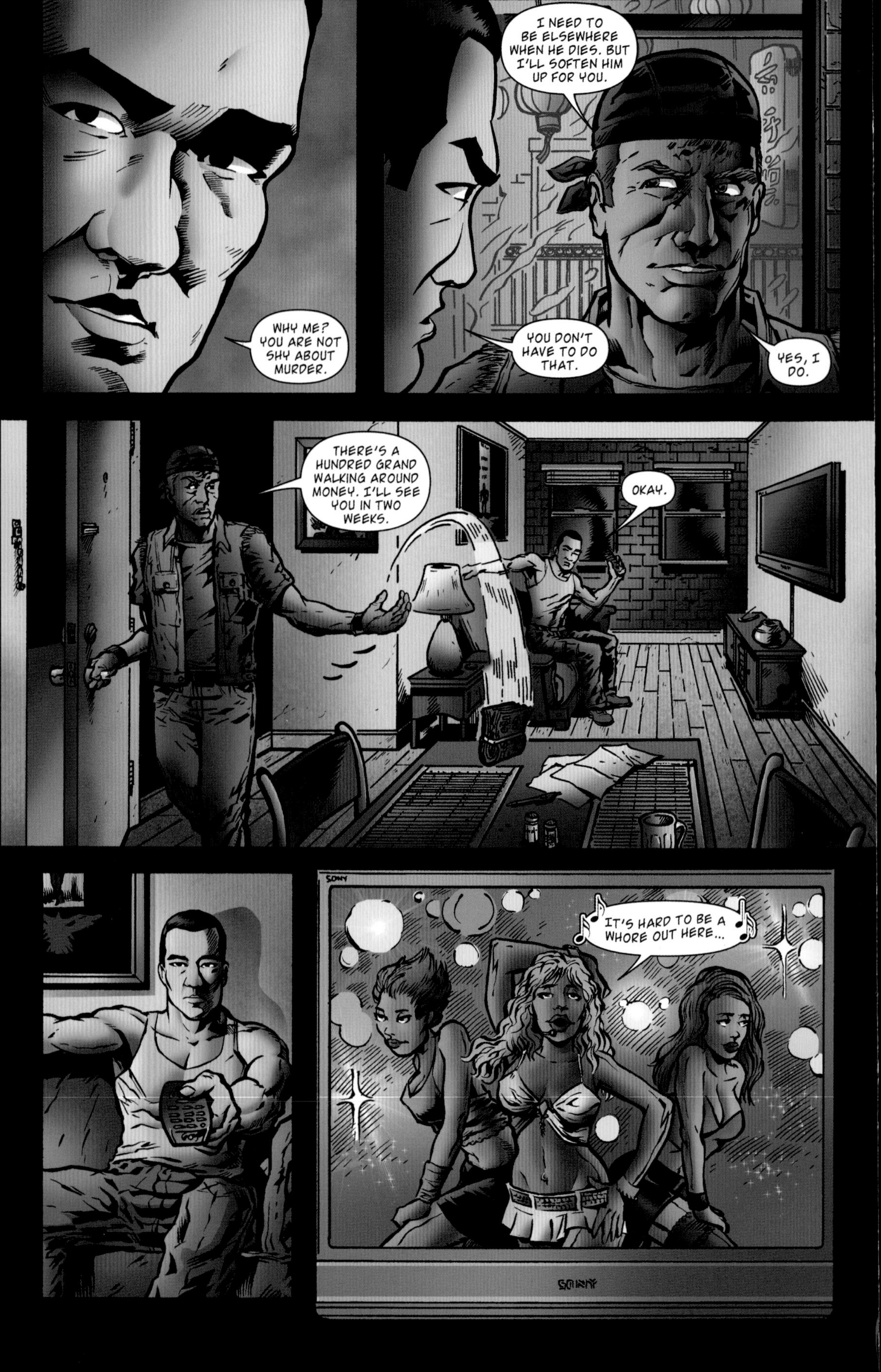
WHY ME? YOU ARE NOT SHY ABOUT MURDER.
I NEED TO BE ELSEWHERE WHEN HE DIES. BUT I'LL SOFTEN HIM UP FOR YOU.
YOU DON'T HAVE TO DO THAT.
YES, I DO.
THERE'S A HUNDRED GRAND WALKING AROUND MONEY. I'LL SEE YOU IN TWO WEEKS.
OKAY.
SONY
IT'S HARD TO BE A WHORE OUT HERE...
SONY

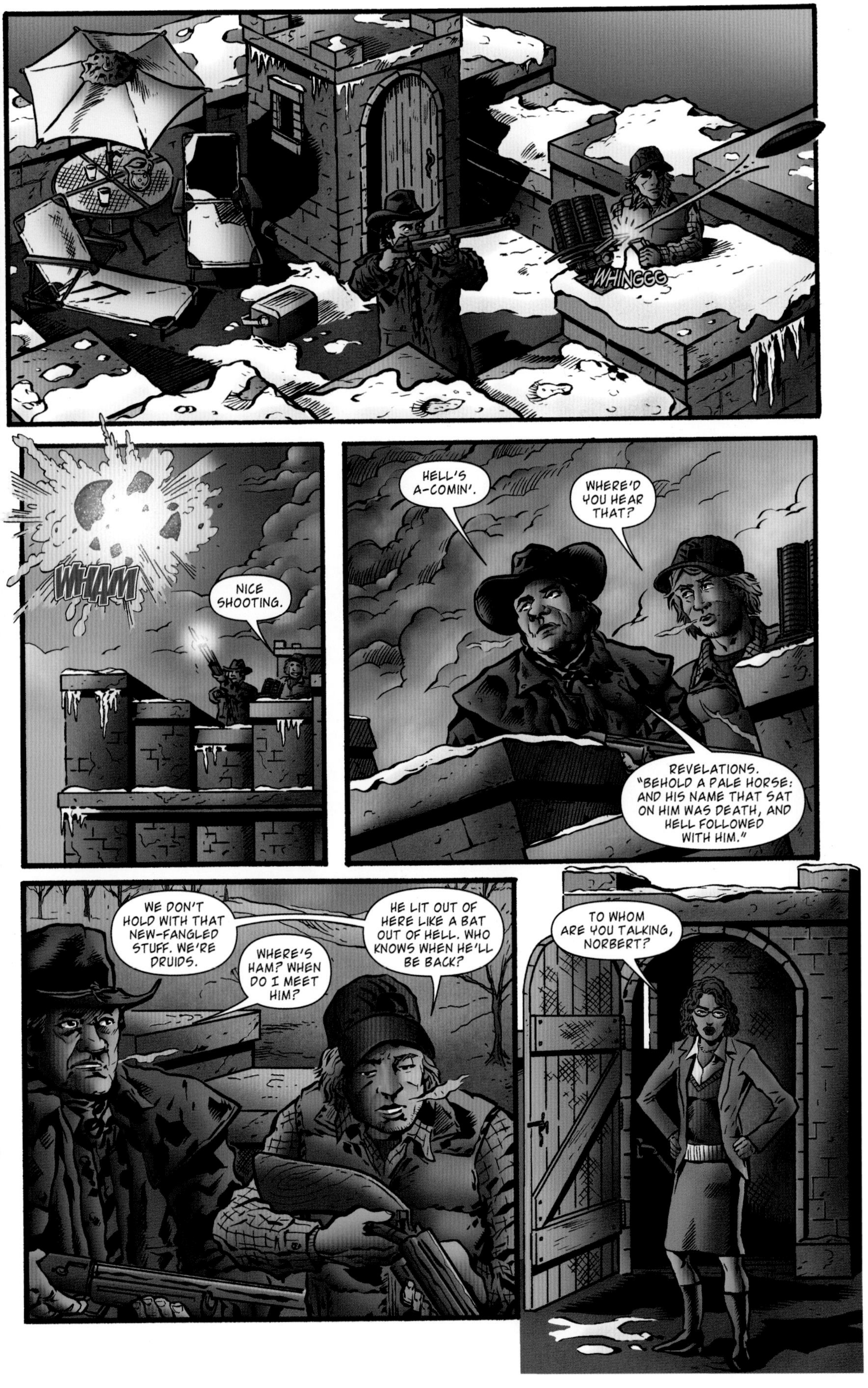
WHINGGG
WHAM
NICE SHOOTING.
HELL'S A-COMIN'.
WHERE'D YOU HEAR THAT?
REVELATIONS. "BEHOLD A PALE HORSE: AND HIS NAME THAT SAT ON HIM WAS DEATH, AND HELL FOLLOWED WITH HIM."
WE DON'T HOLD WITH THAT NEW-FANGLED STUFF. WE'RE DRUIDS.
WHERE'S HAM? WHEN DO I MEET HIM?
HE LIT OUT OF HERE LIKE A BAT OUT OF HELL. WHO KNOWS WHEN HE'LL BE BACK?
TO WHOM ARE YOU TALKING, NORBERT?

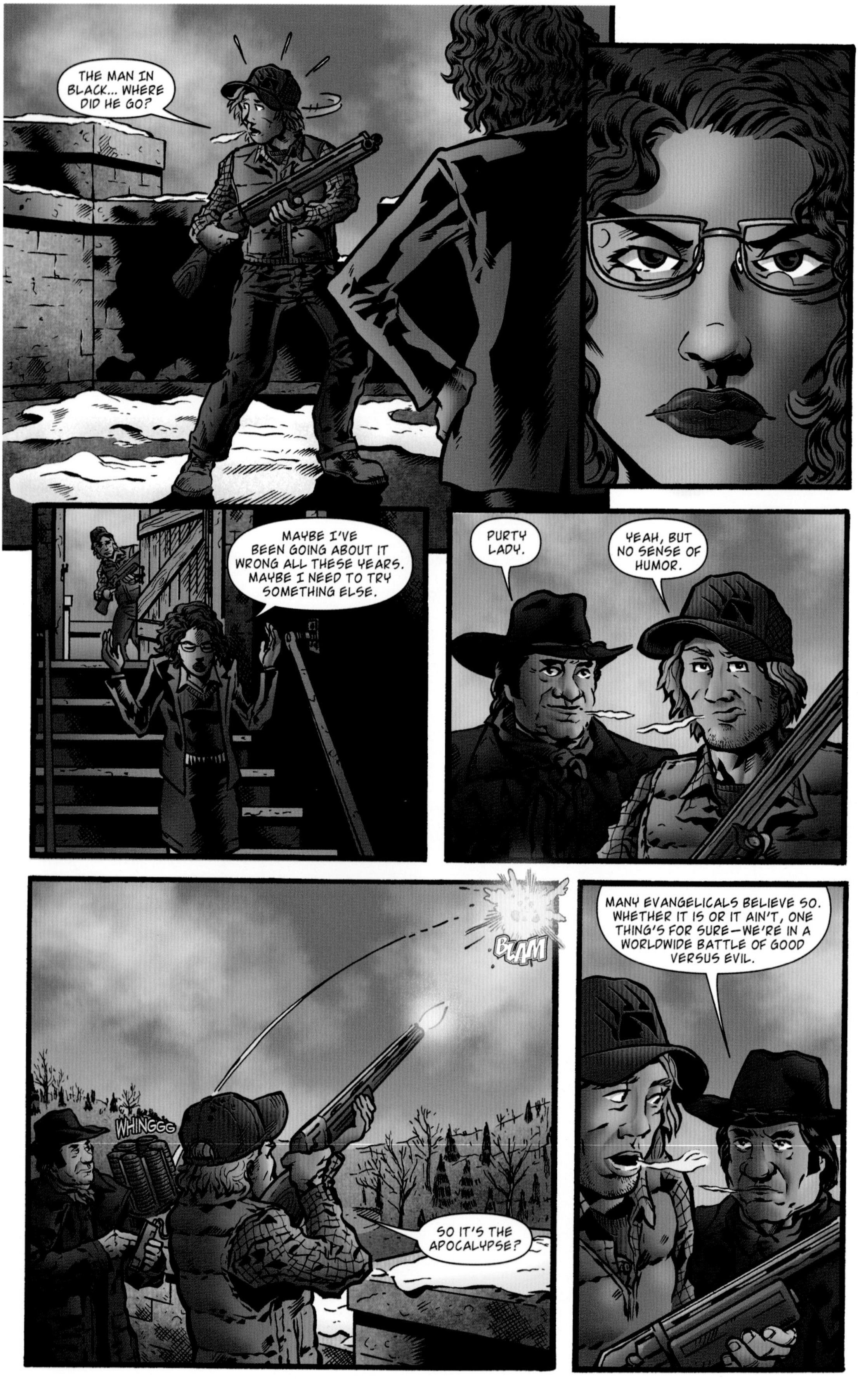
THE MAN IN BLACK... WHERE DID HE GO?
MAYBE I'VE BEEN GOING ABOUT IT WRONG ALL THESE YEARS. MAYBE I NEED TO TRY SOMETHING ELSE.
PURTY LADY.
YEAH, BUT NO SENSE OF HUMOR.
BLAM
WHINGGG
SO IT'S THE APOCALYPSE?
MANY EVANGELICALS BELIEVE SO. WHETHER IT IS OR IT AIN'T, ONE THING'S FOR SURE—WE'RE IN A WORLDWIDE BATTLE OF GOOD VERSUS EVIL.

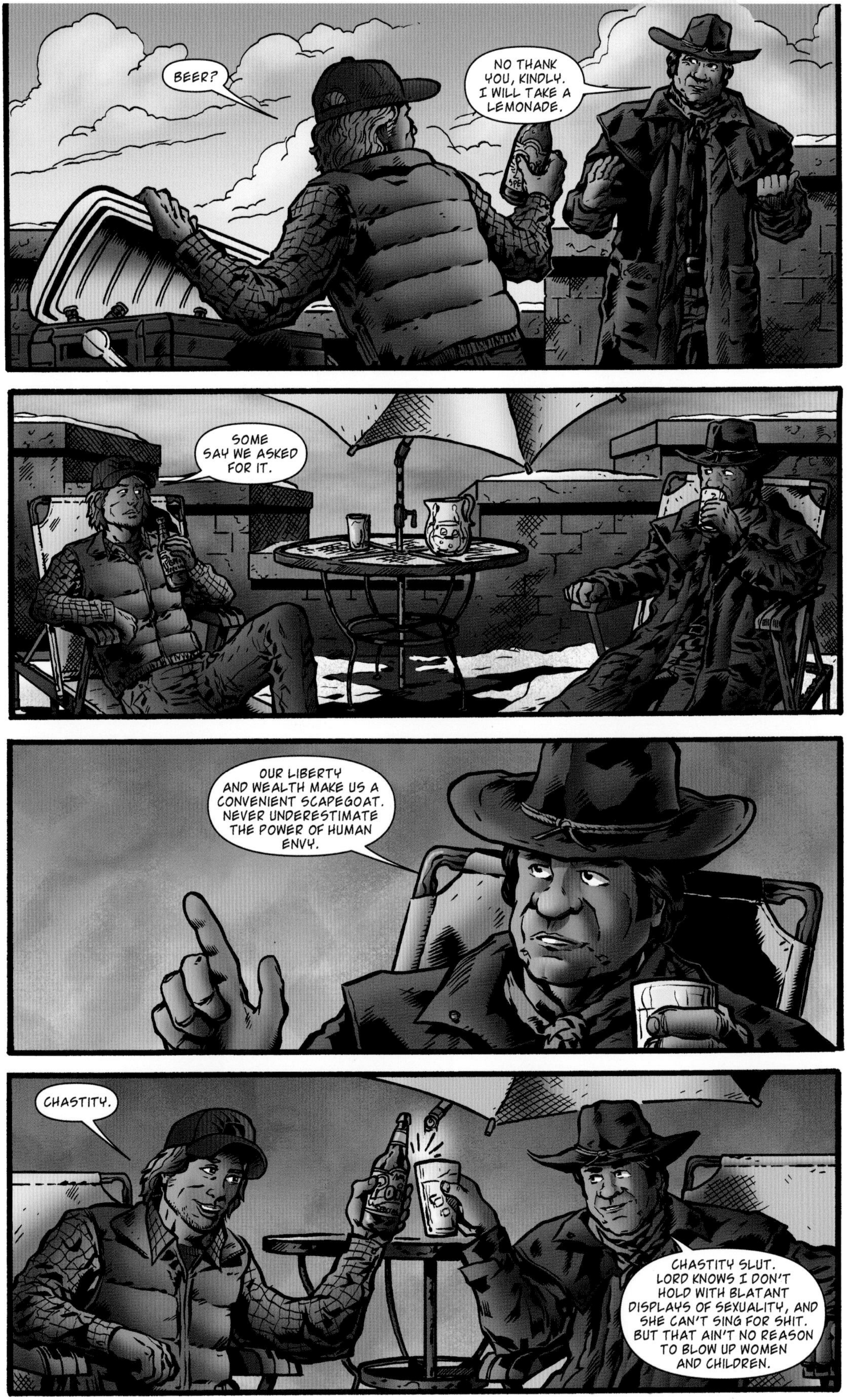
BEER?
NO THANK YOU, KINDLY. I WILL TAKE A LEMONADE.
SOME SAY WE ASKED FOR IT.
OUR LIBERTY AND WEALTH MAKE US A CONVENIENT SCAPEGOAT. NEVER UNDERESTIMATE THE POWER OF HUMAN ENVY.
CHASTITY.
CHASTITY SLUT. LORD KNOWS I DON'T HOLD WITH BLATANT DISPLAYS OF SEXUALITY, AND SHE CAN'T SING FOR SHIT. BUT THAT AIN'T NO REASON TO BLOW UP WOMEN AND CHILDREN.

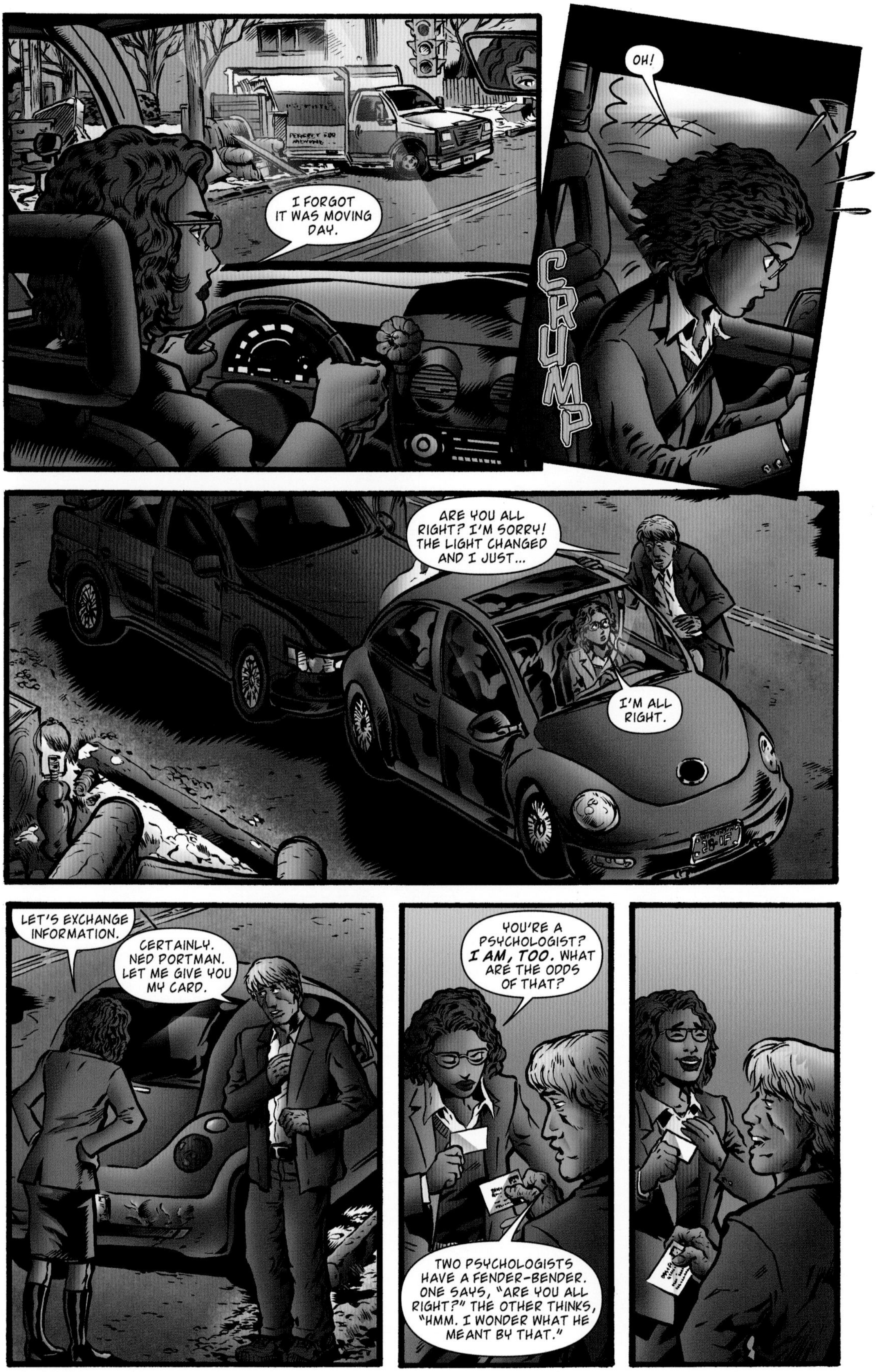
I FORGOT IT WAS MOVING DAY.
OH!
CRUMP
ARE YOU ALL RIGHT? I'M SORRY! THE LIGHT CHANGED AND I JUST...
I'M ALL RIGHT.
LET'S EXCHANGE INFORMATION.
CERTAINLY. NED PORTMAN. LET ME GIVE YOU MY CARD.
YOU'RE A PSYCHOLOGIST? I AM, TOO. WHAT ARE THE ODDS OF THAT?
TWO PSYCHOLOGISTS HAVE A FENDER-BENDER. ONE SAYS, "ARE YOU ALL RIGHT?" THE OTHER THINKS, "HMM. I WONDER WHAT HE MEANT BY THAT."

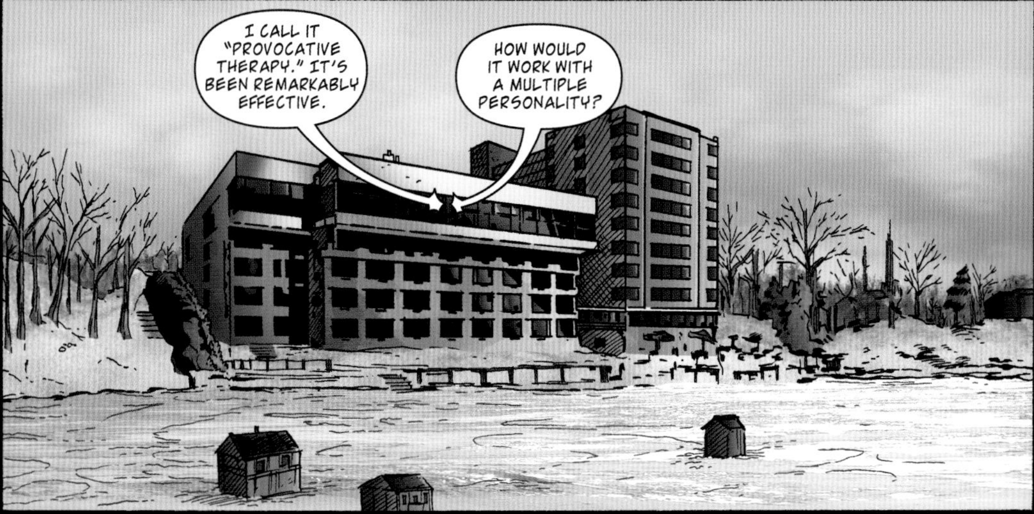
I CALL IT "PROVOCATIVE THERAPY." IT'S BEEN REMARKABLY EFFECTIVE.
HOW WOULD IT WORK WITH A MULTIPLE PERSONALITY?
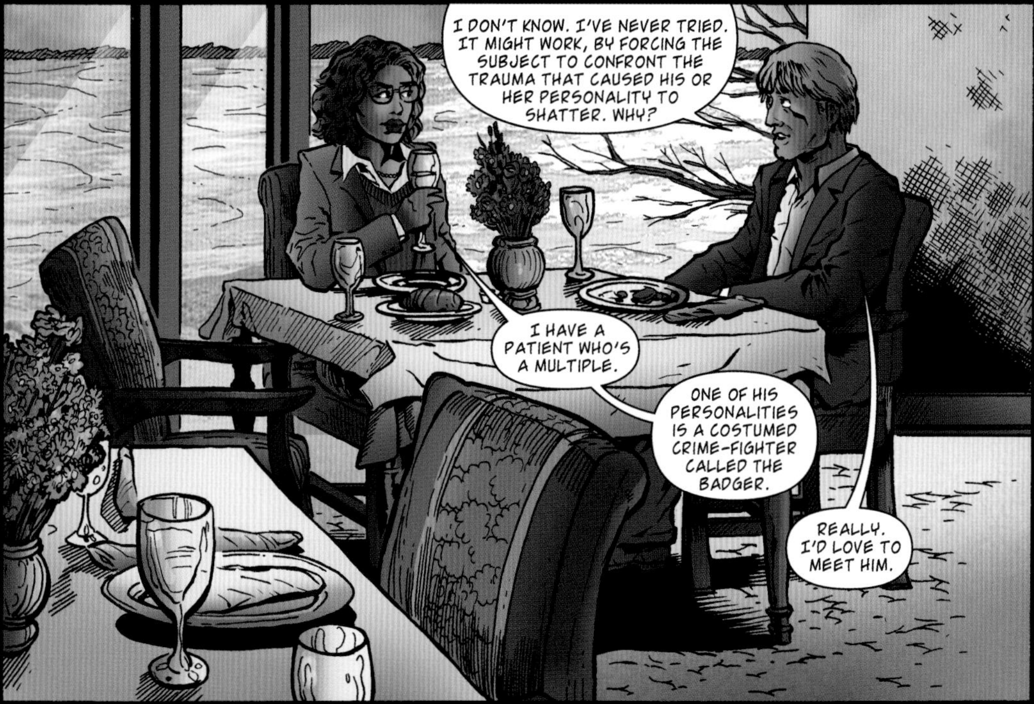
I DON'T KNOW. I'VE NEVER TRIED. IT MIGHT WORK, BY FORCING THE SUBJECT TO CONFRONT THE TRAUMA THAT CAUSED HIS OR HER PERSONALITY TO SHATTER. WHY?
I HAVE A PATIENT WHO'S A MULTIPLE.
ONE OF HIS PERSONALITIES IS A COSTUMED CRIME-FIGHTER CALLED THE BADGER.
REALLY. I'D LOVE TO MEET HIM.
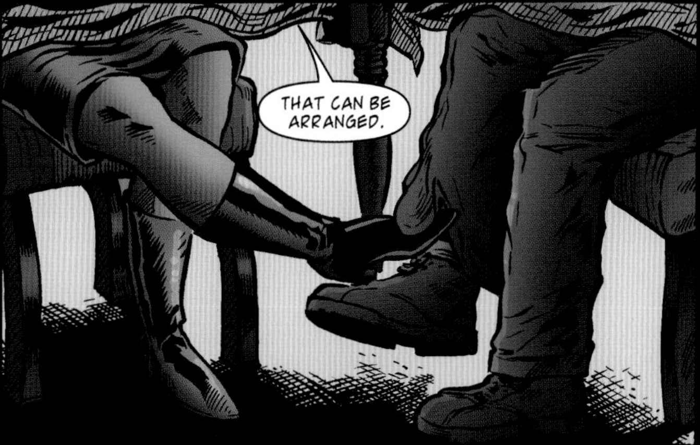
THAT CAN BE ARRANGED.

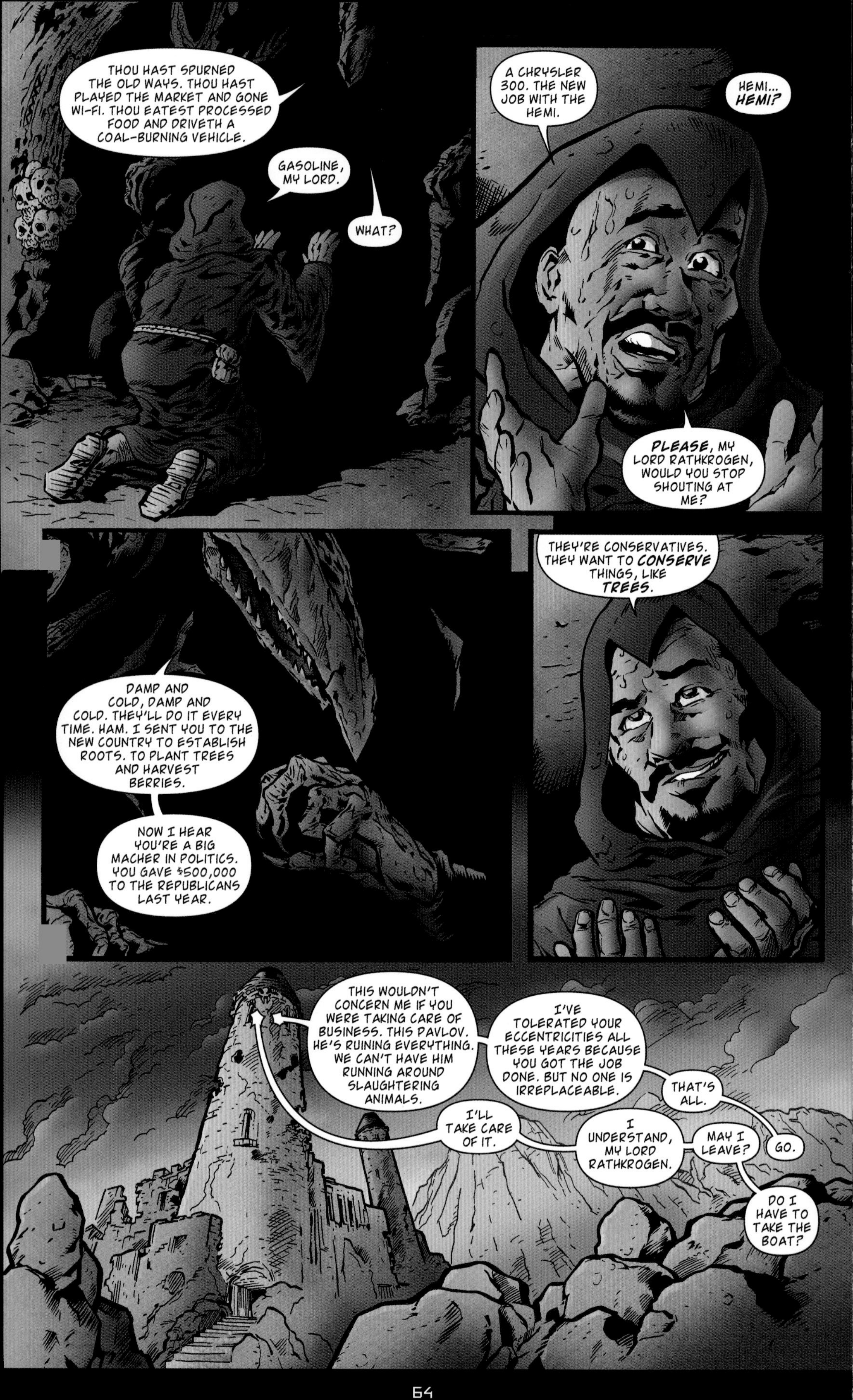

THOU HAST SPURNED THE OLD WAYS. THOU HAST PLAYED THE MARKET AND GONE WI-FI. THOU EATEST PROCESSED FOOD AND DRIVETH A COAL-BURNING VEHICLE.
GASOLINE, MY LORD.
WHAT?
A CHRYSLER 300. THE NEW JOB WITH THE HEMI.
HEMI... **HEMI?**
PLEASE, MY LORD RATHKROGEN, WOULD YOU STOP SHOUTING AT ME?
DAMP AND COLD, DAMP AND COLD. THEY'LL DO IT EVERY TIME. HAM. I SENT YOU TO THE NEW COUNTRY TO ESTABLISH ROOTS. TO PLANT TREES AND HARVEST BERRIES.
NOW I HEAR YOU'RE A BIG MACHER IN POLITICS. YOU GAVE $500,000 TO THE REPUBLICANS LAST YEAR.
THEY'RE CONSERVATIVES. THEY WANT TO **CONSERVE** THINGS, LIKE **TREES**.
THIS WOULDN'T CONCERN ME IF YOU WERE TAKING CARE OF BUSINESS. THIS PAVLOV. HE'S RUINING EVERYTHING. WE CAN'T HAVE HIM RUNNING AROUND SLAUGHTERING ANIMALS.
I'VE TOLERATED YOUR ECCENTRICITIES ALL THESE YEARS BECAUSE YOU GOT THE JOB DONE. BUT NO ONE IS IRREPLACEABLE.
I'LL TAKE CARE OF IT.
I UNDERSTAND, MY LORD RATHKROGEN.
THAT'S ALL.
MAY I LEAVE?
GO.
DO I HAVE TO TAKE THE BOAT?

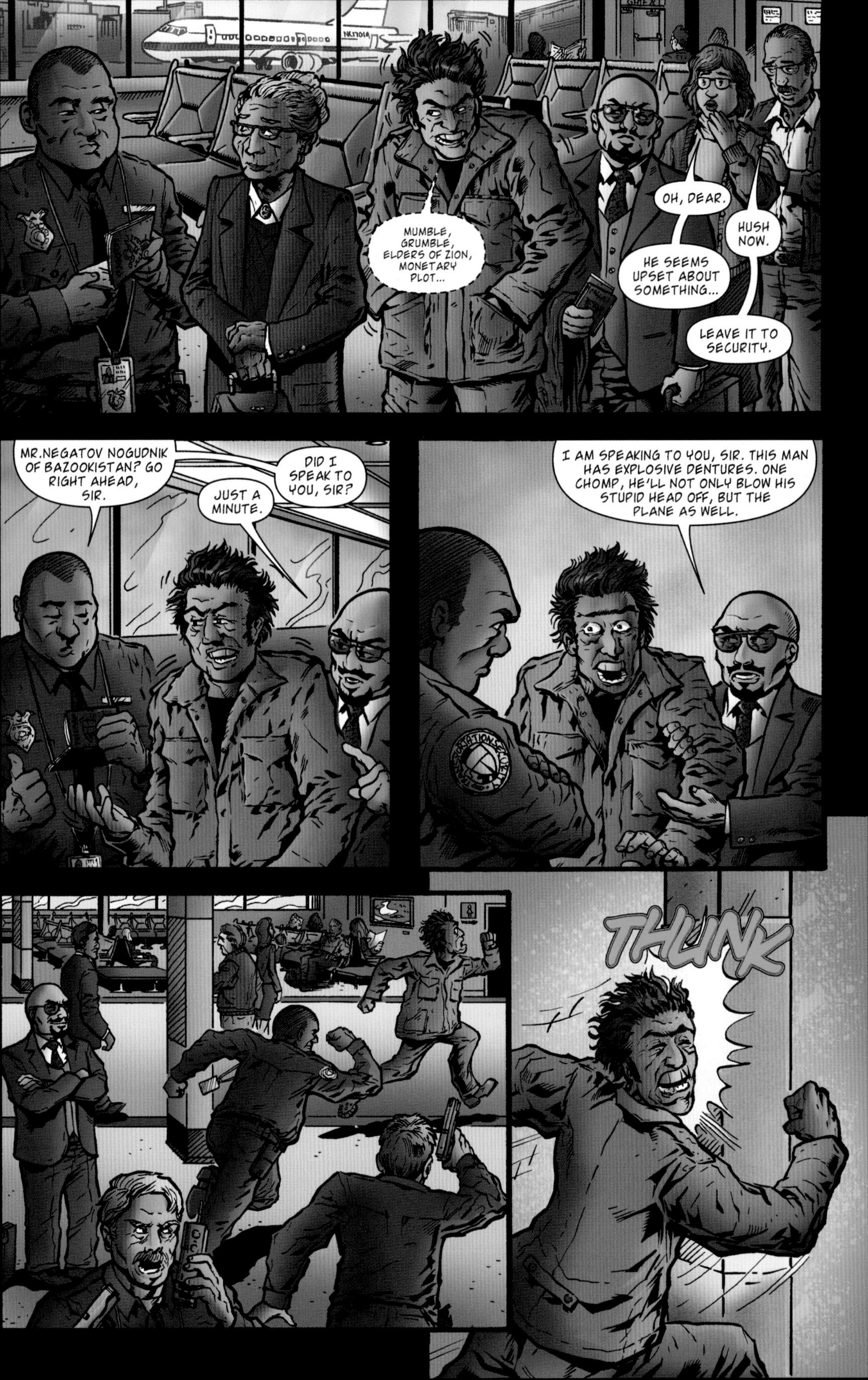
MUMBLE, GRUMBLE, ELDERS OF ZION, MONETARY PLOT...
OH, DEAR.
HE SEEMS UPSET ABOUT SOMETHING...
HUSH NOW.
LEAVE IT TO SECURITY.
MR.NEGATOV NOGUDNIK OF BAZOOKISTAN? GO RIGHT AHEAD, SIR.
JUST A MINUTE.
DID I SPEAK TO YOU, SIR?
I AM SPEAKING TO YOU, SIR. THIS MAN HAS EXPLOSIVE DENTURES. ONE CHOMP, HE'LL NOT ONLY BLOW HIS STUPID HEAD OFF, BUT THE PLANE AS WELL.
THUNK

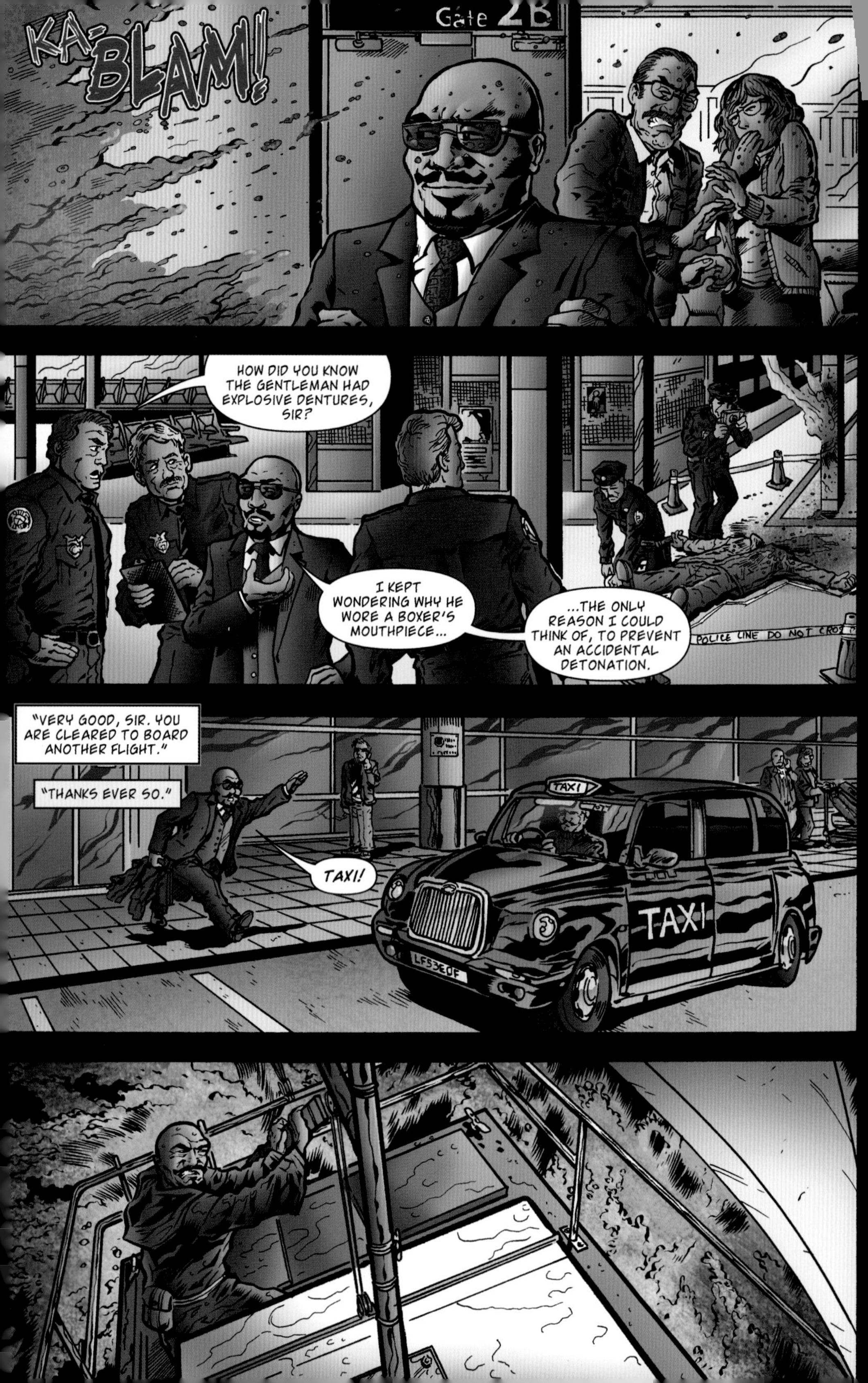
KA-BLAM!
Gate 2B
HOW DID YOU KNOW THE GENTLEMAN HAD EXPLOSIVE DENTURES, SIR?
I KEPT WONDERING WHY HE WORE A BOXER'S MOUTHPIECE...
...THE ONLY REASON I COULD THINK OF, TO PREVENT AN ACCIDENTAL DETONATION.
"VERY GOOD, SIR. YOU ARE CLEARED TO BOARD ANOTHER FLIGHT."
"THANKS EVER SO."
TAXI!
TAXI
TAXI
LF53EOF

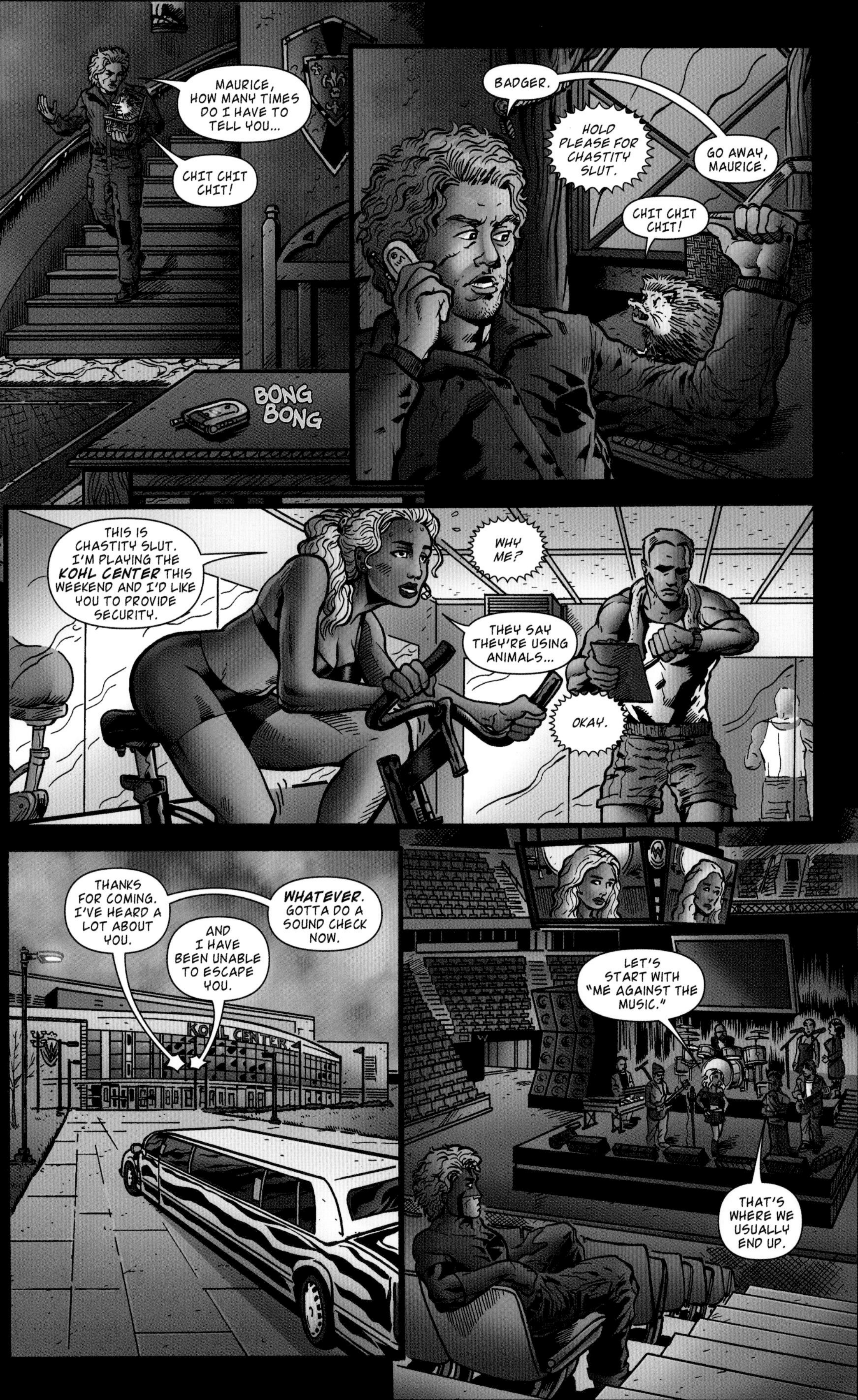
MAURICE, HOW MANY TIMES DO I HAVE TO TELL YOU...
CHIT CHIT CHIT!
BONG BONG
BADGER.
HOLD PLEASE FOR CHASTITY SLUT.
GO AWAY, MAURICE.
CHIT CHIT CHIT!
THIS IS CHASTITY SLUT. I'M PLAYING THE KOHL CENTER THIS WEEKEND AND I'D LIKE YOU TO PROVIDE SECURITY.
WHY ME?
THEY SAY THEY'RE USING ANIMALS...
OKAY.
THANKS FOR COMING. I'VE HEARD A LOT ABOUT YOU.
AND I HAVE BEEN UNABLE TO ESCAPE YOU.
WHATEVER. GOTTA DO A SOUND CHECK NOW.
KOHL CENTER
LET'S START WITH "ME AGAINST THE MUSIC."
THAT'S WHERE WE USUALLY END UP.

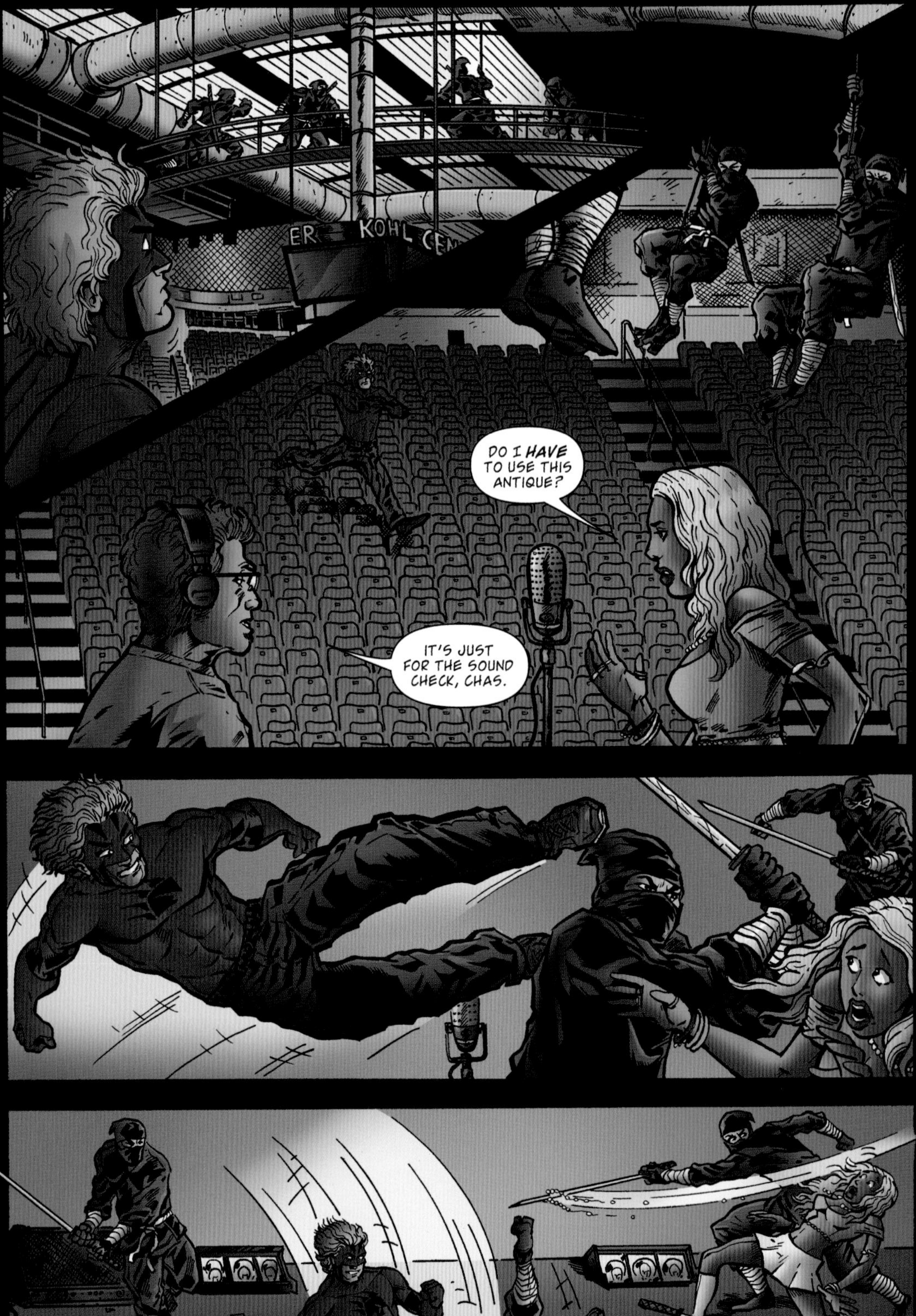
ER KOHL CEN
DO I *HAVE* TO USE THIS ANTIQUE?
IT'S JUST FOR THE SOUND CHECK, CHAS.
WHAM

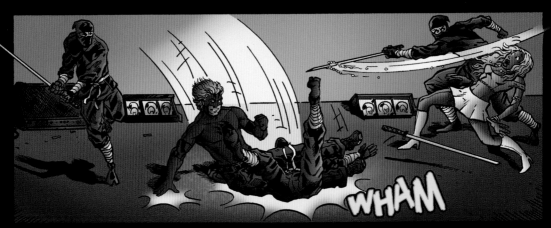

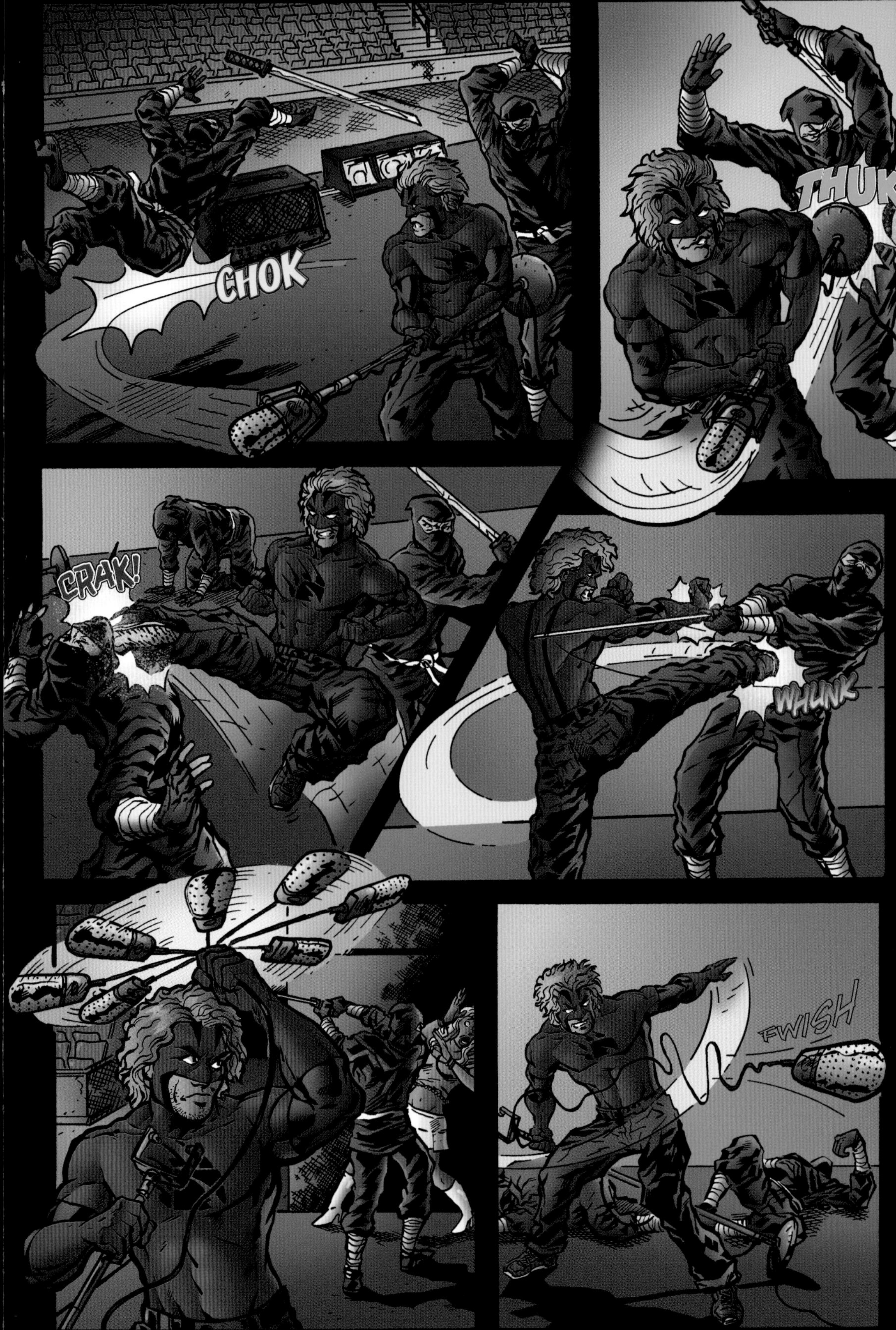
CHOK
THUK
CRAK!
WHUNK
FWISH

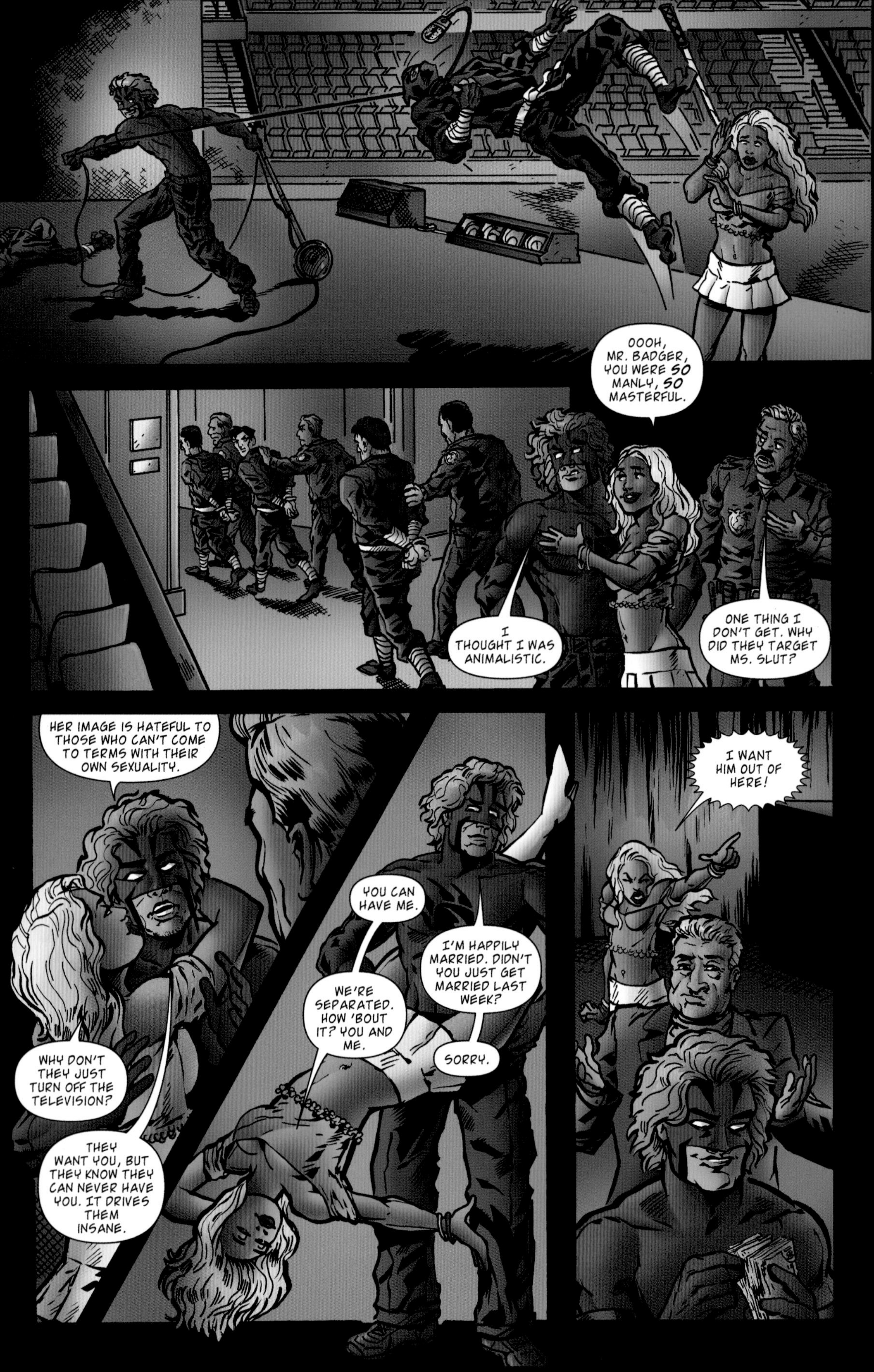
OOOH, MR. BADGER, YOU WERE SO MANLY, SO MASTERFUL.
I THOUGHT I WAS ANIMALISTIC.
ONE THING I DON'T GET. WHY DID THEY TARGET MS. SLUT?
HER IMAGE IS HATEFUL TO THOSE WHO CAN'T COME TO TERMS WITH THEIR OWN SEXUALITY.
WHY DON'T THEY JUST TURN OFF THE TELEVISION?
THEY WANT YOU, BUT THEY KNOW THEY CAN NEVER HAVE YOU. IT DRIVES THEM INSANE.
YOU CAN HAVE ME.
I'M HAPPILY MARRIED. DIDN'T YOU JUST GET MARRIED LAST WEEK?
WE'RE SEPARATED. HOW 'BOUT IT? YOU AND ME.
SORRY.
I WANT HIM OUT OF HERE!

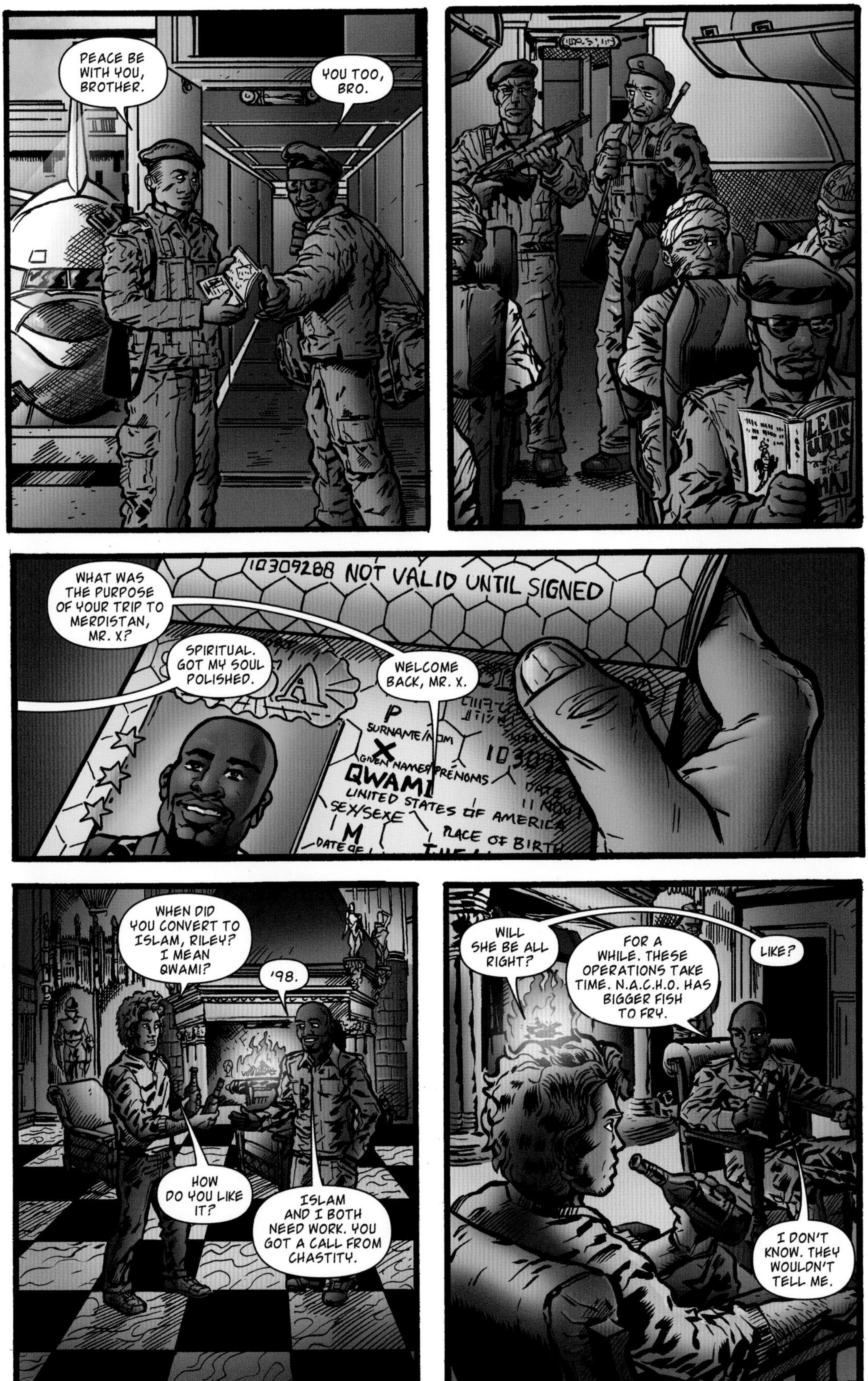
PEACE BE WITH YOU, BROTHER.
YOU TOO, BRO.
LEON URIS THE HAJ
10309288 NOT VALID UNTIL SIGNED
WHAT WAS THE PURPOSE OF YOUR TRIP TO MERDISTAN, MR. X?
SPIRITUAL. GOT MY SOUL POLISHED.
WELCOME BACK, MR. X.
SURNAME/NOM
X
GIVEN NAMES/PRENOMS
QWAMI
UNITED STATES OF AMERICA
SEX/SEXE
M
PLACE OF BIRTH
WHEN DID YOU CONVERT TO ISLAM, RILEY? I MEAN QWAMI?
'98.
HOW DO YOU LIKE IT?
ISLAM AND I BOTH NEED WORK. YOU GOT A CALL FROM CHASTITY.
WILL SHE BE ALL RIGHT?
FOR A WHILE. THESE OPERATIONS TAKE TIME. N.A.C.H.O. HAS BIGGER FISH TO FRY.
LIKE?
I DON'T KNOW. THEY WOULDN'T TELL ME.

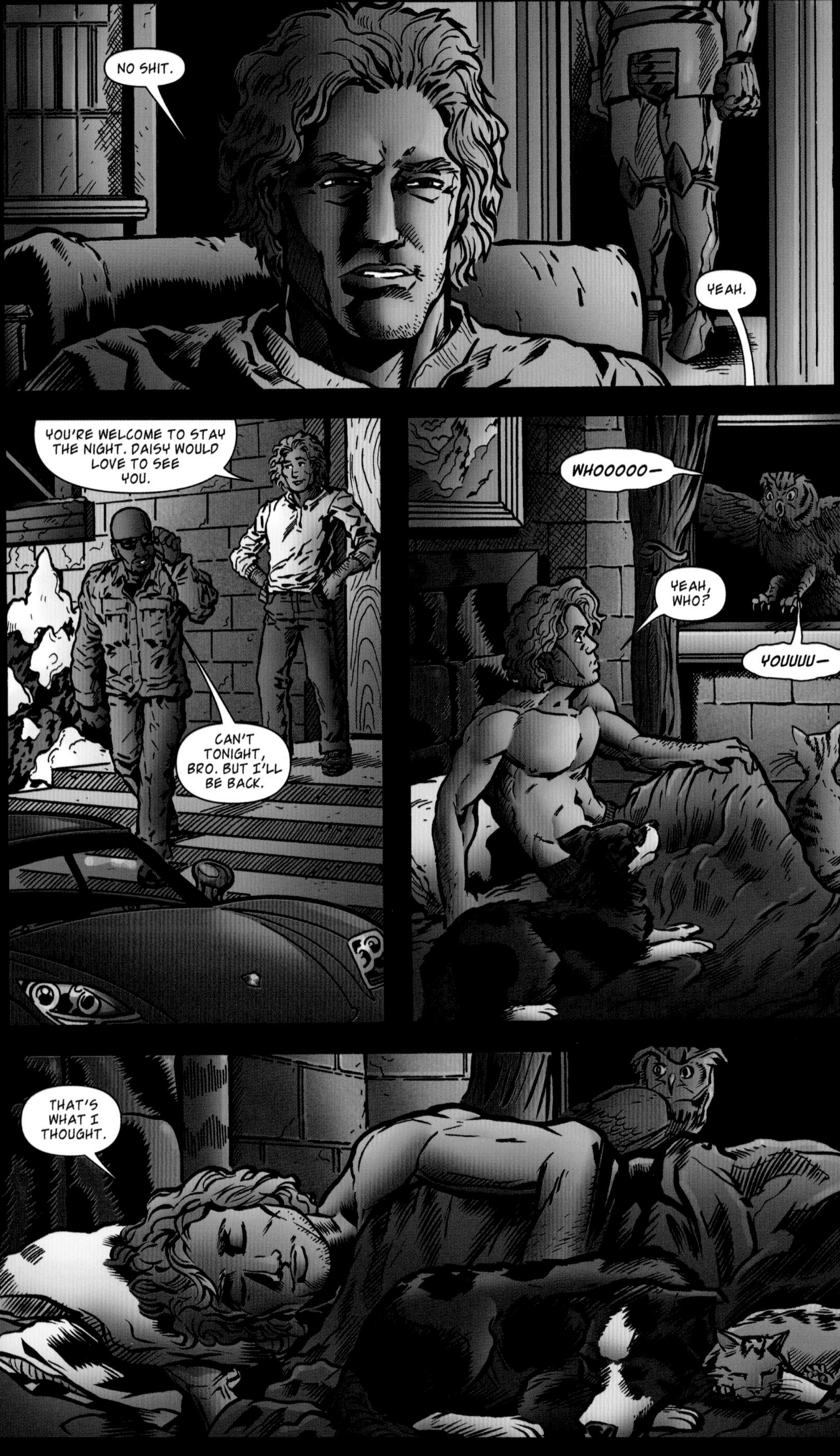
NO SHIT.
YEAH.
YOU'RE WELCOME TO STAY THE NIGHT. DAISY WOULD LOVE TO SEE YOU.
CAN'T TONIGHT, BRO. BUT I'LL BE BACK.
WHOOOOO–
YEAH, WHO?
YOUUUU–
THAT'S WHAT I THOUGHT.

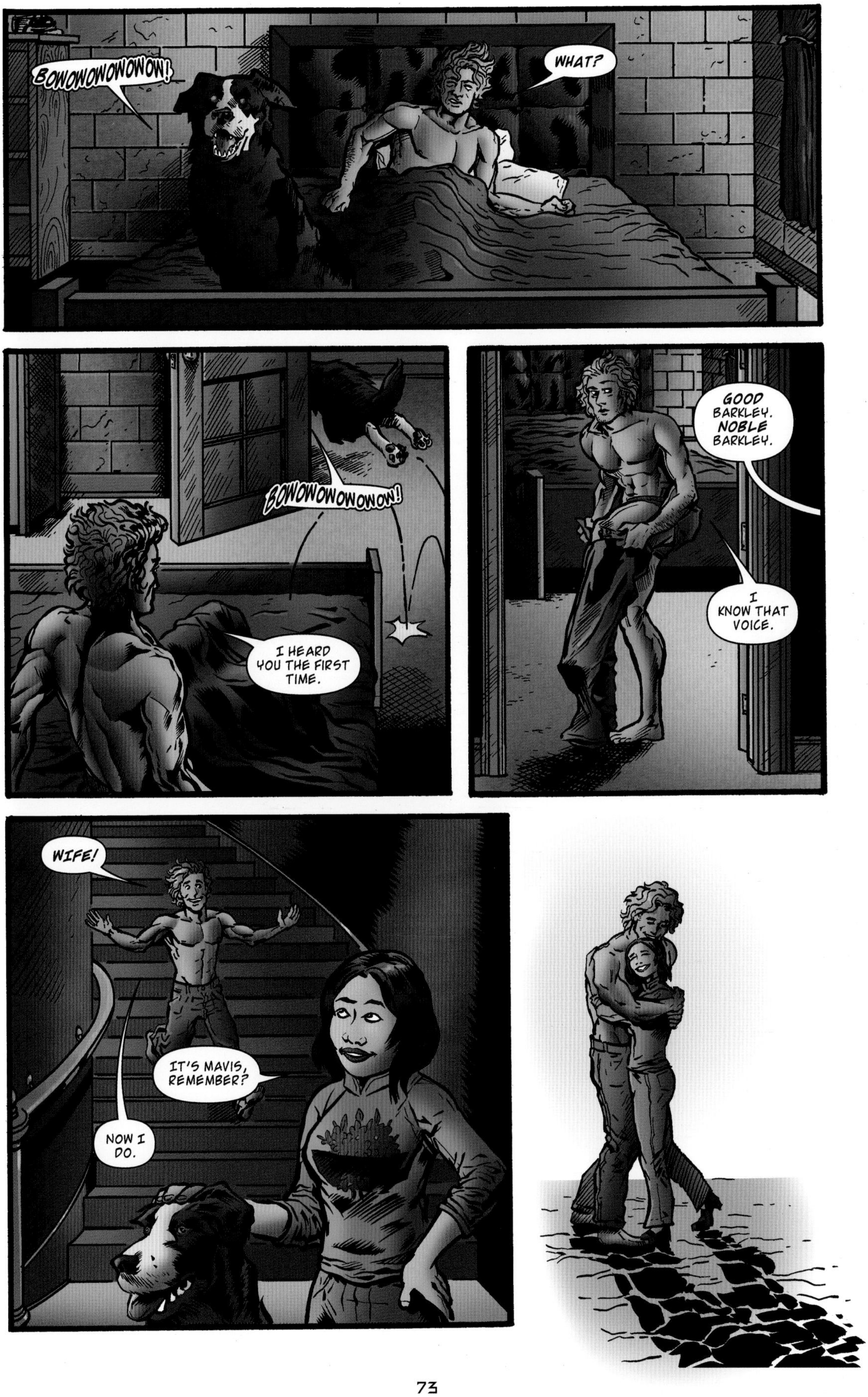
BOWOWOWOWOWOW!
WHAT?
BOWOWOWOWOWOW!
I HEARD YOU THE FIRST TIME.
GOOD BARKLEY. NOBLE BARKLEY.
I KNOW THAT VOICE.
WIFE!
IT'S MAVIS, REMEMBER?
NOW I DO.

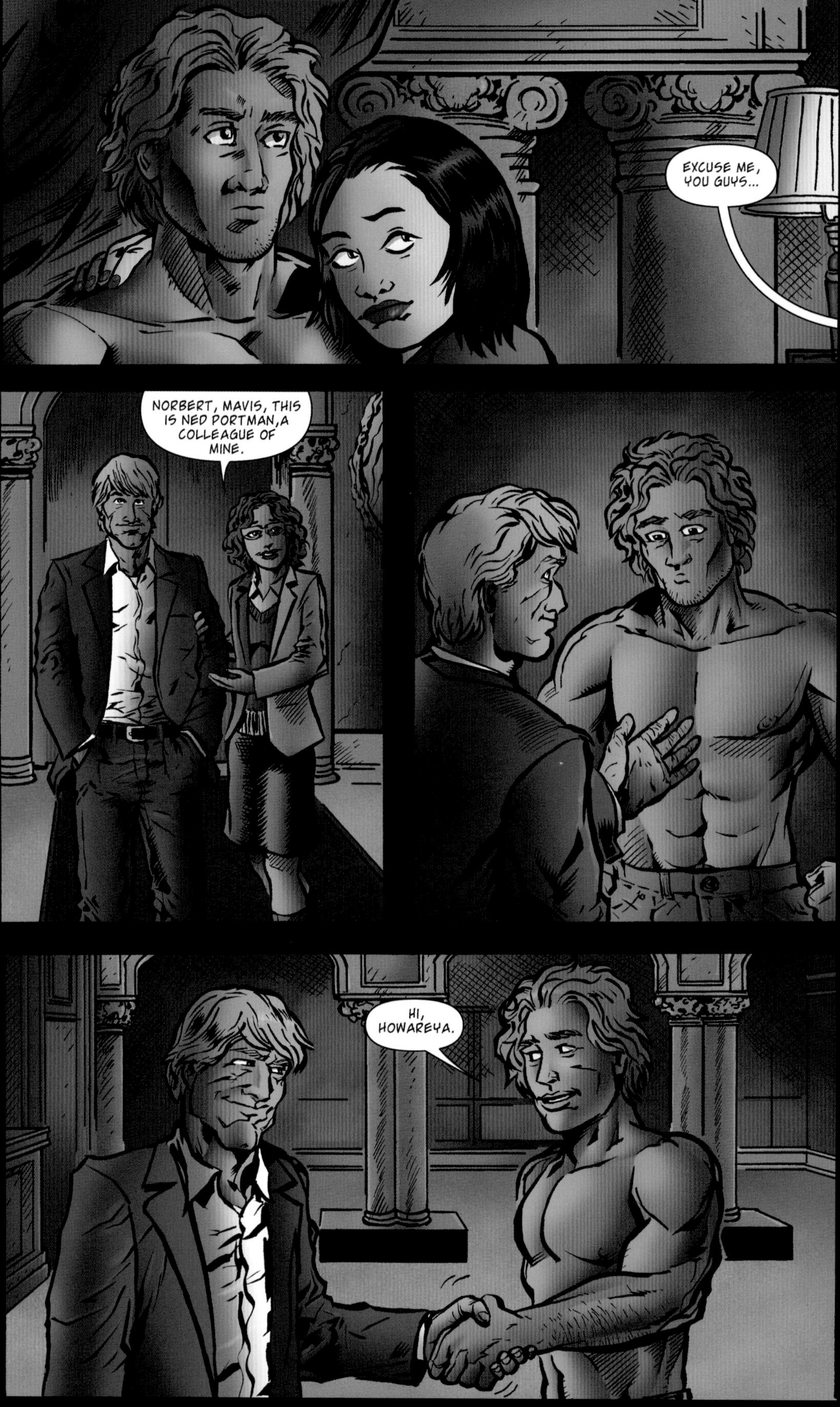
EXCUSE ME, YOU GUYS...
NORBERT, MAVIS, THIS IS NED PORTMAN, A COLLEAGUE OF MINE.
HI, HOWAREYA.

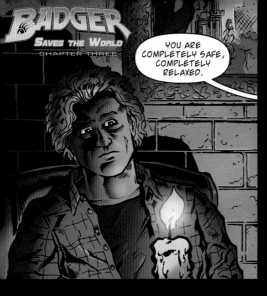

BADGER SAVES THE WORLD
CHAPTER THREE

YOU ARE COMPLETELY SAFE, COMPLETELY RELAXED.

TELL ME ABOUT THE BADGER, NORBERT.

T. TAXUS?

HER NAME IS MYRTLE. SHE FIRST APPEARED TO ME DURING THE GULF WAR...

I THINK SO.

AH.

NORBERT, MYRTLE COULD NOT HAVE BEEN A NORTH AMERICAN BADGER. SHE COULD ONLY HAVE BEEN A *HONEY BADGER.*

WHAT DOES THAT MEAN?

YOU MUST GO TO AFRICA AND FIND OUT.

I'LL BE BACK AS SOON AS I FIGURE OUT WHO I AM.

IF NOT BACK IN TWO WEEKS, I COME LOOKING FOR YOU.

OH NED, THIS IS ALL HAPPENING SO *FAST*...

YOU WANT HIM TO GET *WELL*, DON'T YOU?

OF COURSE.

THEN TRUST ME.

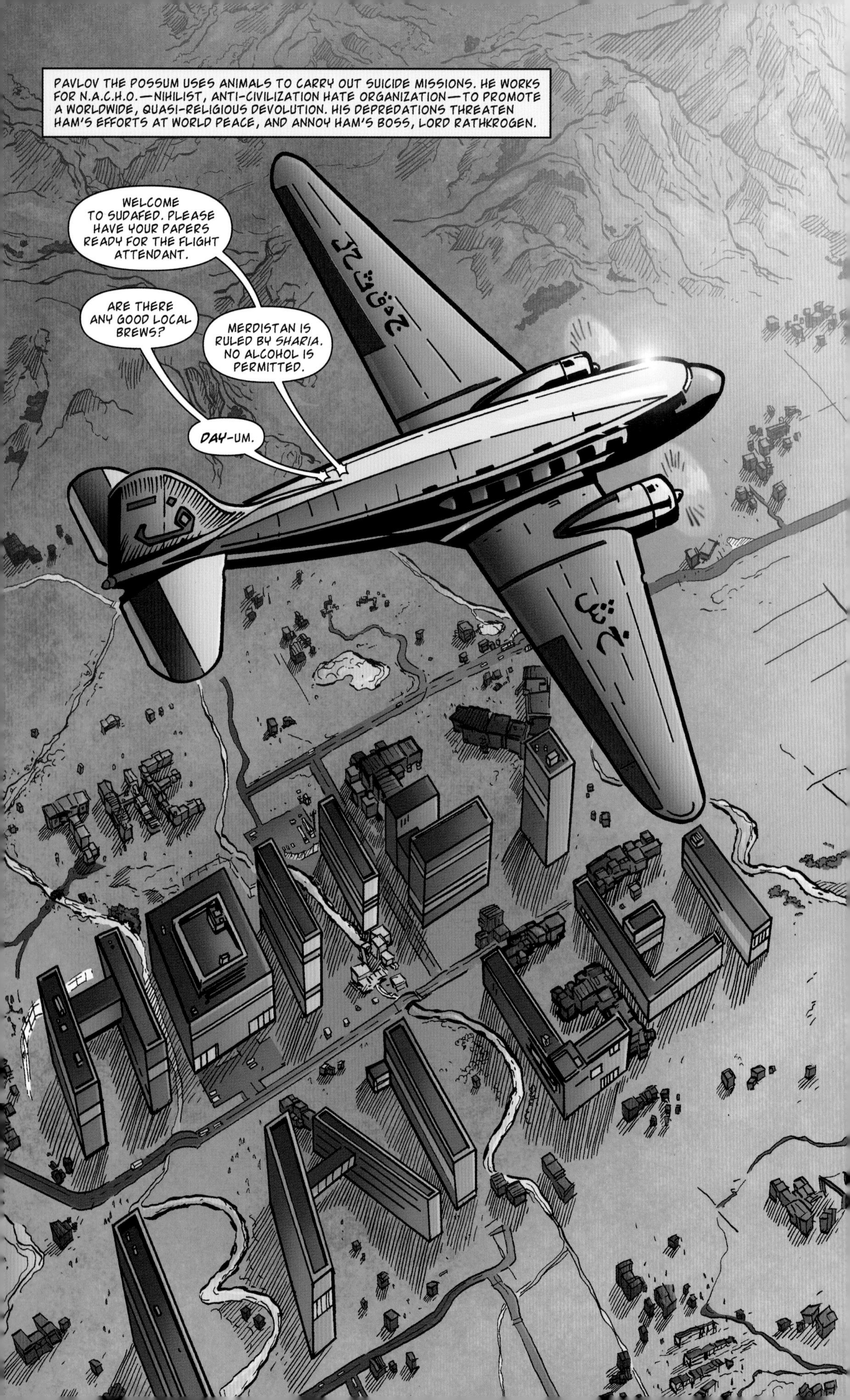
PAVLOV THE POSSUM USES ANIMALS TO CARRY OUT SUICIDE MISSIONS. HE WORKS FOR N.A.C.H.O.—NIHILIST, ANTI-CIVILIZATION HATE ORGANIZATION—TO PROMOTE A WORLDWIDE, QUASI-RELIGIOUS DEVOLUTION. HIS DEPREDATIONS THREATEN HAM'S EFFORTS AT WORLD PEACE, AND ANNOY HAM'S BOSS, LORD RATHKROGEN.
WELCOME TO SUDAFED. PLEASE HAVE YOUR PAPERS READY FOR THE FLIGHT ATTENDANT.
ARE THERE ANY GOOD LOCAL BREWS?
MERDISTAN IS RULED BY *SHARIA*. NO ALCOHOL IS PERMITTED.
***DAY*-UM.**

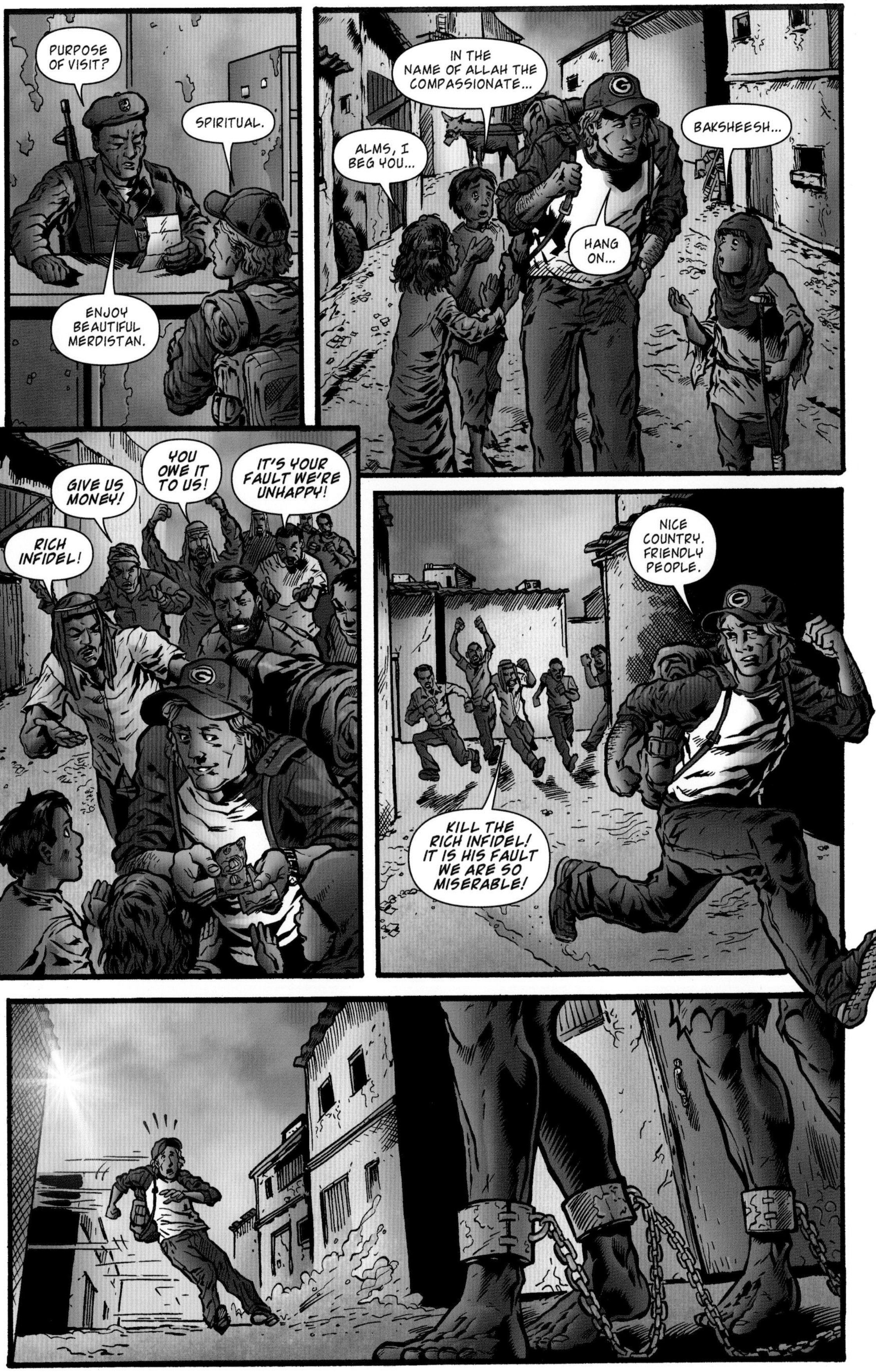
PURPOSE OF VISIT?
SPIRITUAL.
ENJOY BEAUTIFUL MERDISTAN.
IN THE NAME OF ALLAH THE COMPASSIONATE...
ALMS, I BEG YOU...
BAKSHEESH...
HANG ON...
RICH INFIDEL!
GIVE US MONEY!
YOU OWE IT TO US!
IT'S YOUR FAULT WE'RE UNHAPPY!
NICE COUNTRY. FRIENDLY PEOPLE.
KILL THE RICH INFIDEL! IT IS HIS FAULT WE ARE SO MISERABLE!

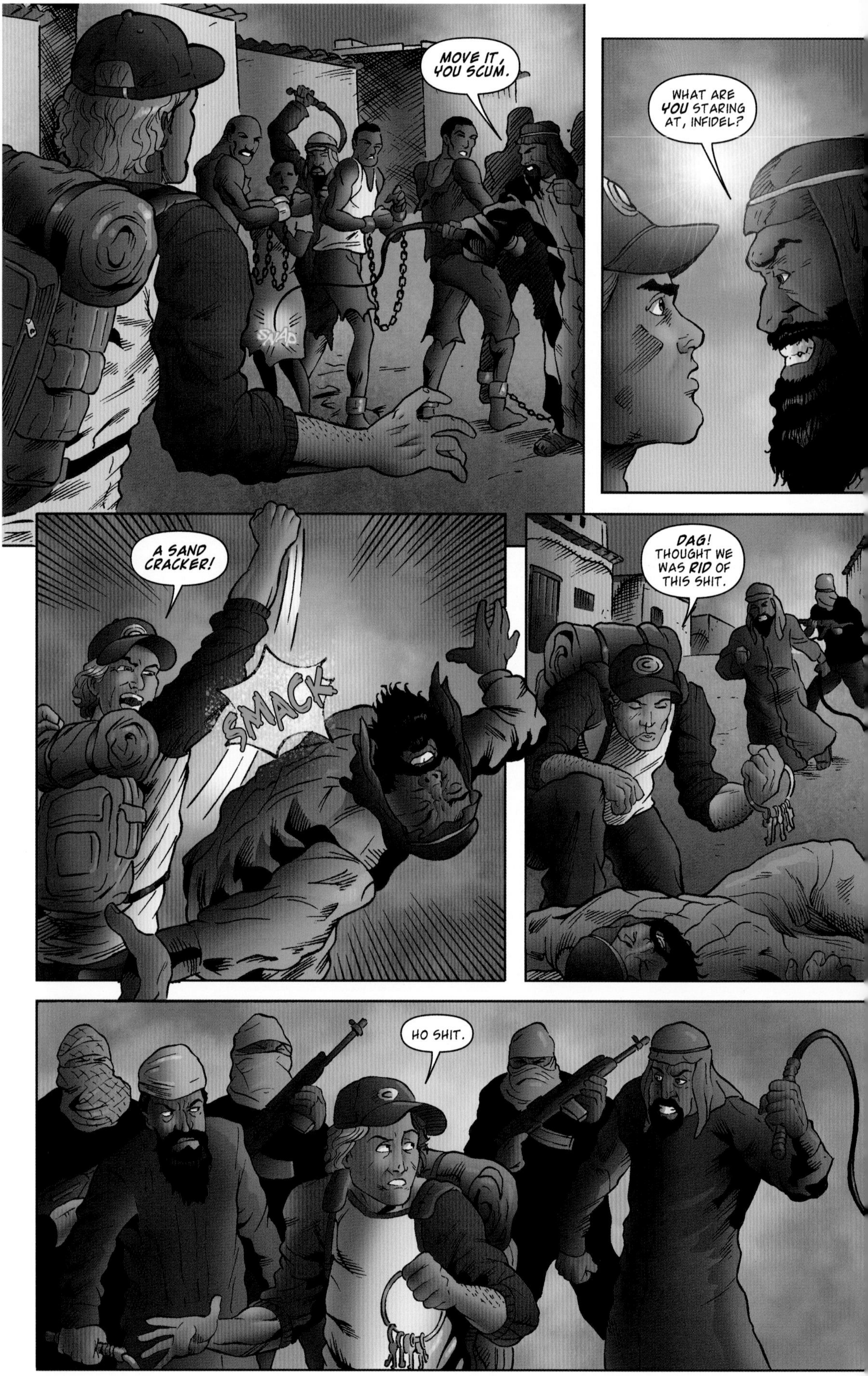
MOVE IT, YOU SCUM.
SWAP
WHAT ARE YOU STARING AT, INFIDEL?
A SAND CRACKER!
SMACK
DAG! THOUGHT WE WAS RID OF THIS SHIT.
HO SHIT.

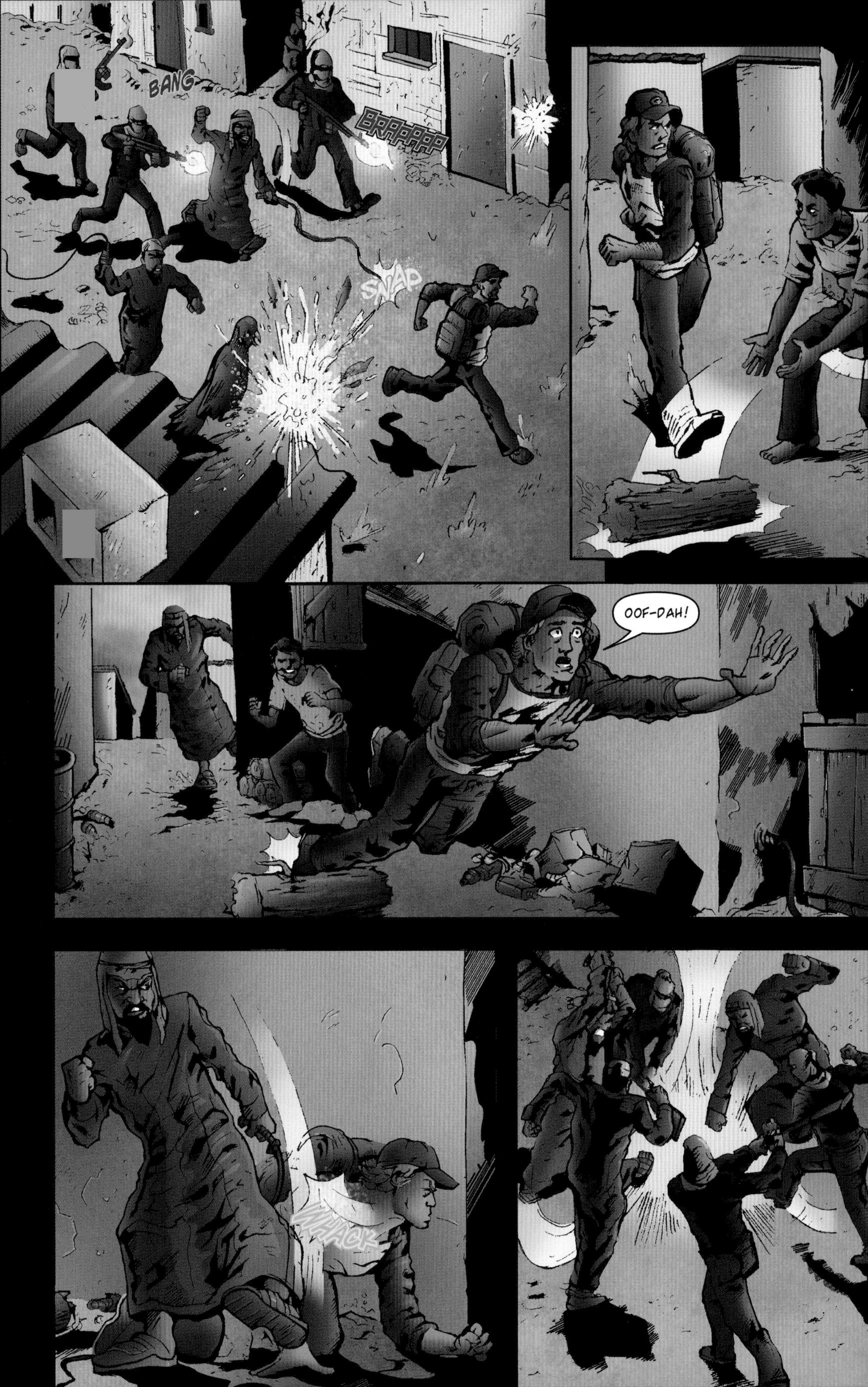
BANG
BRAPPPP
SNAP
OOF-DAH!
WHACK

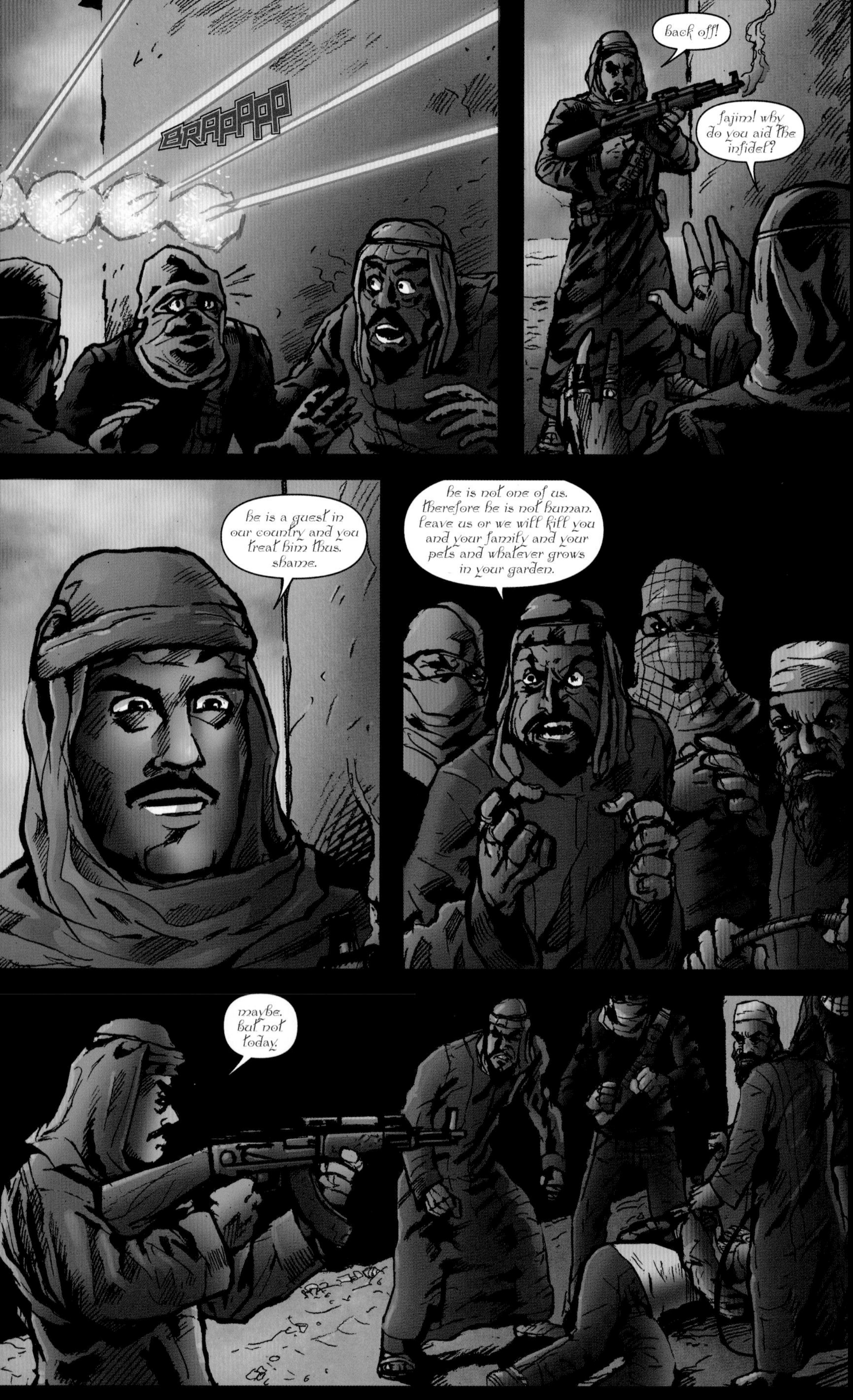
BRAPPPP
back off!
fajim! why do you aid the infidel?
he is a guest in our country and you treat him thus. shame.
he is not one of us. therefore he is not human. leave us or we will kill you and your family and your pets and whatever grows in your garden.
maybe. but not today.

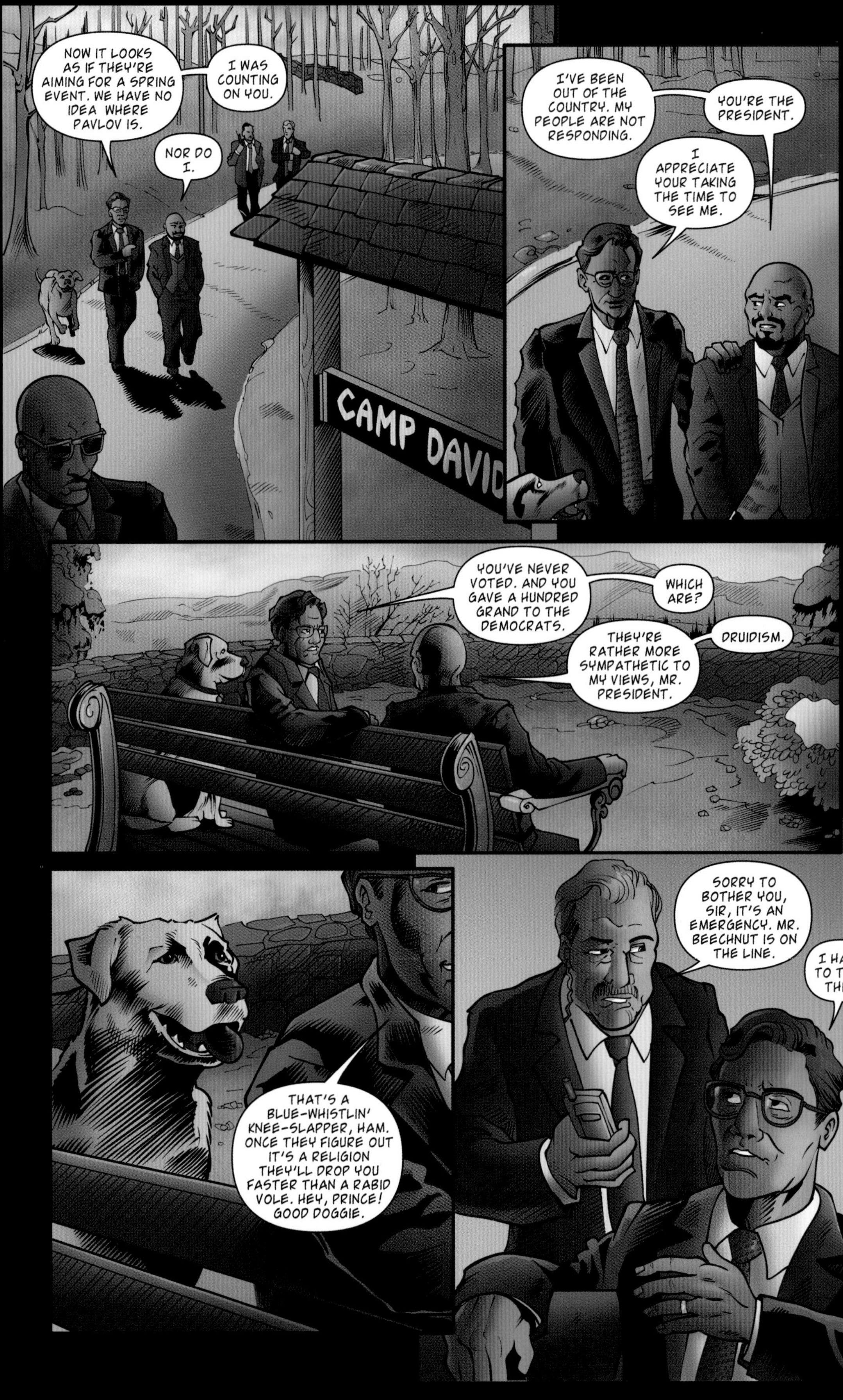
NOW IT LOOKS AS IF THEY'RE AIMING FOR A SPRING EVENT. WE HAVE NO IDEA WHERE PAVLOV IS.
I WAS COUNTING ON YOU.
NOR DO I.
CAMP DAVID
I'VE BEEN OUT OF THE COUNTRY. MY PEOPLE ARE NOT RESPONDING.
YOU'RE THE PRESIDENT.
I APPRECIATE YOUR TAKING THE TIME TO SEE ME.
YOU'VE NEVER VOTED. AND YOU GAVE A HUNDRED GRAND TO THE DEMOCRATS.
WHICH ARE?
THEY'RE RATHER MORE SYMPATHETIC TO MY VIEWS, MR. PRESIDENT.
DRUIDISM.
THAT'S A BLUE-WHISTLIN' KNEE-SLAPPER, HAM. ONCE THEY FIGURE OUT IT'S A RELIGION THEY'LL DROP YOU FASTER THAN A RABID VOLE. HEY, PRINCE! GOOD DOGGIE.
SORRY TO BOTHER YOU, SIR, IT'S AN EMERGENCY. MR. BEECHNUT IS ON THE LINE.
I HAVE TO TAKE THIS.

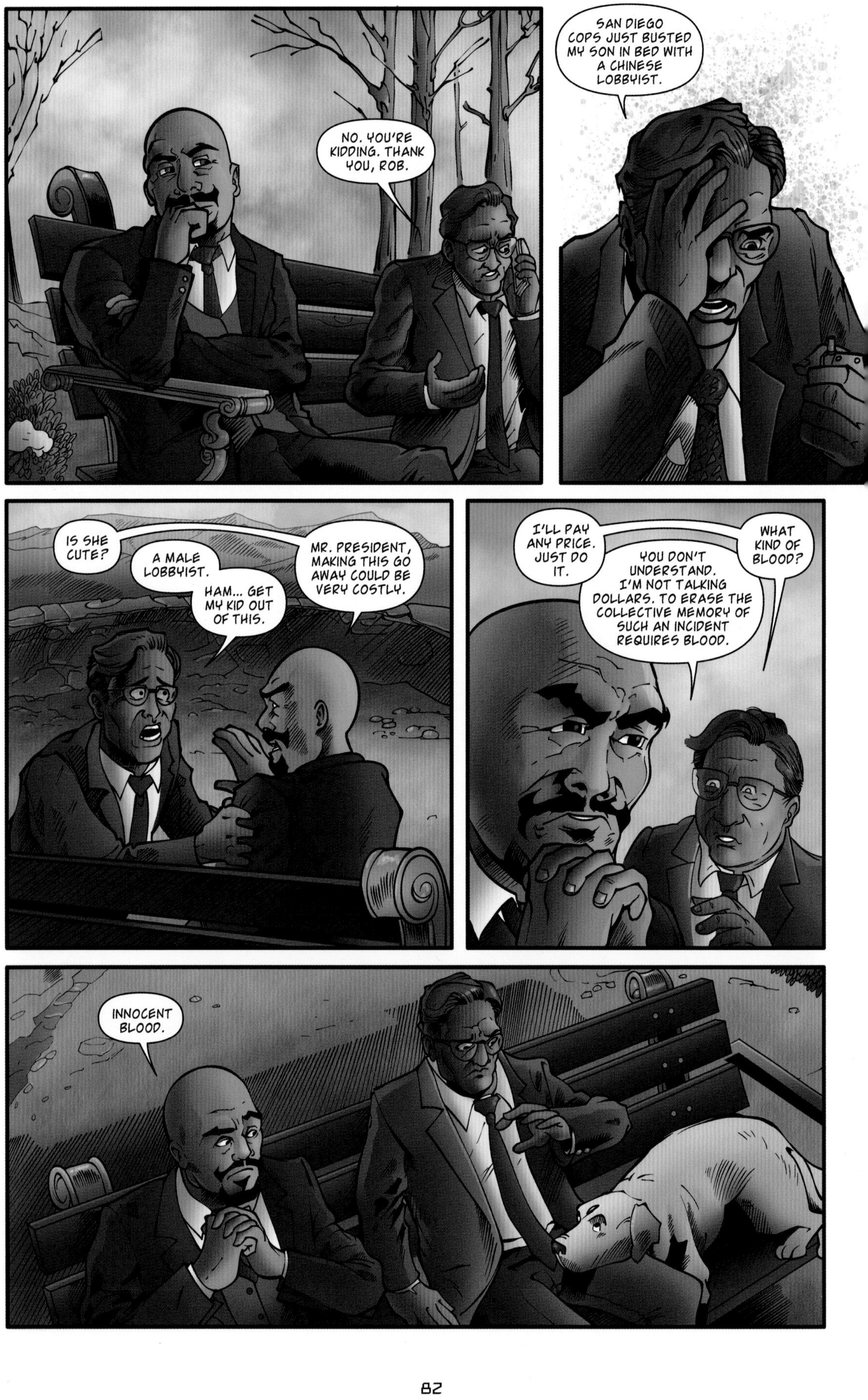
NO. YOU'RE KIDDING. THANK YOU, ROB.
SAN DIEGO COPS JUST BUSTED MY SON IN BED WITH A CHINESE LOBBYIST.
IS SHE CUTE?
A MALE LOBBYIST.
HAM... GET MY KID OUT OF THIS.
MR. PRESIDENT, MAKING THIS GO AWAY COULD BE VERY COSTLY.
I'LL PAY ANY PRICE. JUST DO IT.
YOU DON'T UNDERSTAND. I'M NOT TALKING DOLLARS. TO ERASE THE COLLECTIVE MEMORY OF SUCH AN INCIDENT REQUIRES BLOOD.
WHAT KIND OF BLOOD?
INNOCENT BLOOD.

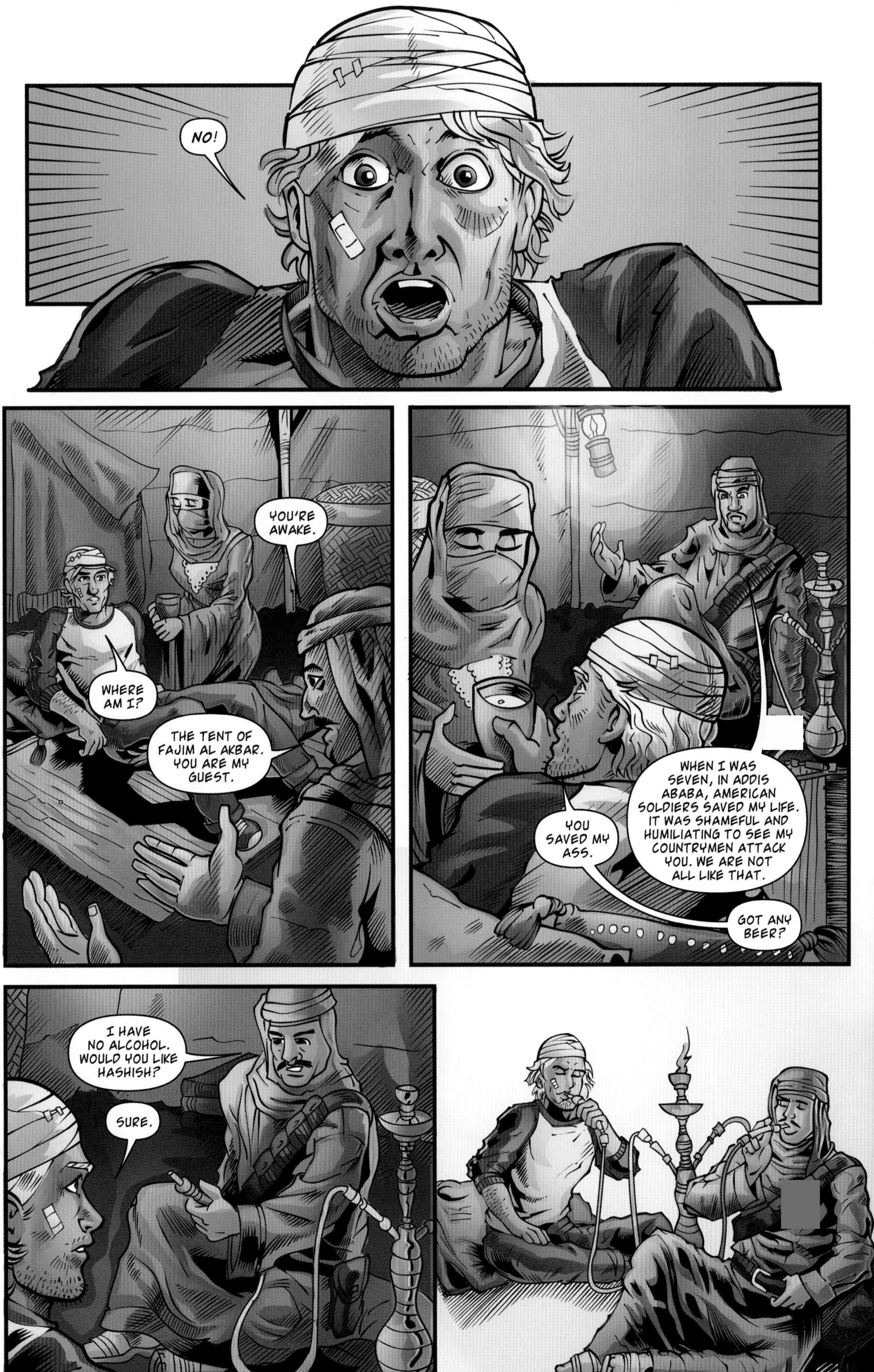
NO!
YOU'RE AWAKE.
WHERE AM I?
THE TENT OF FAJIM AL AKBAR. YOU ARE MY GUEST.
YOU SAVED MY ASS.
WHEN I WAS SEVEN, IN ADDIS ABABA, AMERICAN SOLDIERS SAVED MY LIFE. IT WAS SHAMEFUL AND HUMILIATING TO SEE MY COUNTRYMEN ATTACK YOU. WE ARE NOT ALL LIKE THAT.
GOT ANY BEER?
I HAVE NO ALCOHOL. WOULD YOU LIKE HASHISH?
SURE.

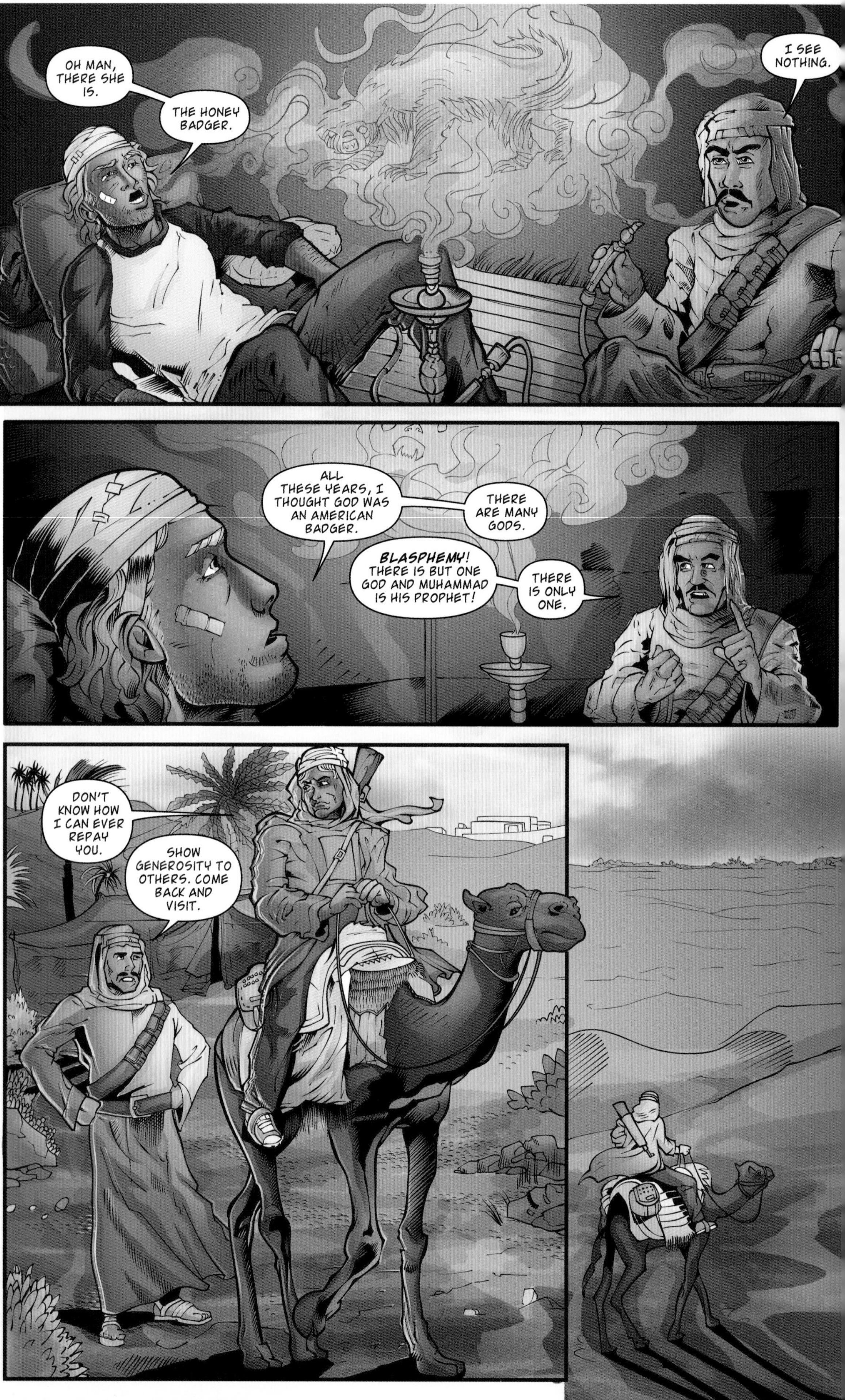
OH MAN, THERE SHE IS.
THE HONEY BADGER.
I SEE NOTHING.
ALL THESE YEARS, I THOUGHT GOD WAS AN AMERICAN BADGER.
THERE ARE MANY GODS.
BLASPHEMY! THERE IS BUT ONE GOD AND MUHAMMAD IS HIS PROPHET!
THERE IS ONLY ONE.
DON'T KNOW HOW I CAN EVER REPAY YOU.
SHOW GENEROSITY TO OTHERS. COME BACK AND VISIT.

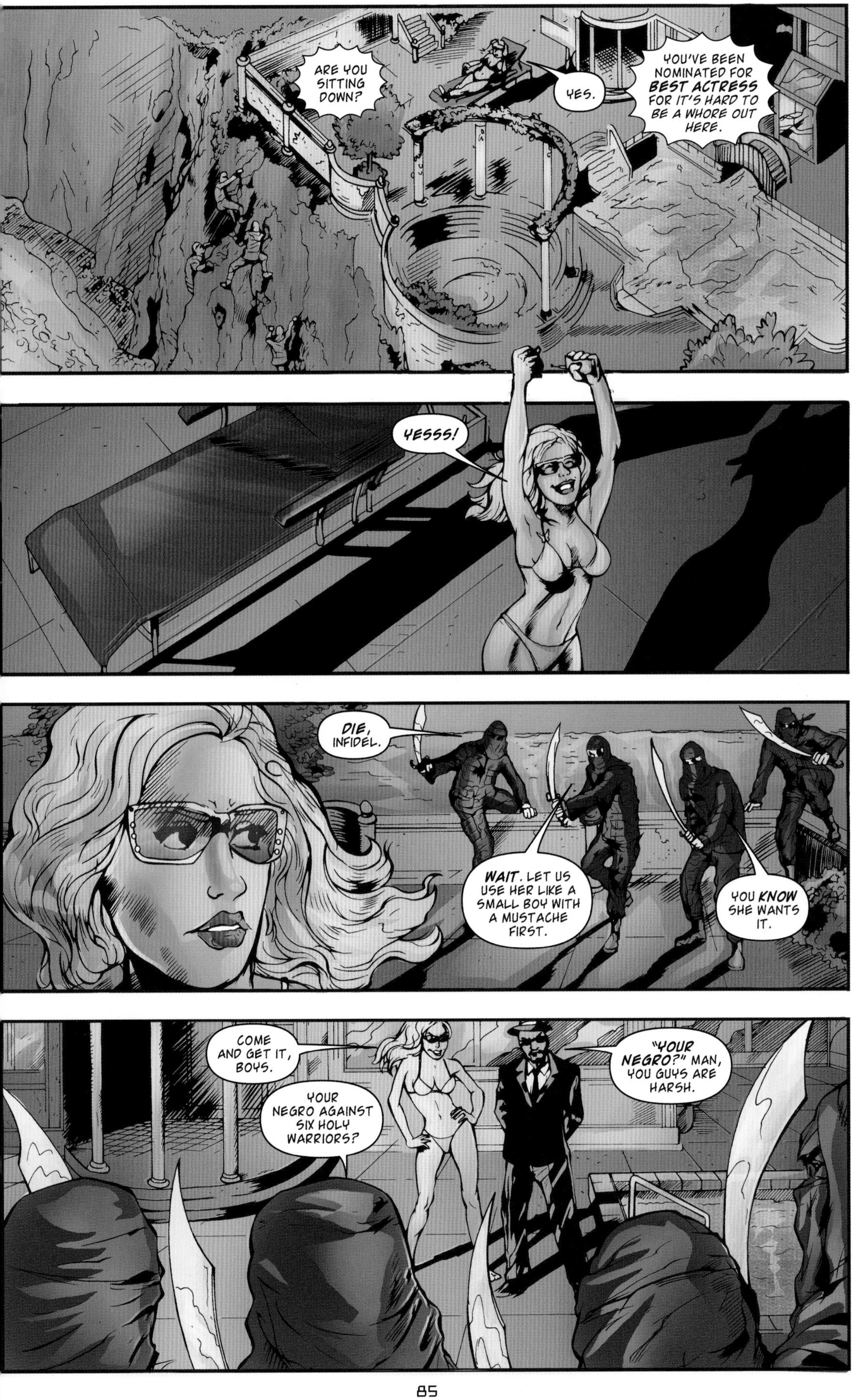
ARE YOU SITTING DOWN?
YES.
YOU'VE BEEN NOMINATED FOR BEST ACTRESS FOR IT'S HARD TO BE A WHORE OUT HERE.
YESSS!
DIE, INFIDEL.
WAIT. LET US USE HER LIKE A SMALL BOY WITH A MUSTACHE FIRST.
YOU KNOW SHE WANTS IT.
COME AND GET IT, BOYS.
YOUR NEGRO AGAINST SIX HOLY WARRIORS?
"YOUR NEGRO?" MAN, YOU GUYS ARE HARSH.

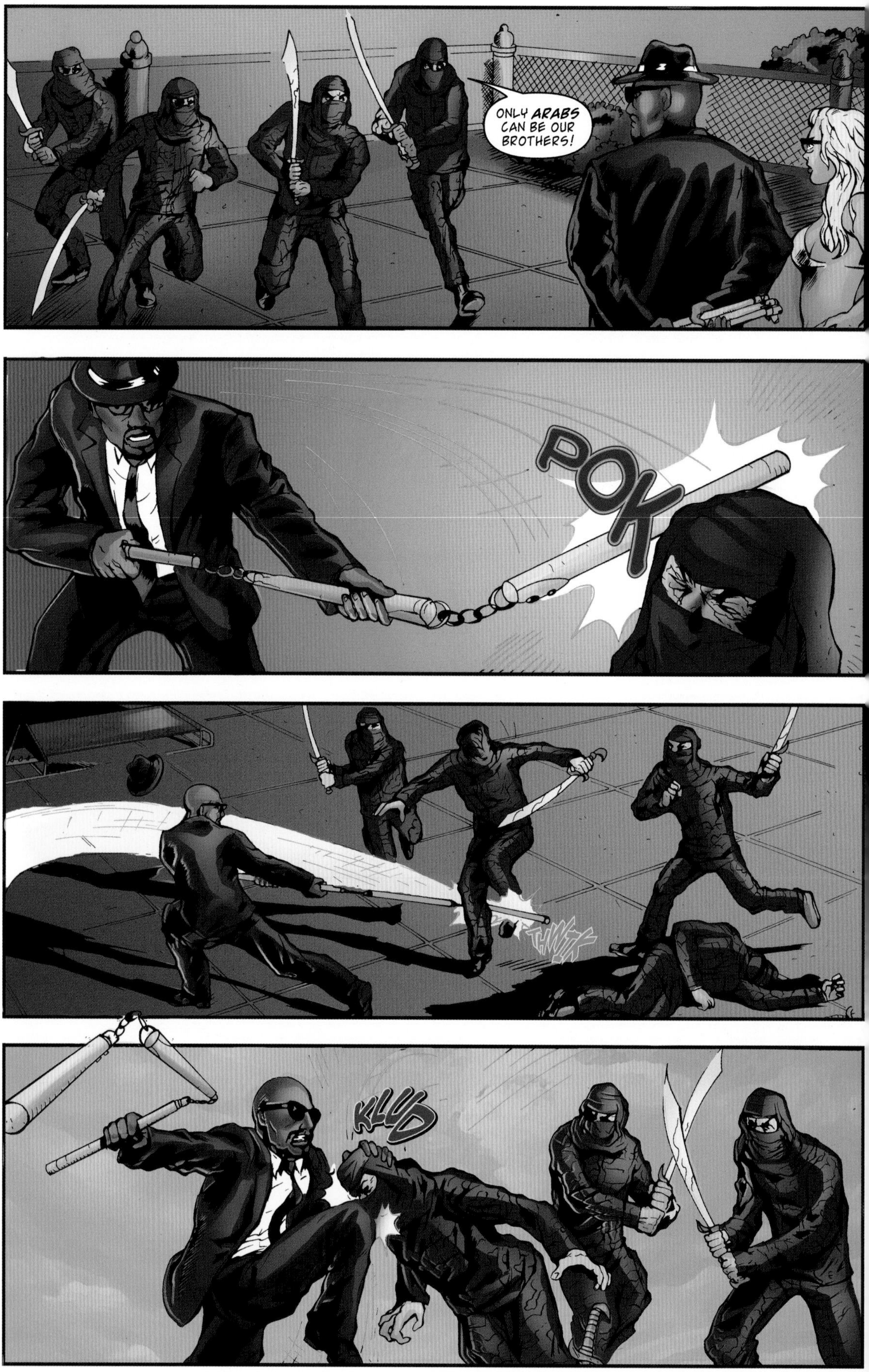
ONLY ARABS CAN BE OUR BROTHERS!
POK
THWIK
KLUD

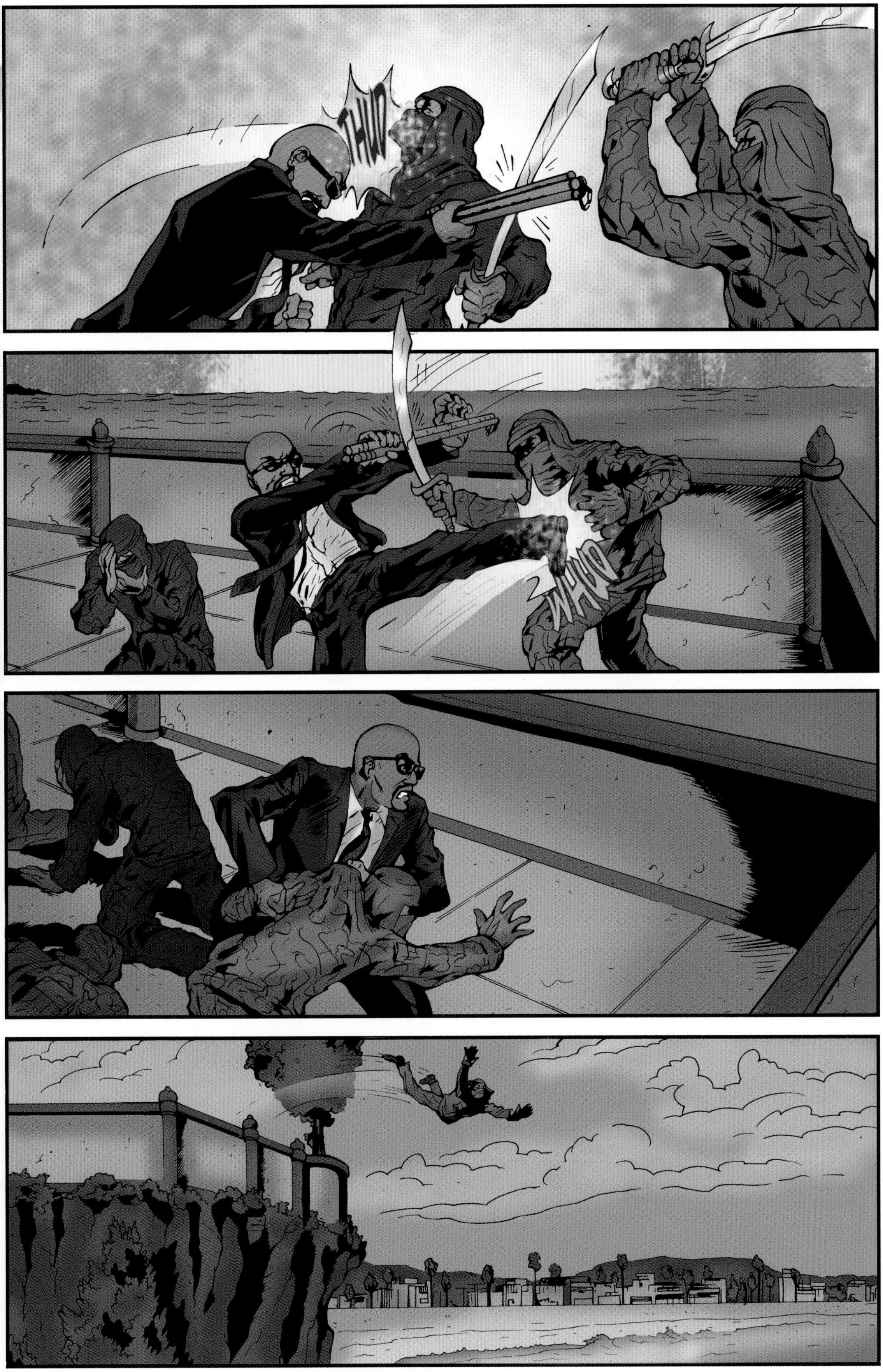
THUD
WHUD

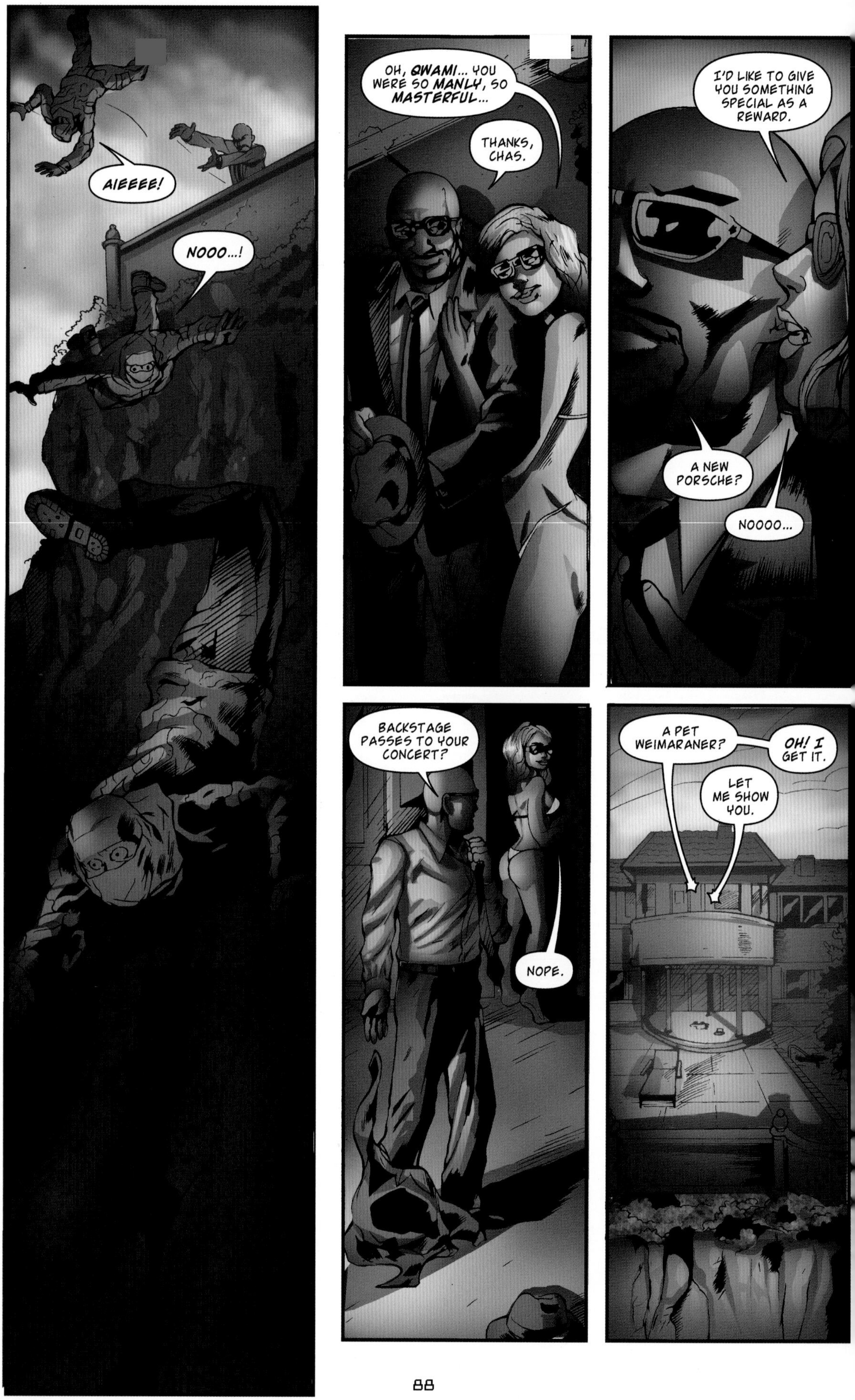
AIEEEE!
NOOO...!
OH, QWAMI... YOU WERE SO MANLY, SO MASTERFUL...
THANKS, CHAS.
I'D LIKE TO GIVE YOU SOMETHING SPECIAL AS A REWARD.
A NEW PORSCHE?
NOOOO...
BACKSTAGE PASSES TO YOUR CONCERT?
NOPE.
A PET WEIMARANER?
OH! I GET IT.
LET ME SHOW YOU.

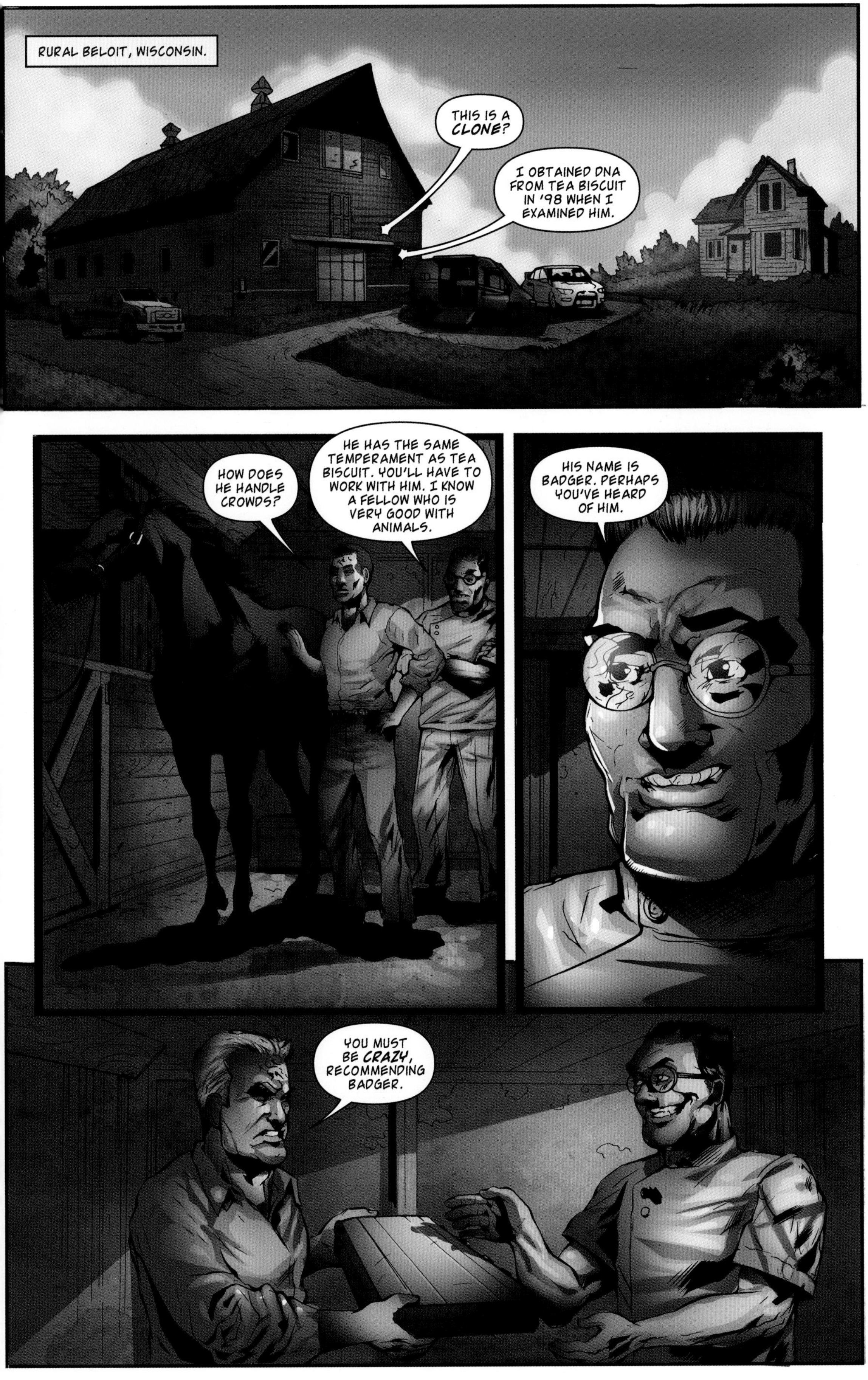
RURAL BELOIT, WISCONSIN.
THIS IS A CLONE?
I OBTAINED DNA FROM TEA BISCUIT IN '98 WHEN I EXAMINED HIM.
HOW DOES HE HANDLE CROWDS?
HE HAS THE SAME TEMPERAMENT AS TEA BISCUIT. YOU'LL HAVE TO WORK WITH HIM. I KNOW A FELLOW WHO IS VERY GOOD WITH ANIMALS.
HIS NAME IS BADGER. PERHAPS YOU'VE HEARD OF HIM.
YOU MUST BE CRAZY, RECOMMENDING BADGER.

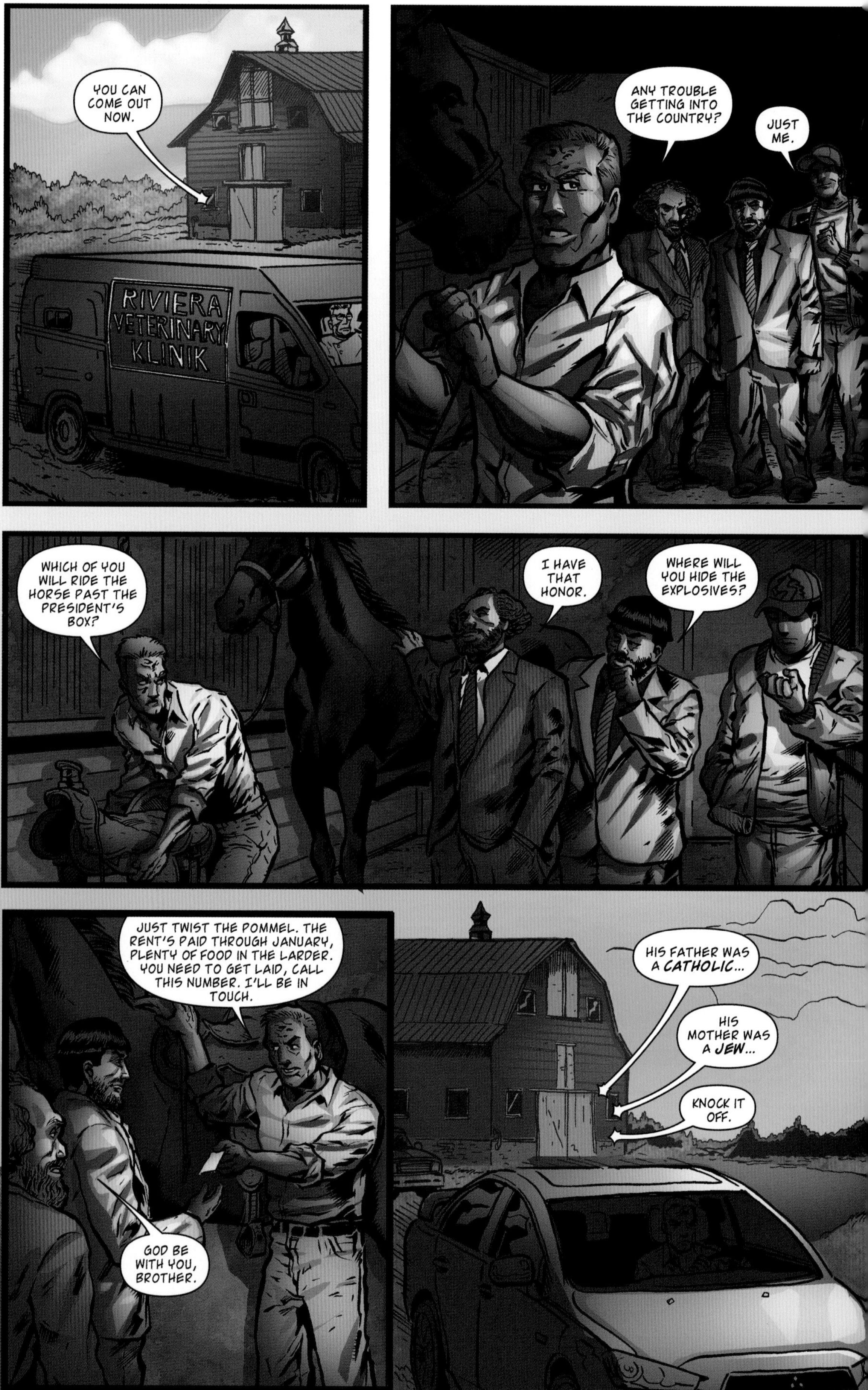
YOU CAN COME OUT NOW.
RIVIERA VETERINARY KLINIK
ANY TROUBLE GETTING INTO THE COUNTRY?
JUST ME.
WHICH OF YOU WILL RIDE THE HORSE PAST THE PRESIDENT'S BOX?
I HAVE THAT HONOR.
WHERE WILL YOU HIDE THE EXPLOSIVES?
JUST TWIST THE POMMEL. THE RENT'S PAID THROUGH JANUARY, PLENTY OF FOOD IN THE LARDER. YOU NEED TO GET LAID, CALL THIS NUMBER. I'LL BE IN TOUCH.
GOD BE WITH YOU, BROTHER.
HIS FATHER WAS A ***CATHOLIC***...
HIS MOTHER WAS A ***JEW***...
KNOCK IT OFF.

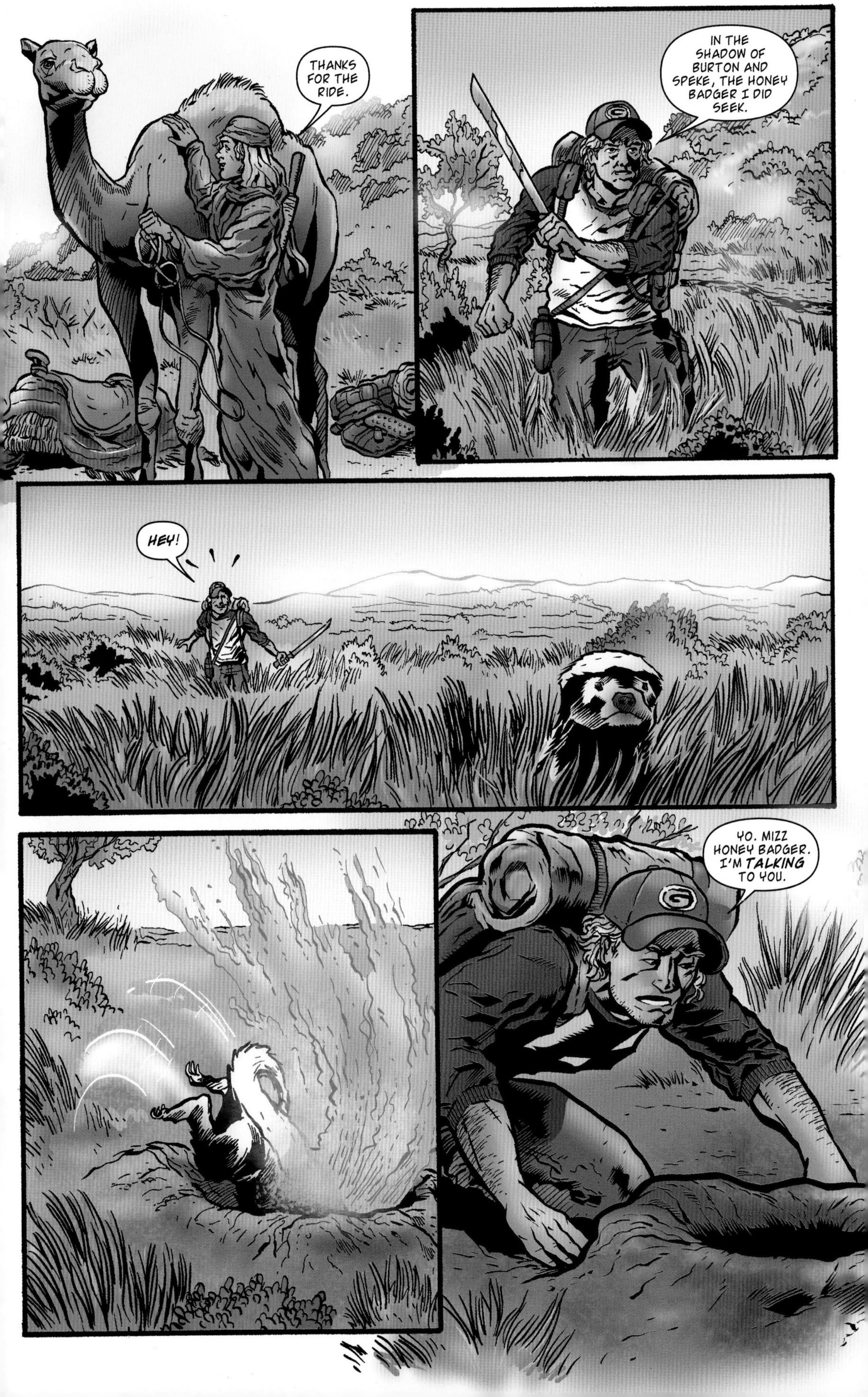
THANKS FOR THE RIDE.
IN THE SHADOW OF BURTON AND SPEKE, THE HONEY BADGER I DID SEEK.
HEY!
YO. MIZZ HONEY BADGER. I'M *TALKING* TO YOU.

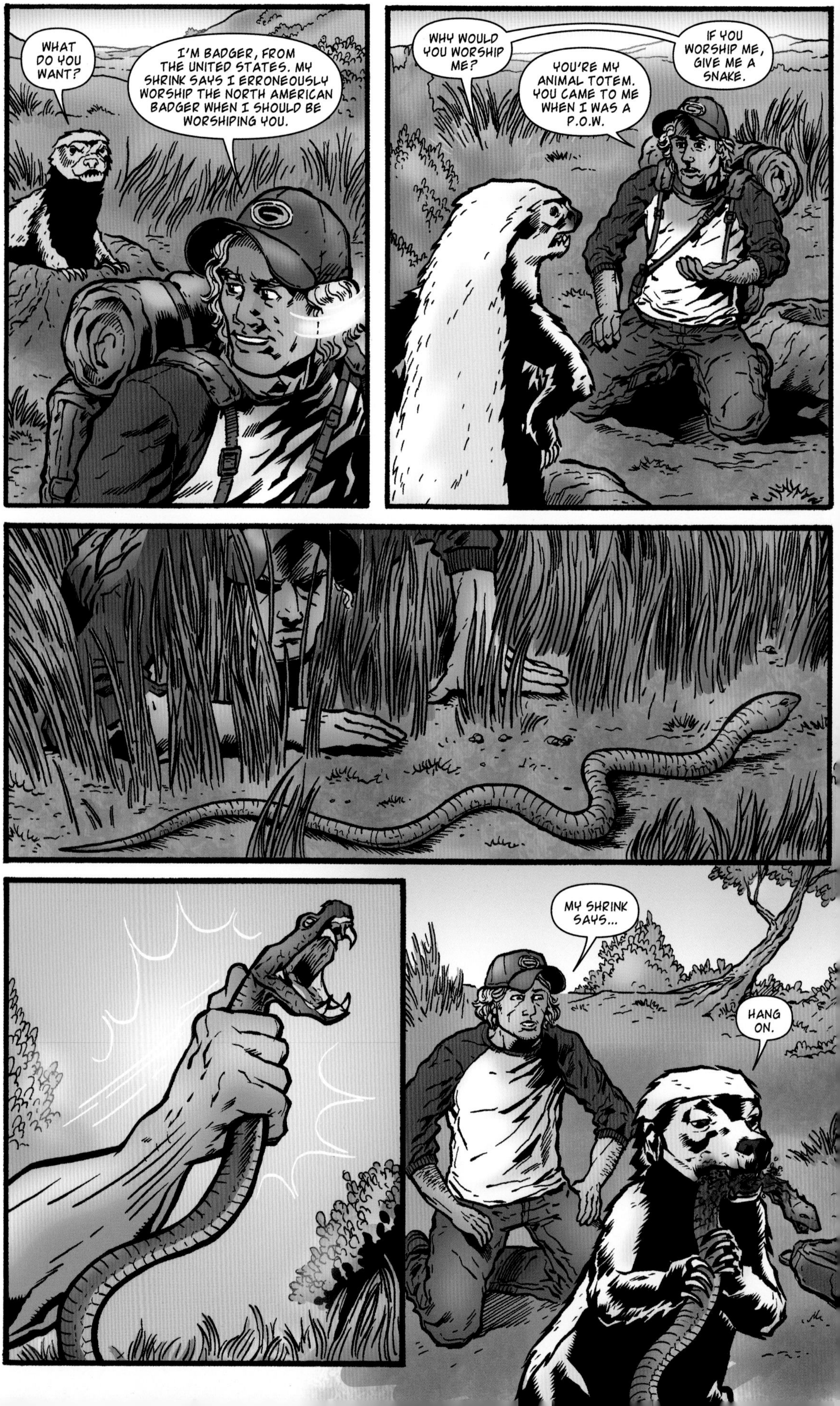
WHAT DO YOU WANT?
I'M BADGER, FROM THE UNITED STATES. MY SHRINK SAYS I ERRONEOUSLY WORSHIP THE NORTH AMERICAN BADGER WHEN I SHOULD BE WORSHIPING YOU.
WHY WOULD YOU WORSHIP ME?
YOU'RE MY ANIMAL TOTEM. YOU CAME TO ME WHEN I WAS A P.O.W.
IF YOU WORSHIP ME, GIVE ME A SNAKE.
MY SHRINK SAYS...
HANG ON.

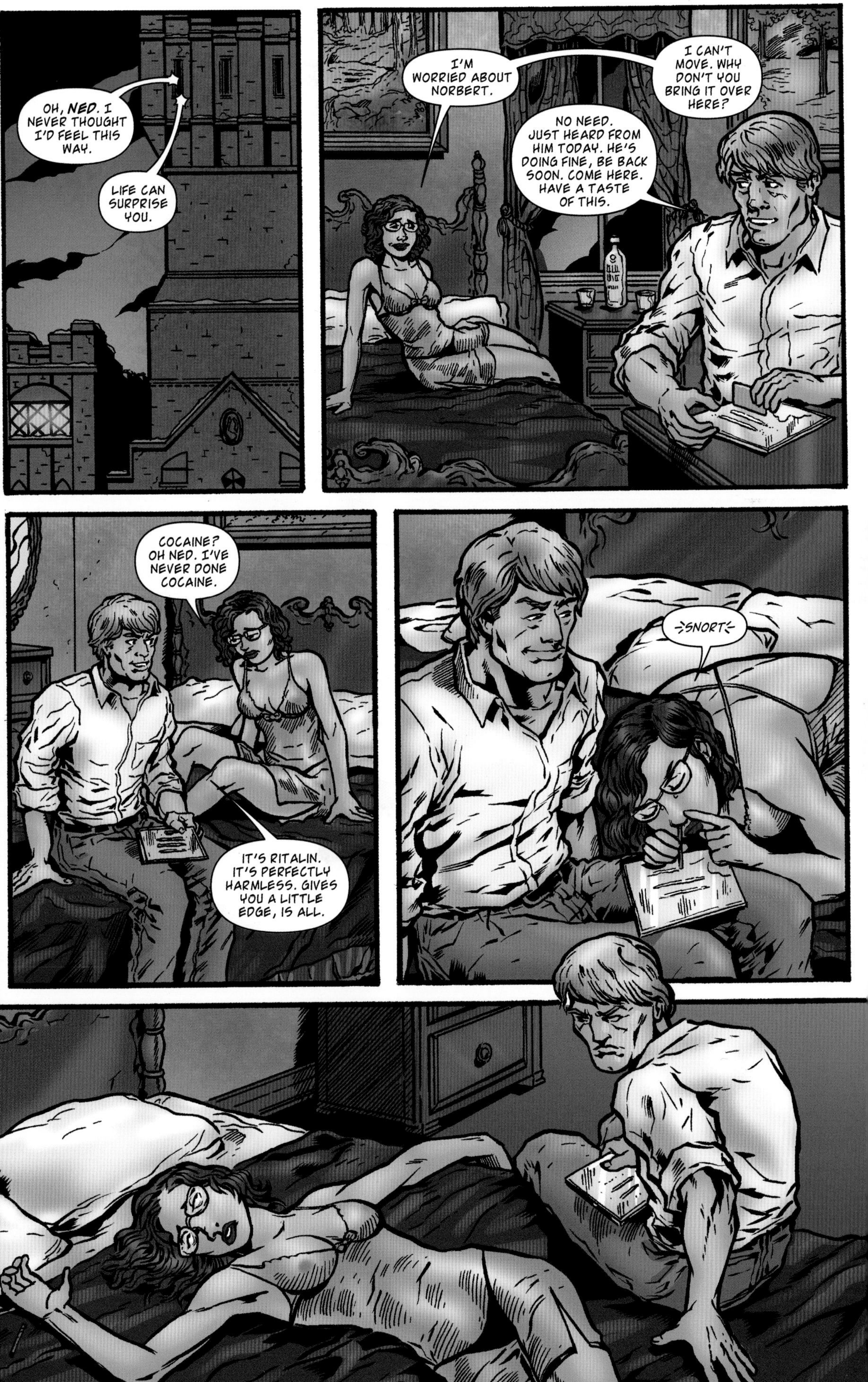

OH, NED. I NEVER THOUGHT I'D FEEL THIS WAY.
LIFE CAN SURPRISE YOU.
I'M WORRIED ABOUT NORBERT.
NO NEED. JUST HEARD FROM HIM TODAY. HE'S DOING FINE, BE BACK SOON. COME HERE. HAVE A TASTE OF THIS.
I CAN'T MOVE. WHY DON'T YOU BRING IT OVER HERE?
COCAINE? OH NED. I'VE NEVER DONE COCAINE.
IT'S RITALIN. IT'S PERFECTLY HARMLESS. GIVES YOU A LITTLE EDGE, IS ALL.
SNORT

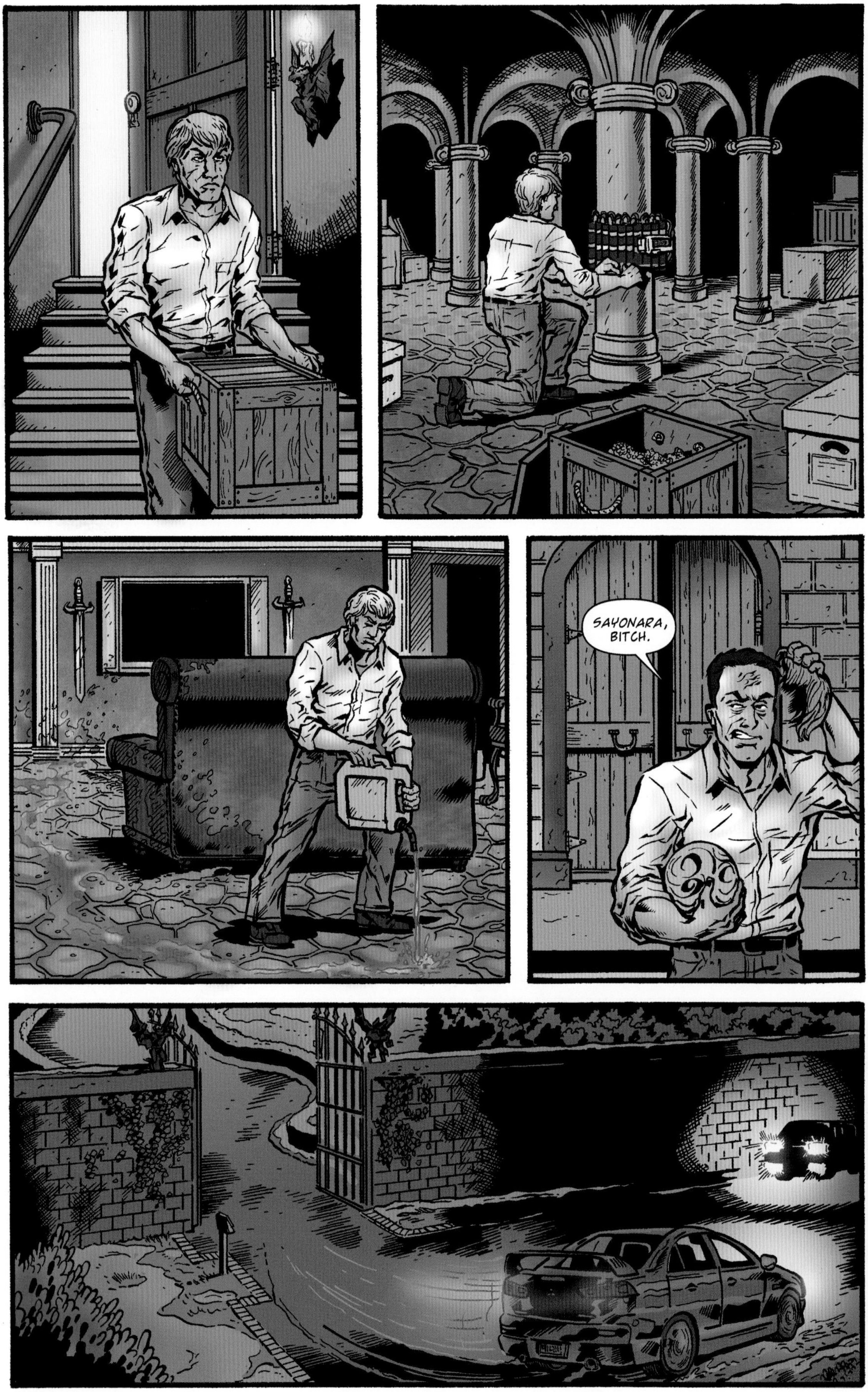
SAYONARA, BITCH.

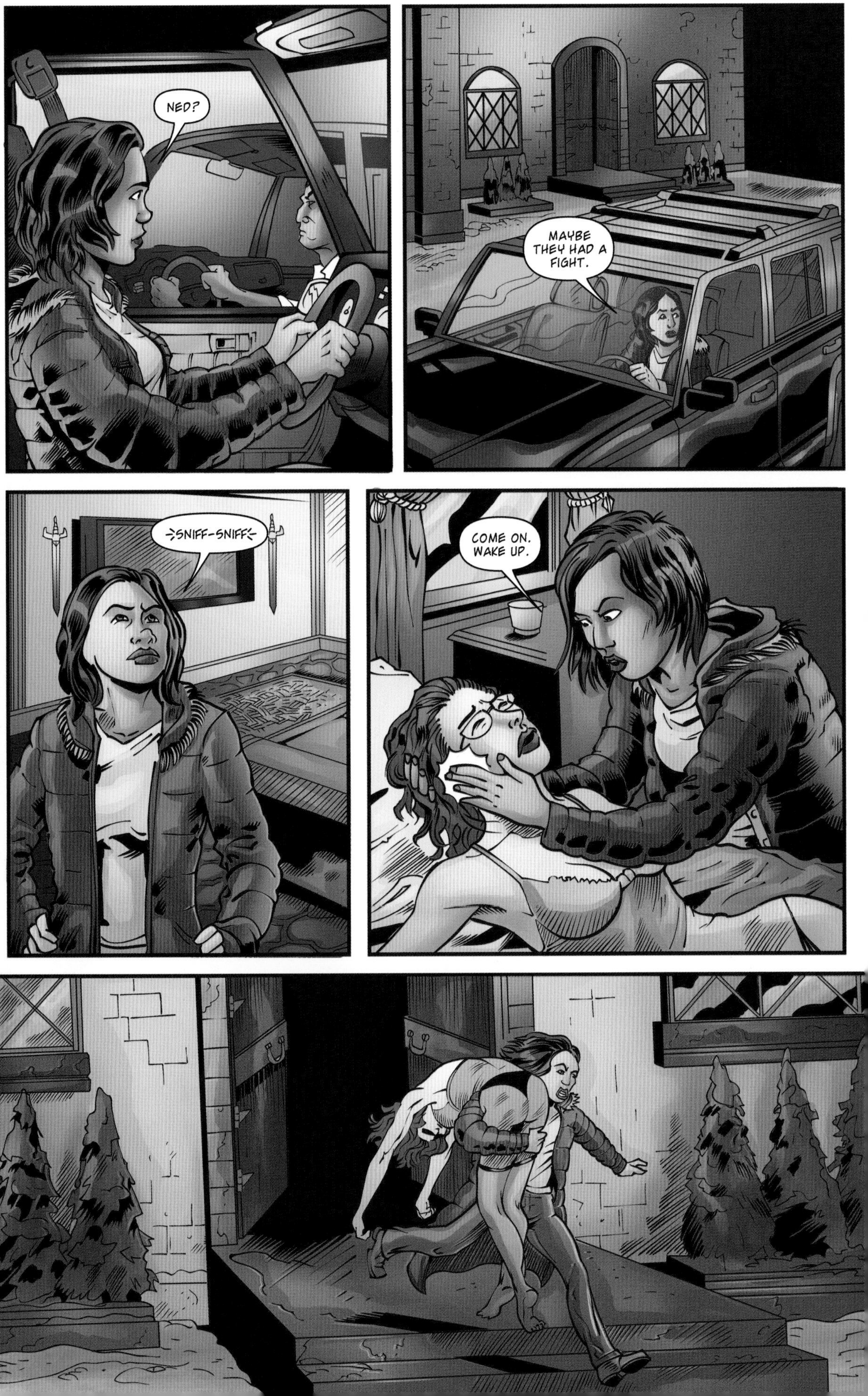
NED?
MAYBE THEY HAD A FIGHT.
-SNIFF-SNIFF-
COME ON. WAKE UP.

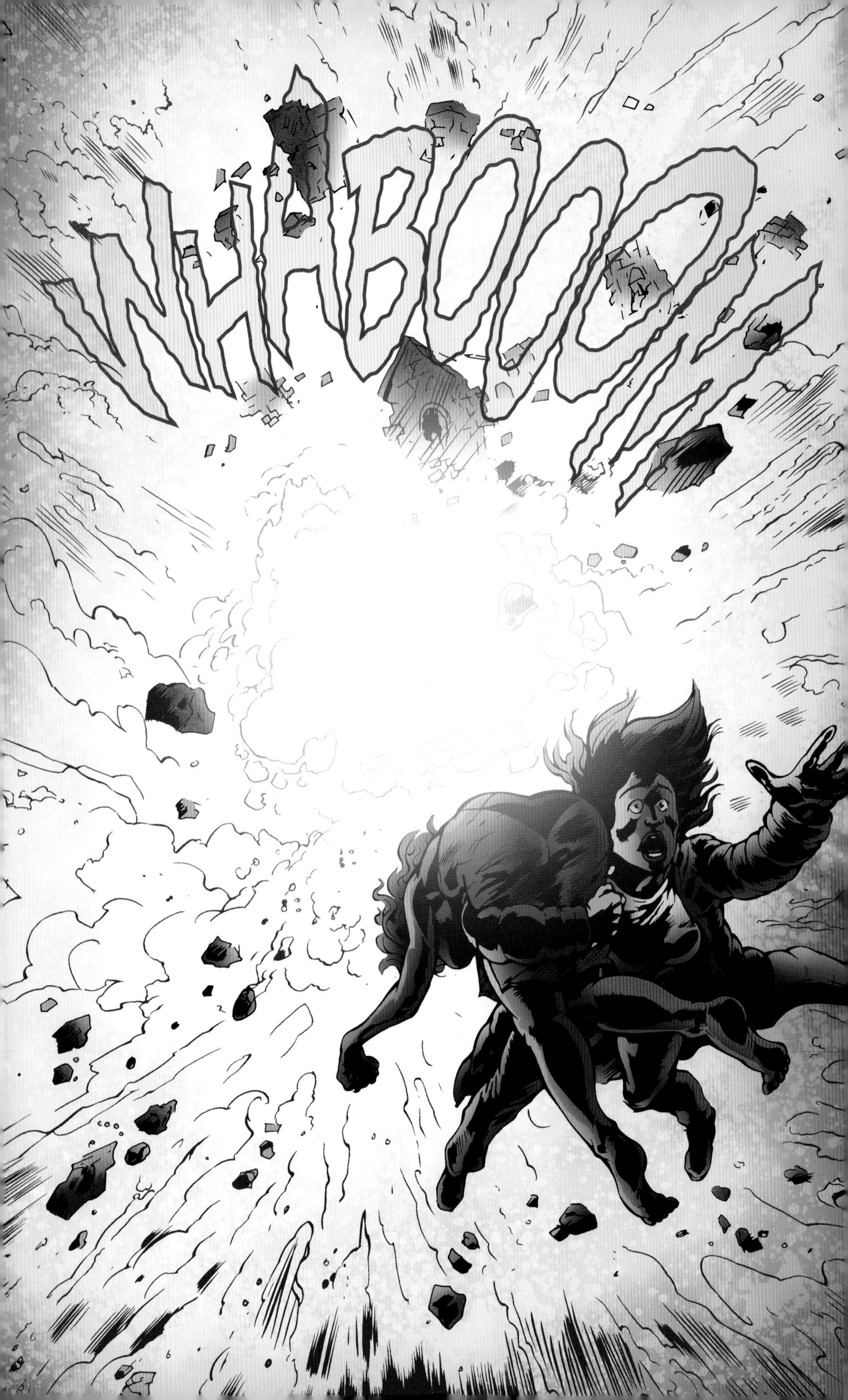
WHABOOOM

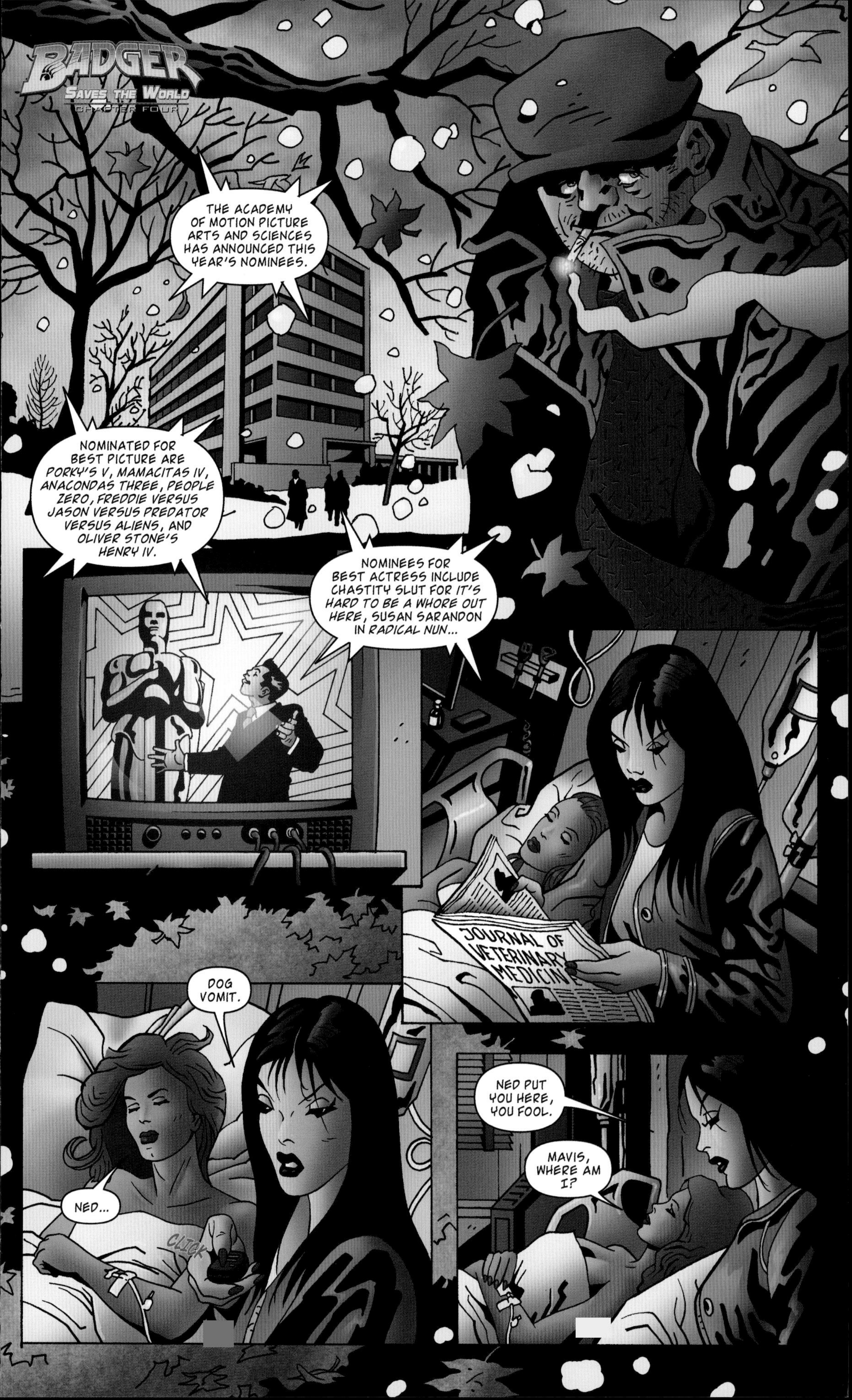
BADGER
SAVES THE WORLD
CHAPTER FOUR
THE ACADEMY OF MOTION PICTURE ARTS AND SCIENCES HAS ANNOUNCED THIS YEAR'S NOMINEES.
NOMINATED FOR BEST PICTURE ARE PORKY'S V, MAMACITAS IV, ANACONDAS THREE, PEOPLE ZERO, FREDDIE VERSUS JASON VERSUS PREDATOR VERSUS ALIENS, AND OLIVER STONE'S HENRY IV.
NOMINEES FOR BEST ACTRESS INCLUDE CHASTITY SLUT FOR IT'S HARD TO BE A WHORE OUT HERE, SUSAN SARANDON IN RADICAL NUN...
JOURNAL OF VETERINARY MEDICINE
DOG VOMIT.
NED...
CLICK
NED PUT YOU HERE, YOU FOOL.
MAVIS, WHERE AM I?

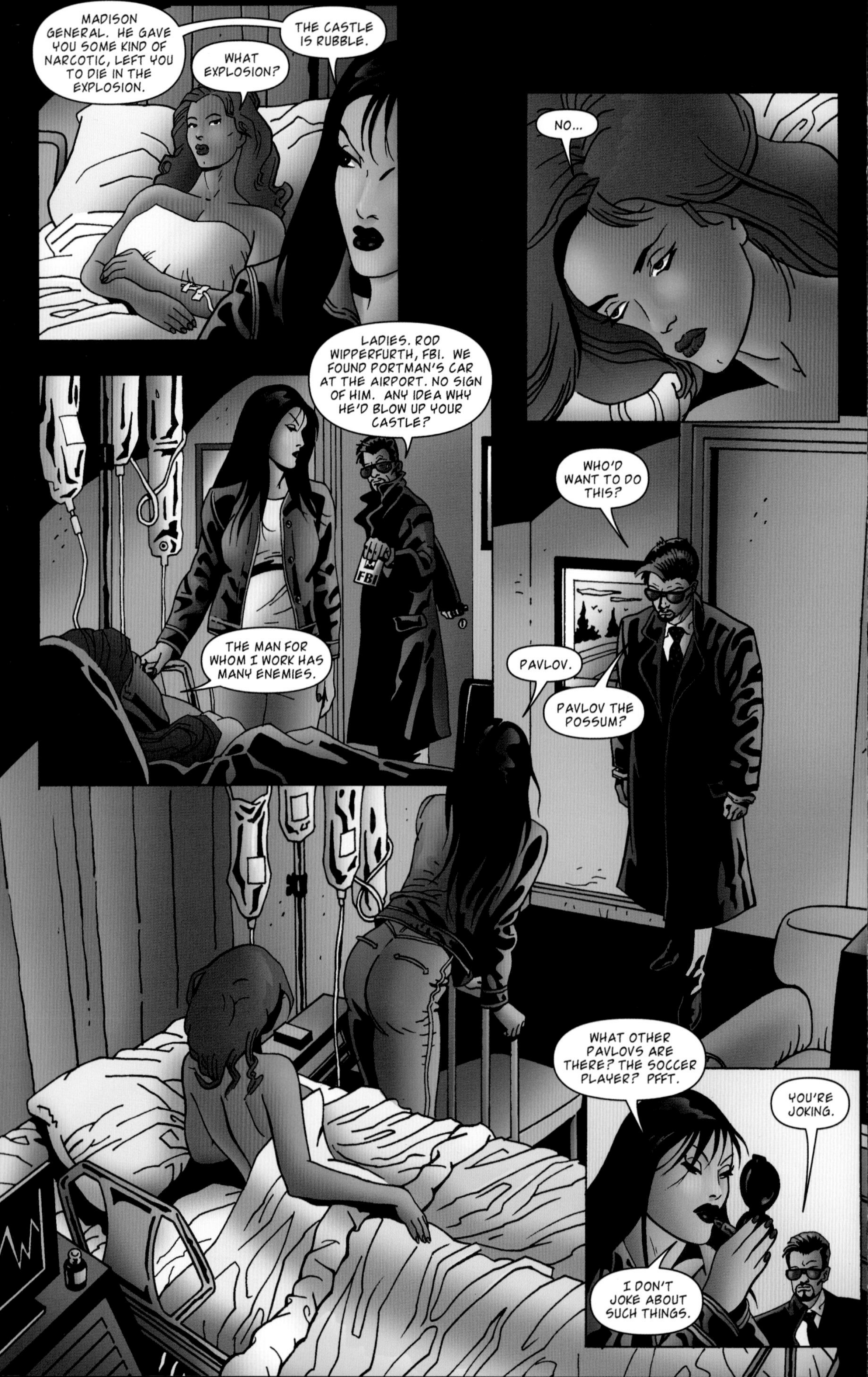
MADISON GENERAL. HE GAVE YOU SOME KIND OF NARCOTIC, LEFT YOU TO DIE IN THE EXPLOSION.
WHAT EXPLOSION?
THE CASTLE IS RUBBLE.
NO...
LADIES. ROD WIPPERFURTH, FBI. WE FOUND PORTMAN'S CAR AT THE AIRPORT. NO SIGN OF HIM. ANY IDEA WHY HE'D BLOW UP YOUR CASTLE?
FBI
THE MAN FOR WHOM I WORK HAS MANY ENEMIES.
WHO'D WANT TO DO THIS?
PAVLOV.
PAVLOV THE POSSUM?
WHAT OTHER PAVLOVS ARE THERE? THE SOCCER PLAYER? PFFT.
YOU'RE JOKING.
I DON'T JOKE ABOUT SUCH THINGS.

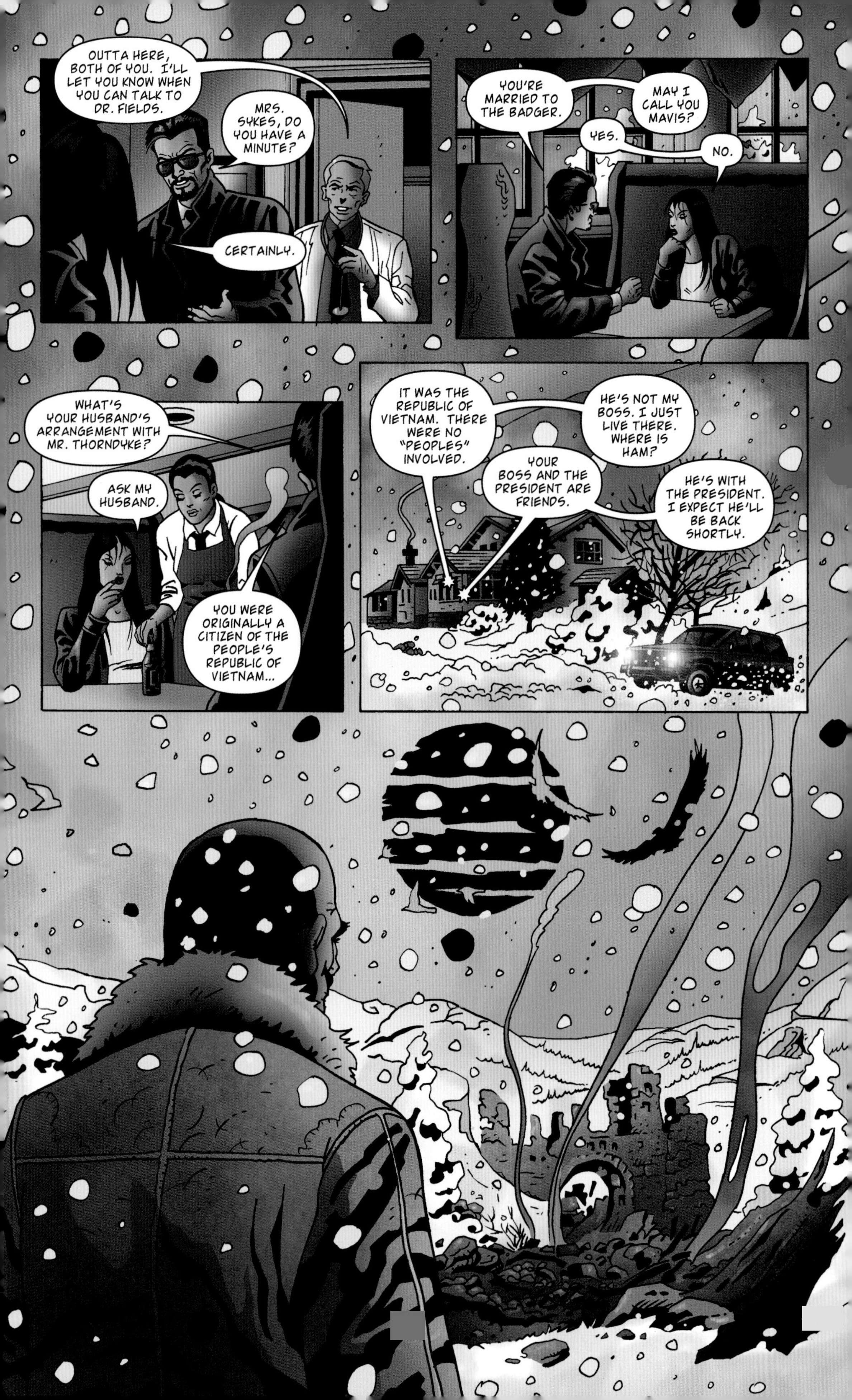
OUTTA HERE, BOTH OF YOU. I'LL LET YOU KNOW WHEN YOU CAN TALK TO DR. FIELDS.
MRS. SYKES, DO YOU HAVE A MINUTE?
CERTAINLY.
YOU'RE MARRIED TO THE BADGER.
MAY I CALL YOU MAVIS?
YES.
NO.
WHAT'S YOUR HUSBAND'S ARRANGEMENT WITH MR. THORNDYKE?
ASK MY HUSBAND.
YOU WERE ORIGINALLY A CITIZEN OF THE PEOPLE'S REPUBLIC OF VIETNAM...
IT WAS THE REPUBLIC OF VIETNAM. THERE WERE NO "PEOPLES" INVOLVED.
YOUR BOSS AND THE PRESIDENT ARE FRIENDS.
HE'S NOT MY BOSS. I JUST LIVE THERE. WHERE IS HAM?
HE'S WITH THE PRESIDENT. I EXPECT HE'LL BE BACK SHORTLY.

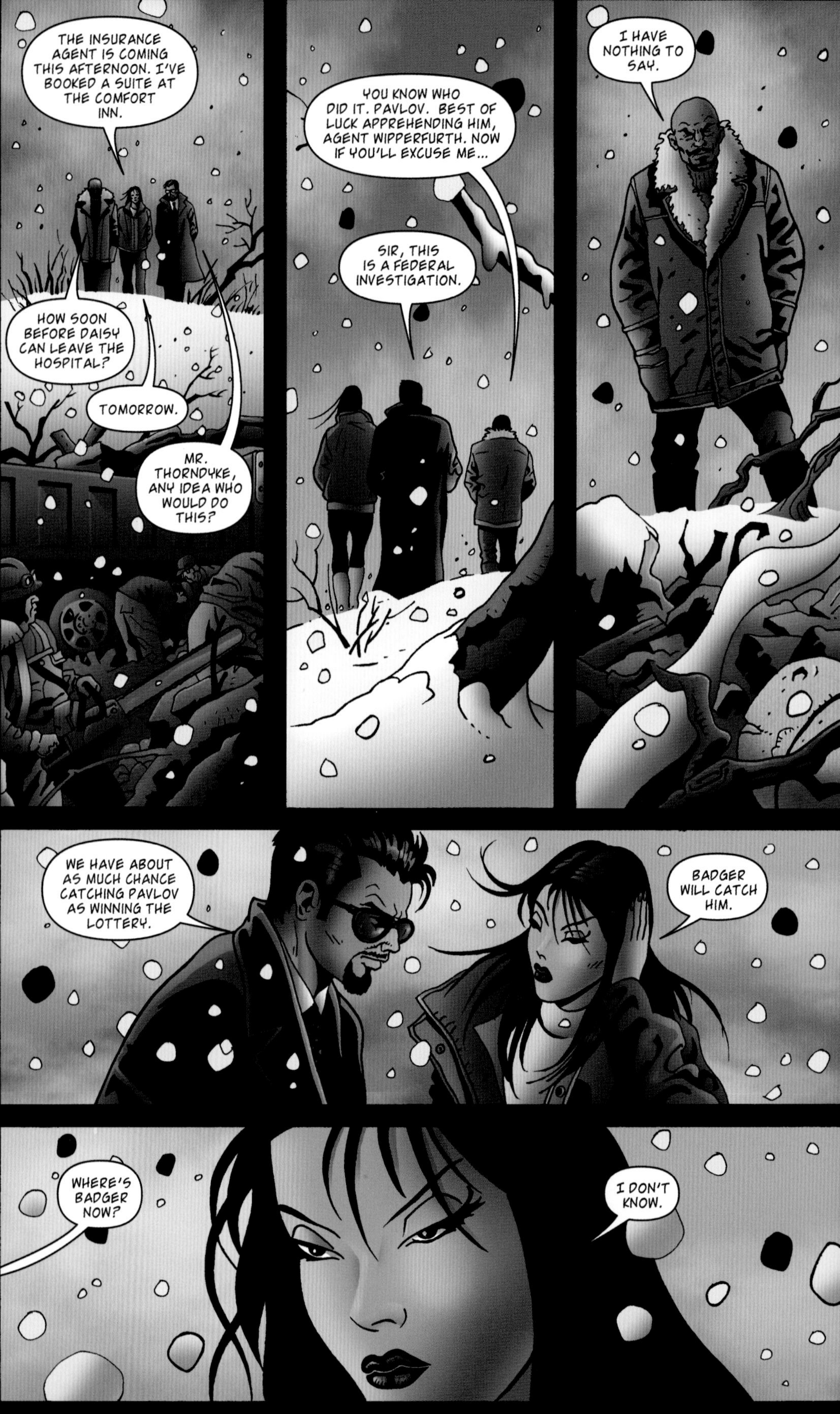
THE INSURANCE AGENT IS COMING THIS AFTERNOON. I'VE BOOKED A SUITE AT THE COMFORT INN.
HOW SOON BEFORE DAISY CAN LEAVE THE HOSPITAL?
TOMORROW.
MR. THORNDYKE, ANY IDEA WHO WOULD DO THIS?
YOU KNOW WHO DID IT. PAVLOV. BEST OF LUCK APPREHENDING HIM, AGENT WIPPERFURTH. NOW IF YOU'LL EXCUSE ME...
SIR, THIS IS A FEDERAL INVESTIGATION.
I HAVE NOTHING TO SAY.
WE HAVE ABOUT AS MUCH CHANCE CATCHING PAVLOV AS WINNING THE LOTTERY.
BADGER WILL CATCH HIM.
WHERE'S BADGER NOW?
I DON'T KNOW.

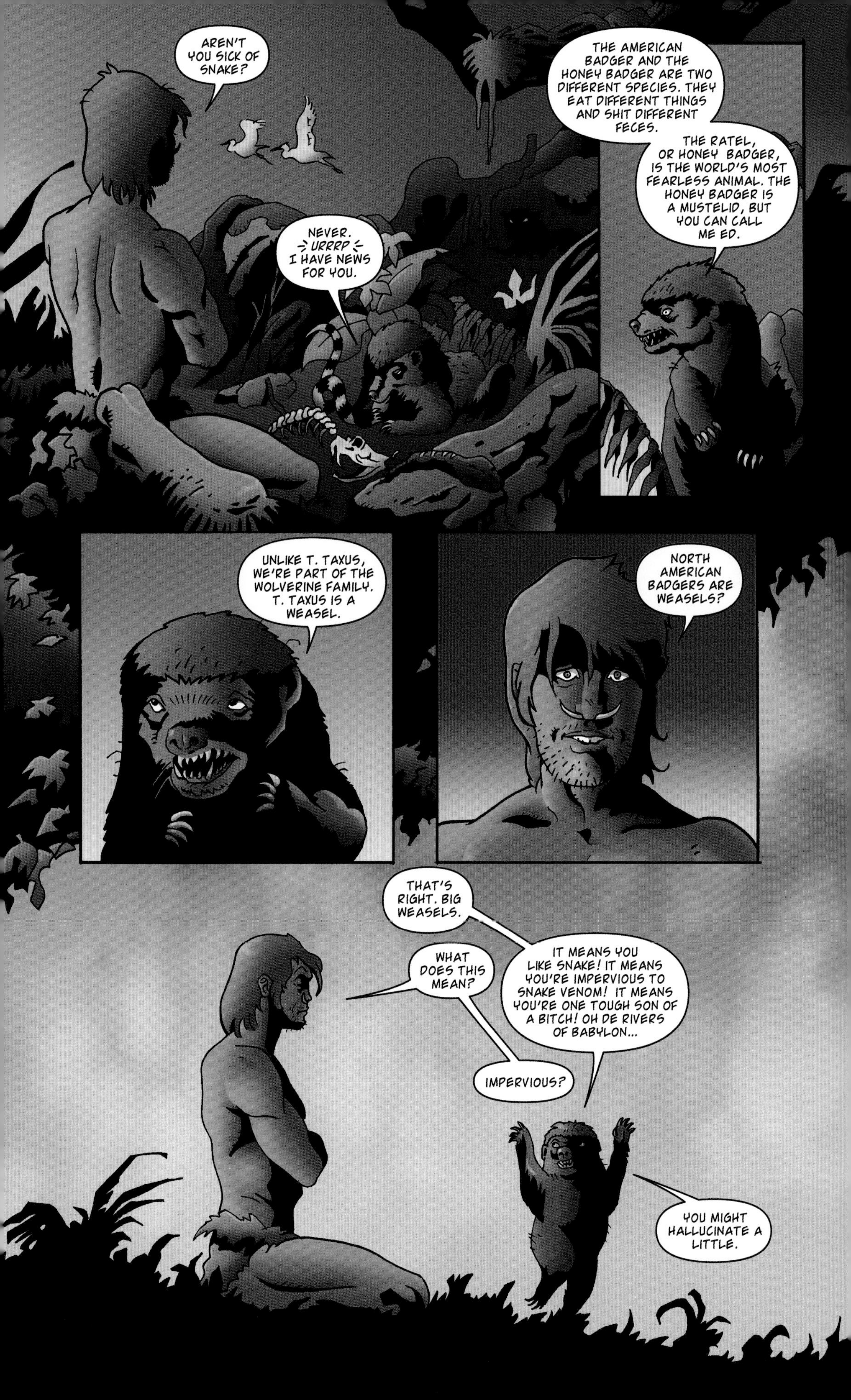
AREN'T YOU SICK OF SNAKE?
NEVER. URRRP I HAVE NEWS FOR YOU.
THE AMERICAN BADGER AND THE HONEY BADGER ARE TWO DIFFERENT SPECIES. THEY EAT DIFFERENT THINGS AND SHIT DIFFERENT FECES.
THE RATEL, OR HONEY BADGER, IS THE WORLD'S MOST FEARLESS ANIMAL. THE HONEY BADGER IS A MUSTELID, BUT YOU CAN CALL ME ED.
UNLIKE T. TAXUS, WE'RE PART OF THE WOLVERINE FAMILY. T. TAXUS IS A WEASEL.
NORTH AMERICAN BADGERS ARE WEASELS?
THAT'S RIGHT. BIG WEASELS.
WHAT DOES THIS MEAN?
IT MEANS YOU LIKE SNAKE! IT MEANS YOU'RE IMPERVIOUS TO SNAKE VENOM! IT MEANS YOU'RE ONE TOUGH SON OF A BITCH! OH DE RIVERS OF BABYLON...
IMPERVIOUS?
YOU MIGHT HALLUCINATE A LITTLE.

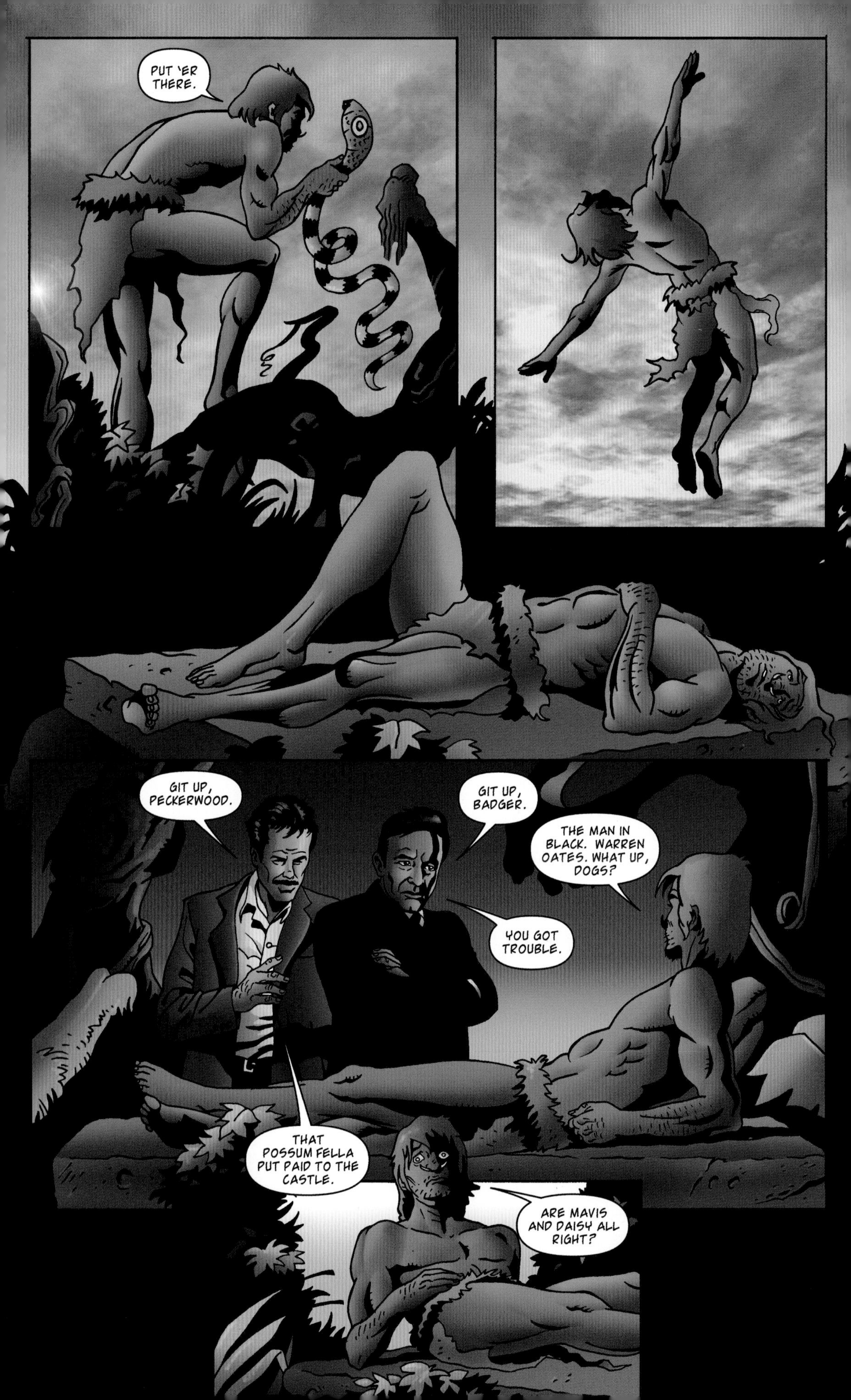
PUT 'ER THERE.
GIT UP, PECKERWOOD.
GIT UP, BADGER.
THE MAN IN BLACK. WARREN OATES. WHAT UP, DOGS?
YOU GOT TROUBLE.
THAT POSSUM FELLA PUT PAID TO THE CASTLE.
ARE MAVIS AND DAISY ALL RIGHT?

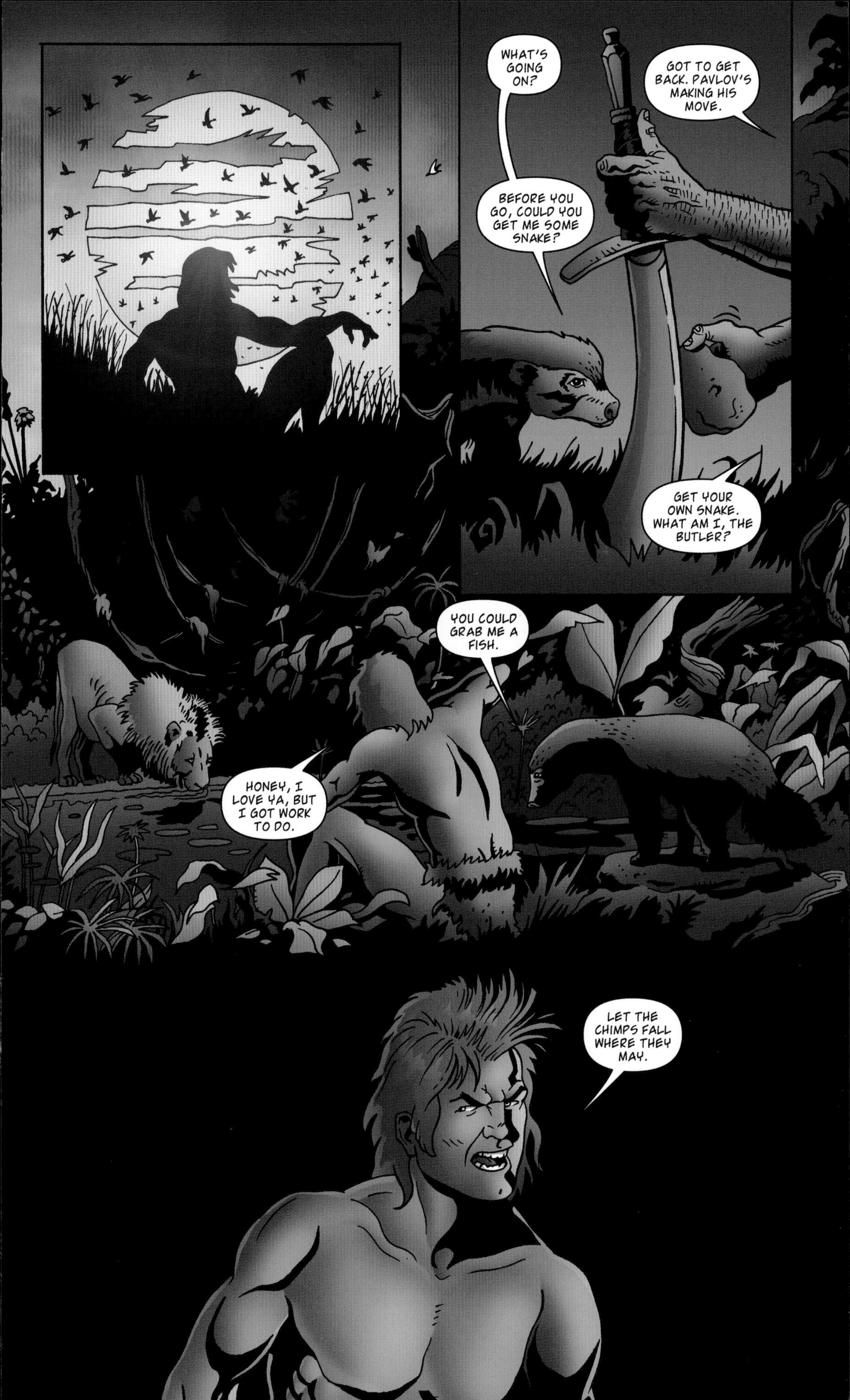

WHAT'S GOING ON?
GOT TO GET BACK. PAVLOV'S MAKING HIS MOVE.
BEFORE YOU GO, COULD YOU GET ME SOME SNAKE?
GET YOUR OWN SNAKE. WHAT AM I, THE BUTLER?
YOU COULD GRAB ME A FISH.
HONEY, I LOVE YA, BUT I GOT WORK TO DO.
LET THE CHIMPS FALL WHERE THEY MAY.

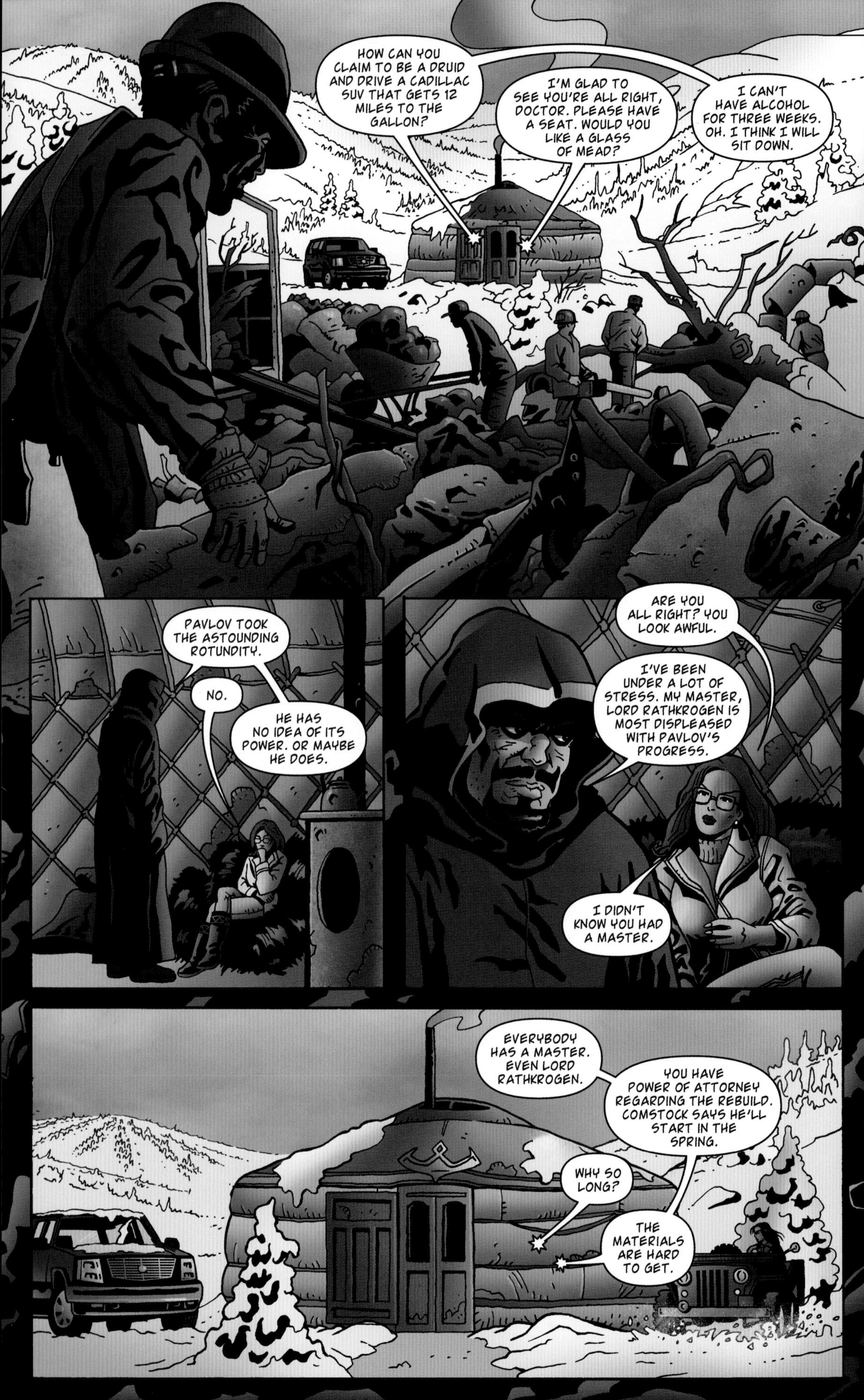

HOW CAN YOU CLAIM TO BE A DRUID AND DRIVE A CADILLAC SUV THAT GETS 12 MILES TO THE GALLON?
I'M GLAD TO SEE YOU'RE ALL RIGHT, DOCTOR. PLEASE HAVE A SEAT. WOULD YOU LIKE A GLASS OF MEAD?
I CAN'T HAVE ALCOHOL FOR THREE WEEKS. OH. I THINK I WILL SIT DOWN.
PAVLOV TOOK THE ASTOUNDING ROTUNDITY.
NO.
HE HAS NO IDEA OF ITS POWER. OR MAYBE HE DOES.
ARE YOU ALL RIGHT? YOU LOOK AWFUL.
I'VE BEEN UNDER A LOT OF STRESS. MY MASTER, LORD RATHKROGEN IS MOST DISPLEASED WITH PAVLOV'S PROGRESS.
I DIDN'T KNOW YOU HAD A MASTER.
EVERYBODY HAS A MASTER. EVEN LORD RATHKROGEN.
YOU HAVE POWER OF ATTORNEY REGARDING THE REBUILD. COMSTOCK SAYS HE'LL START IN THE SPRING.
WHY SO LONG?
THE MATERIALS ARE HARD TO GET.

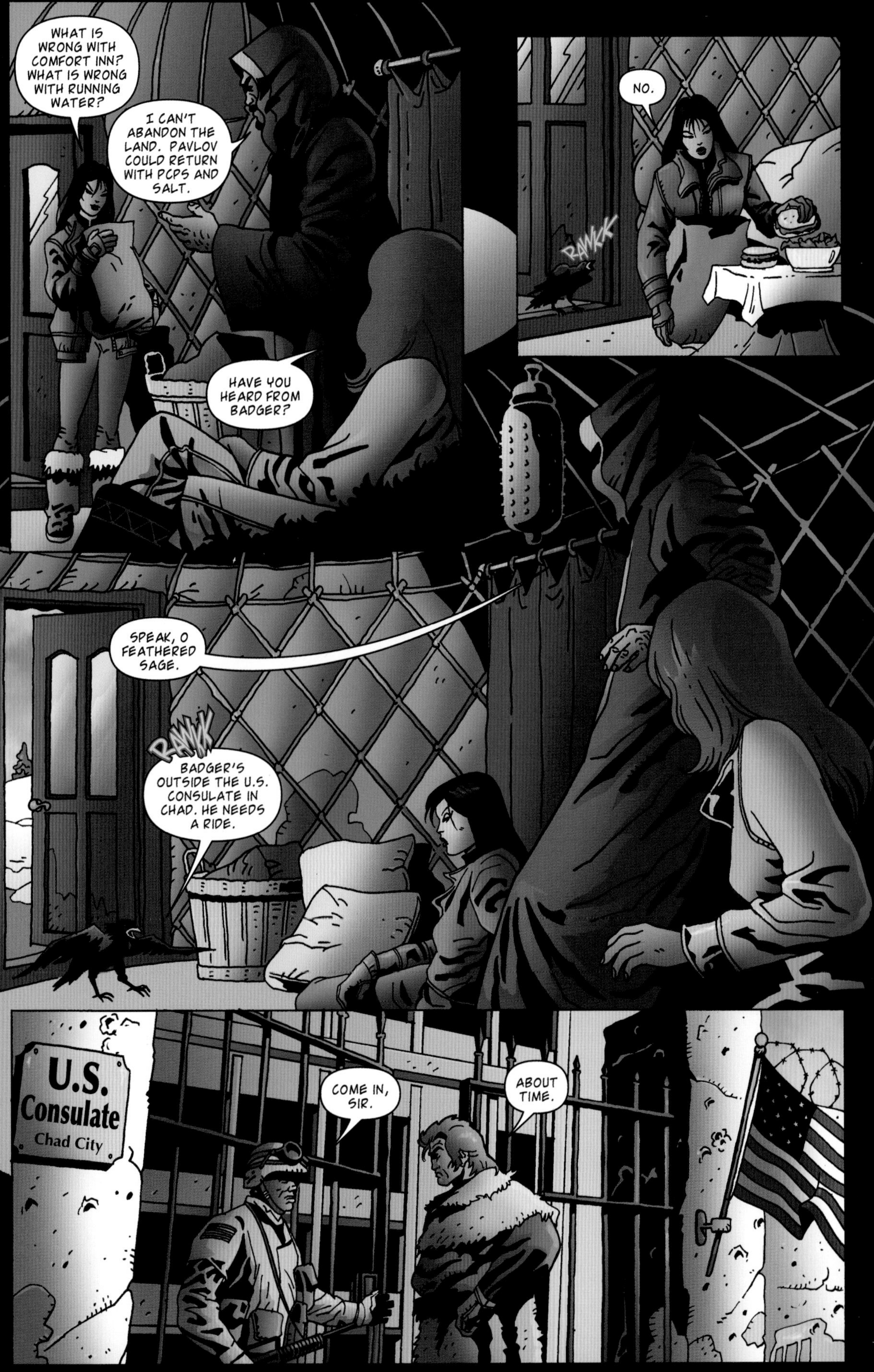
WHAT IS WRONG WITH COMFORT INN? WHAT IS WRONG WITH RUNNING WATER?
I CAN'T ABANDON THE LAND. PAVLOV COULD RETURN WITH PCPS AND SALT.
NO.
RAWKK
HAVE YOU HEARD FROM BADGER?
SPEAK, O FEATHERED SAGE.
RAWKK
BADGER'S OUTSIDE THE U.S. CONSULATE IN CHAD. HE NEEDS A RIDE.
U.S. Consulate Chad City
COME IN, SIR.
ABOUT TIME.

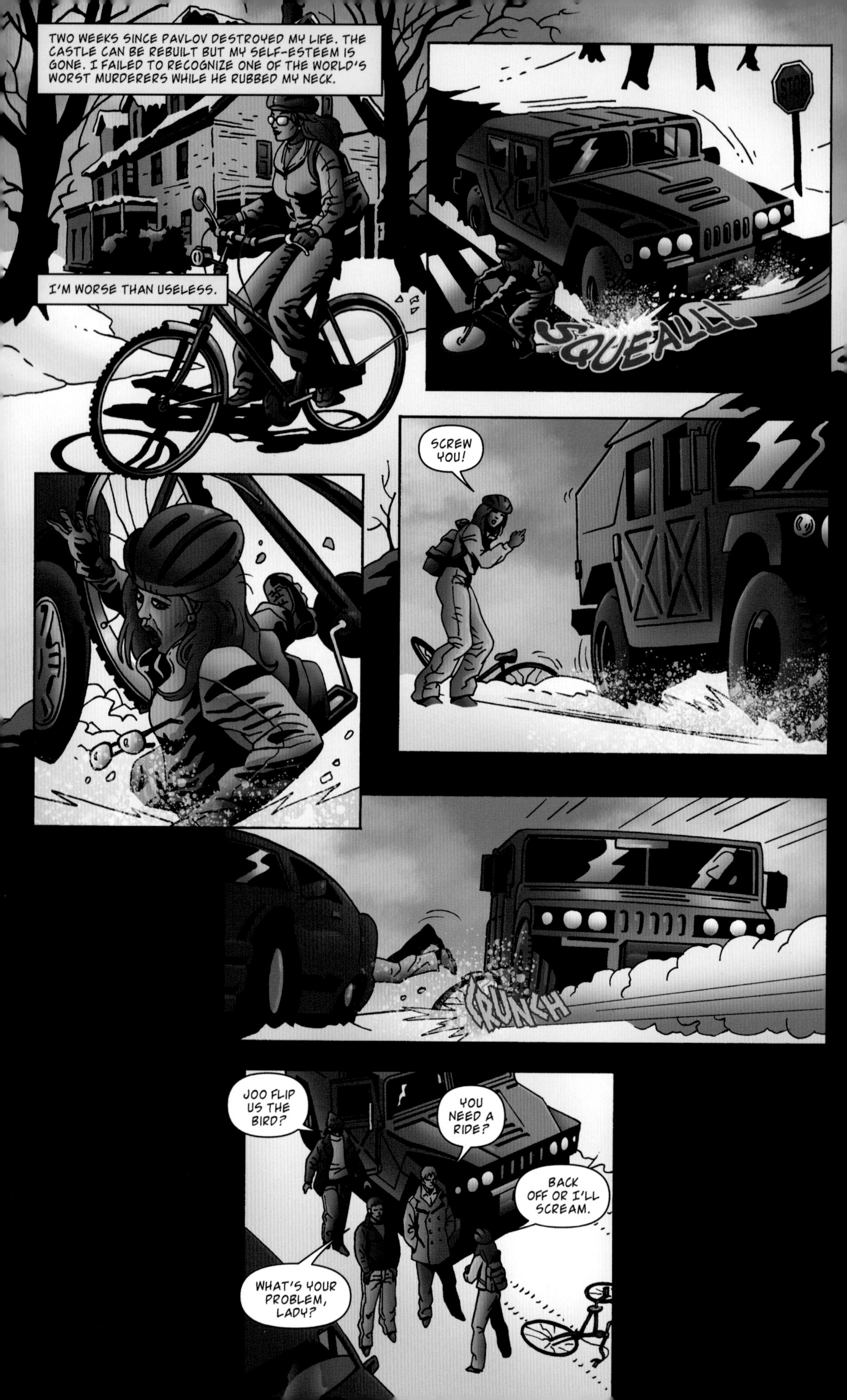
TWO WEEKS SINCE PAVLOV DESTROYED MY LIFE. THE CASTLE CAN BE REBUILT BUT MY SELF-ESTEEM IS GONE. I FAILED TO RECOGNIZE ONE OF THE WORLD'S WORST MURDERERS WHILE HE RUBBED MY NECK.
I'M WORSE THAN USELESS.
STOP
SQUEALLL
SCREW YOU!
CRUNCH
JOO FLIP US THE BIRD?
YOU NEED A RIDE?
BACK OFF OR I'LL SCREAM.
WHAT'S YOUR PROBLEM, LADY?

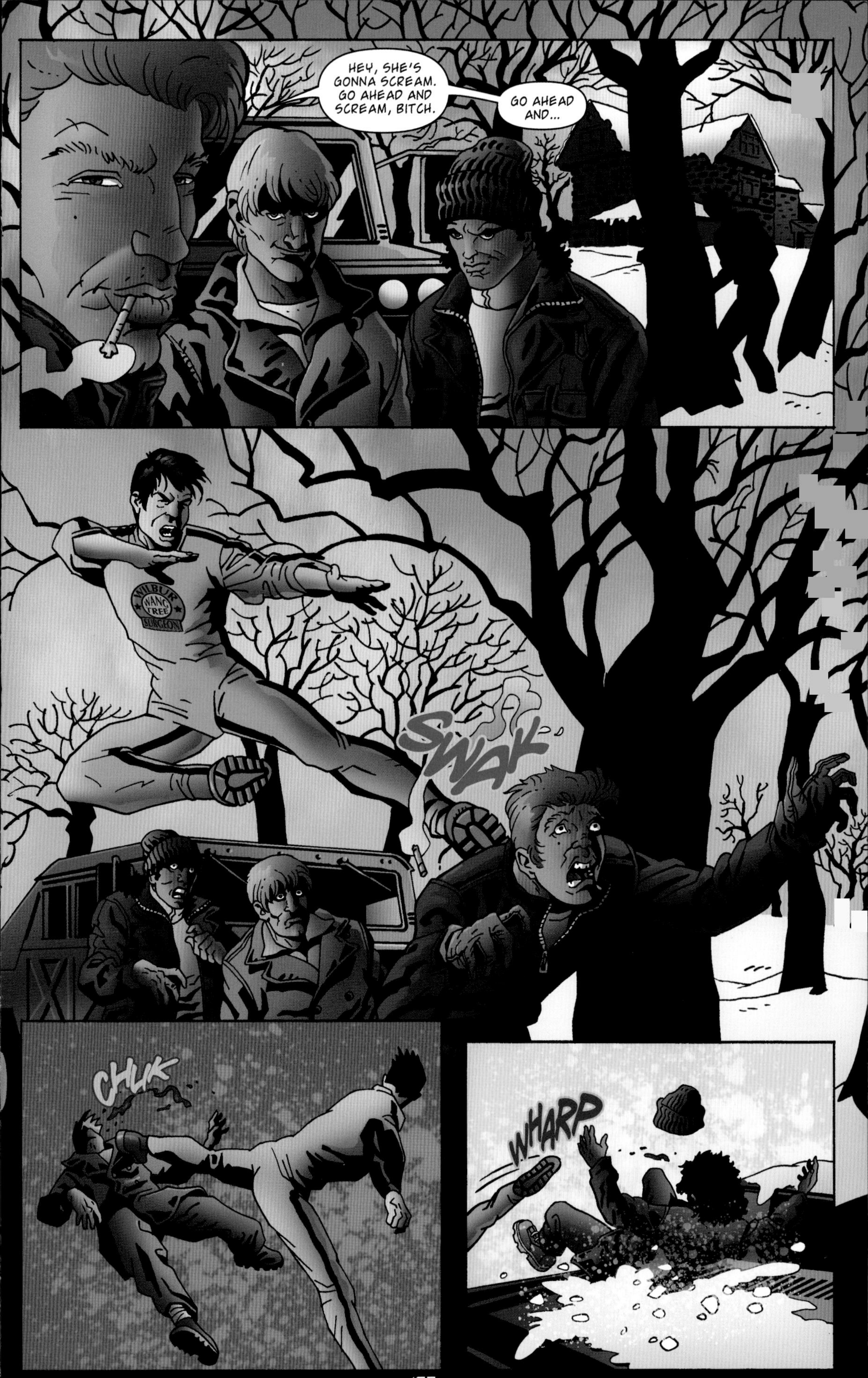
HEY, SHE'S GONNA SCREAM. GO AHEAD AND SCREAM, BITCH.
GO AHEAD AND...
SWAK
CHUK
WHARP

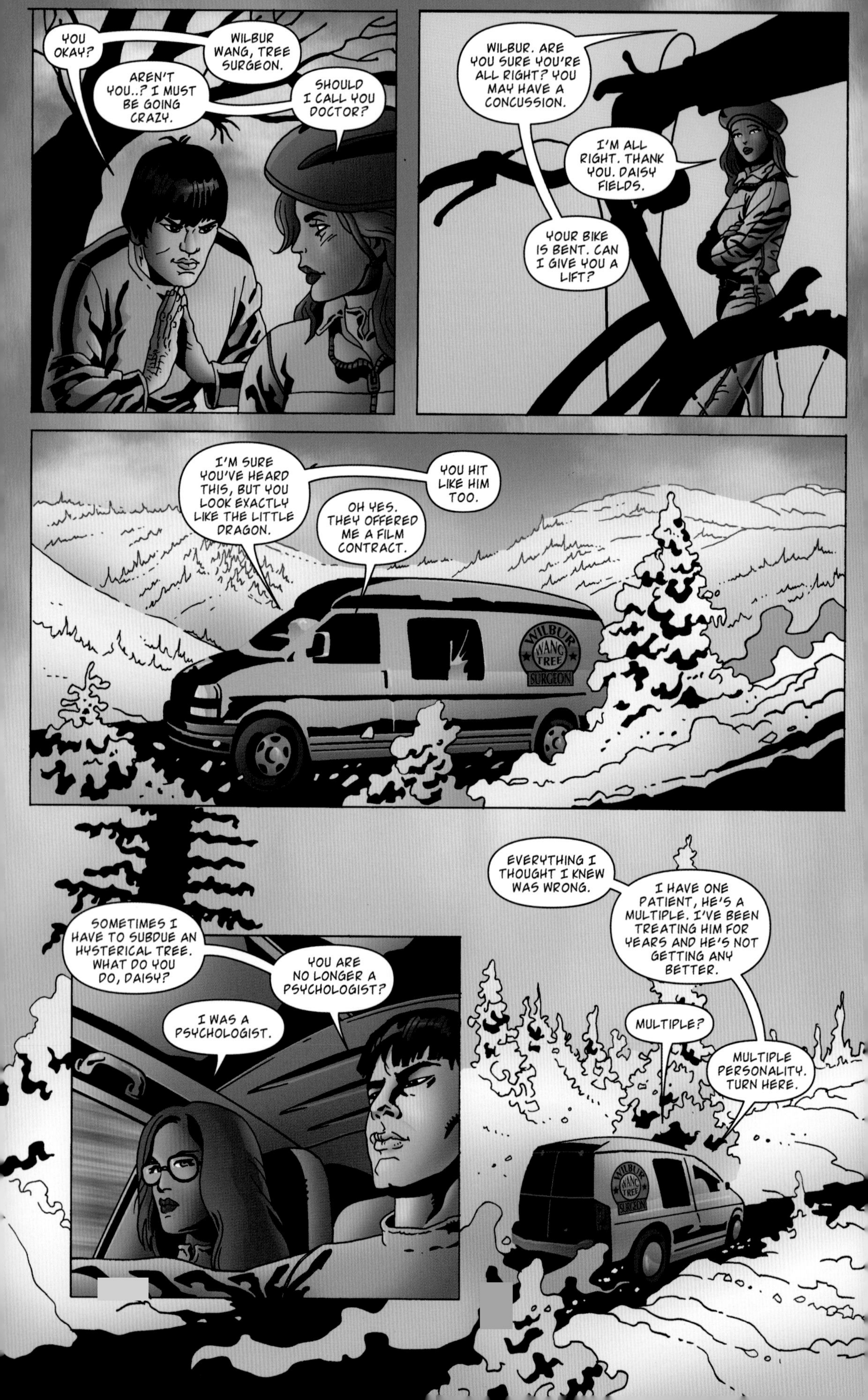

YOU OKAY?
WILBUR WANG, TREE SURGEON.
AREN'T YOU..? I MUST BE GOING CRAZY.
SHOULD I CALL YOU DOCTOR?
WILBUR. ARE YOU SURE YOU'RE ALL RIGHT? YOU MAY HAVE A CONCUSSION.
I'M ALL RIGHT. THANK YOU. DAISY FIELDS.
YOUR BIKE IS BENT. CAN I GIVE YOU A LIFT?
I'M SURE YOU'VE HEARD THIS, BUT YOU LOOK EXACTLY LIKE THE LITTLE DRAGON.
YOU HIT LIKE HIM TOO.
OH YES. THEY OFFERED ME A FILM CONTRACT.
WILBUR WANG TREE SURGEON
SOMETIMES I HAVE TO SUBDUE AN HYSTERICAL TREE. WHAT DO YOU DO, DAISY?
I WAS A PSYCHOLOGIST.
YOU ARE NO LONGER A PSYCHOLOGIST?
EVERYTHING I THOUGHT I KNEW WAS WRONG.
I HAVE ONE PATIENT, HE'S A MULTIPLE. I'VE BEEN TREATING HIM FOR YEARS AND HE'S NOT GETTING ANY BETTER.
MULTIPLE?
MULTIPLE PERSONALITY. TURN HERE.
WILBUR WANG TREE SURGEON

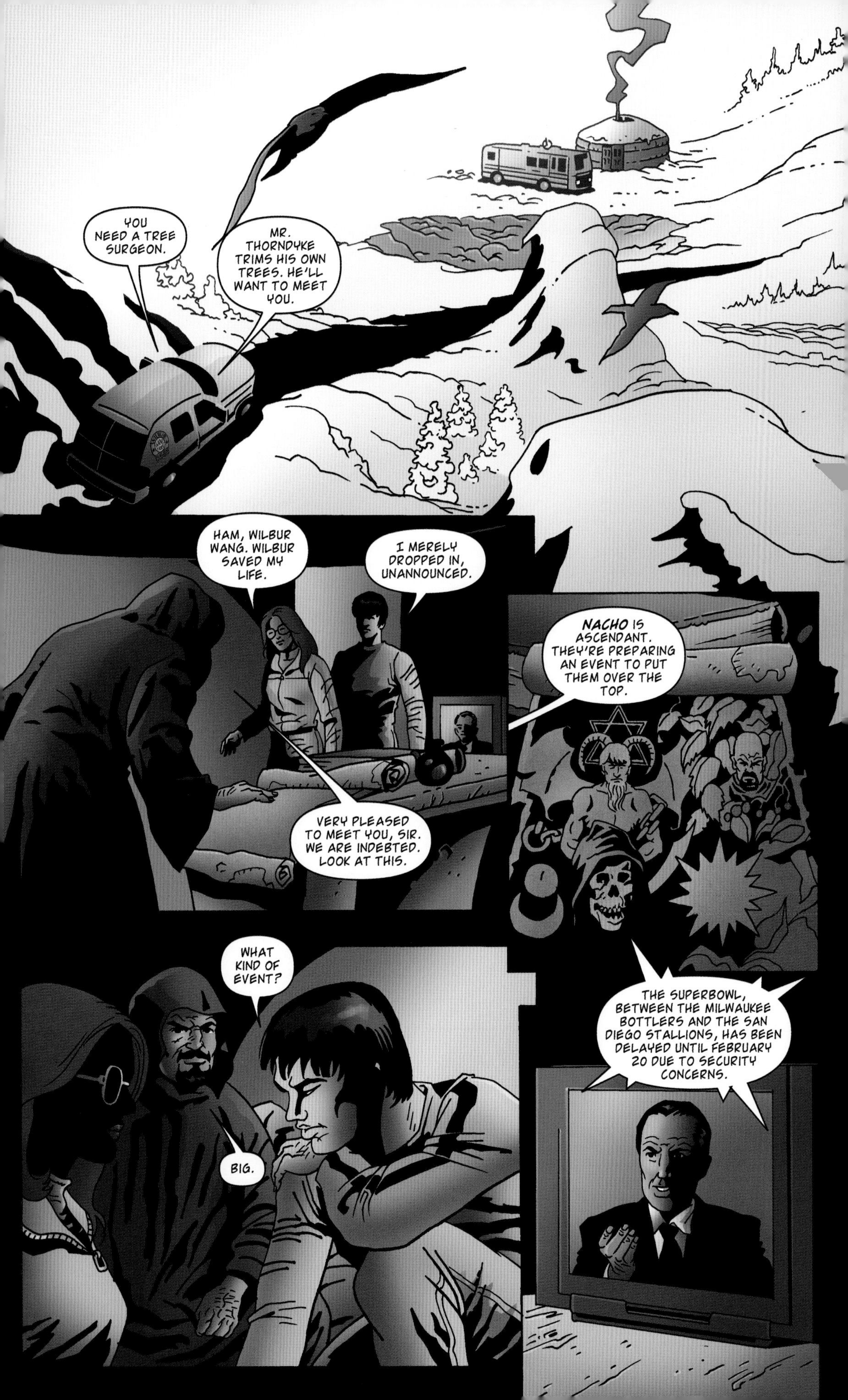
YOU NEED A TREE SURGEON.
MR. THORNDYKE TRIMS HIS OWN TREES. HE'LL WANT TO MEET YOU.
HAM, WILBUR WANG. WILBUR SAVED MY LIFE.
I MERELY DROPPED IN, UNANNOUNCED.
VERY PLEASED TO MEET YOU, SIR. WE ARE INDEBTED. LOOK AT THIS.
NACHO IS ASCENDANT. THEY'RE PREPARING AN EVENT TO PUT THEM OVER THE TOP.
WHAT KIND OF EVENT?
BIG.
THE SUPERBOWL, BETWEEN THE MILWAUKEE BOTTLERS AND THE SAN DIEGO STALLIONS, HAS BEEN DELAYED UNTIL FEBRUARY 20 DUE TO SECURITY CONCERNS.

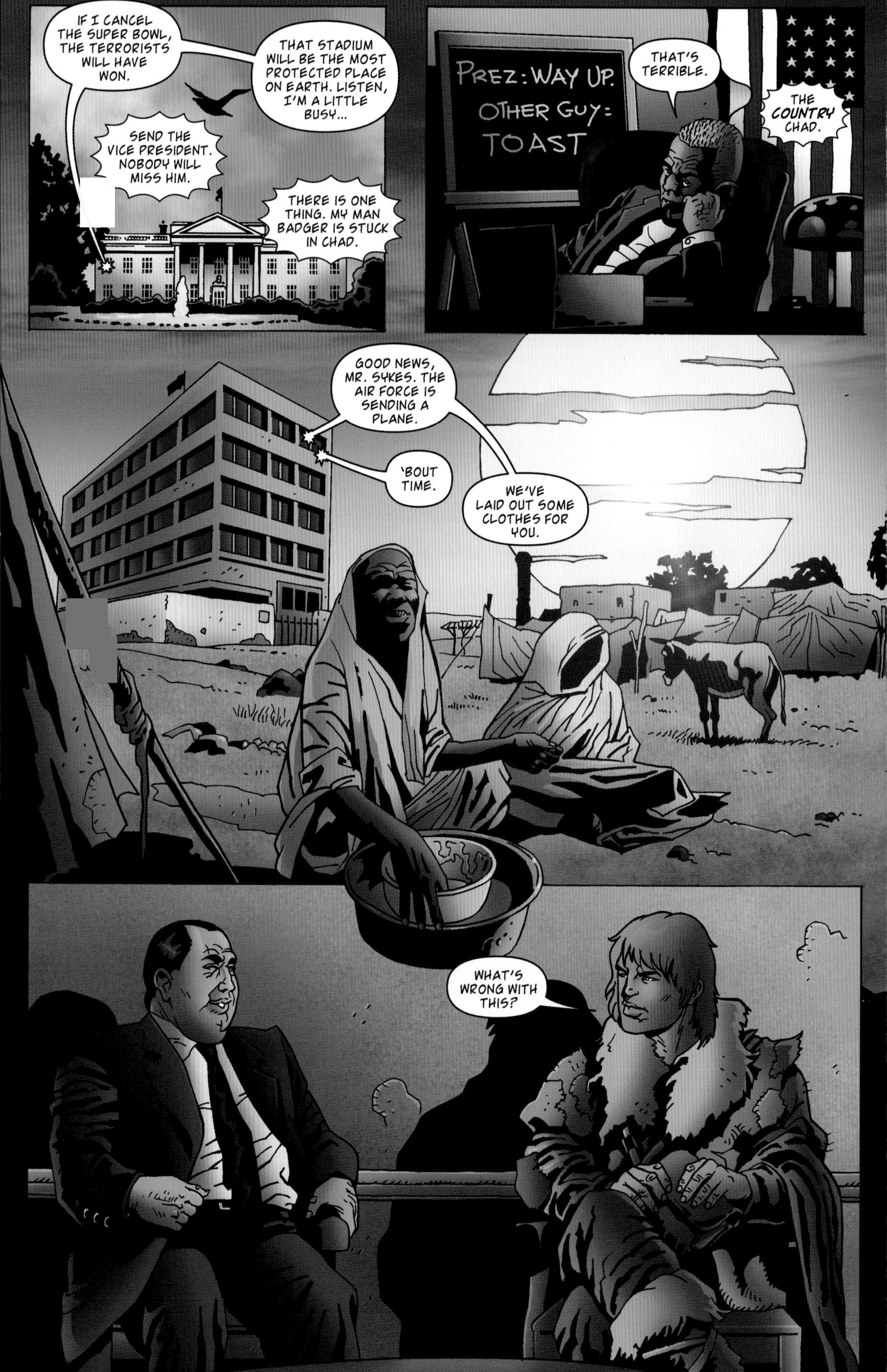
IF I CANCEL THE SUPER BOWL, THE TERRORISTS WILL HAVE WON.
THAT STADIUM WILL BE THE MOST PROTECTED PLACE ON EARTH. LISTEN, I'M A LITTLE BUSY...
SEND THE VICE PRESIDENT. NOBODY WILL MISS HIM.
THERE IS ONE THING. MY MAN BADGER IS STUCK IN CHAD.
PREZ: WAY UP. OTHER GUY: TOAST
THAT'S TERRIBLE.
THE COUNTRY CHAD.
GOOD NEWS, MR. SYKES. THE AIR FORCE IS SENDING A PLANE.
'BOUT TIME.
WE'VE LAID OUT SOME CLOTHES FOR YOU.
WHAT'S WRONG WITH THIS?

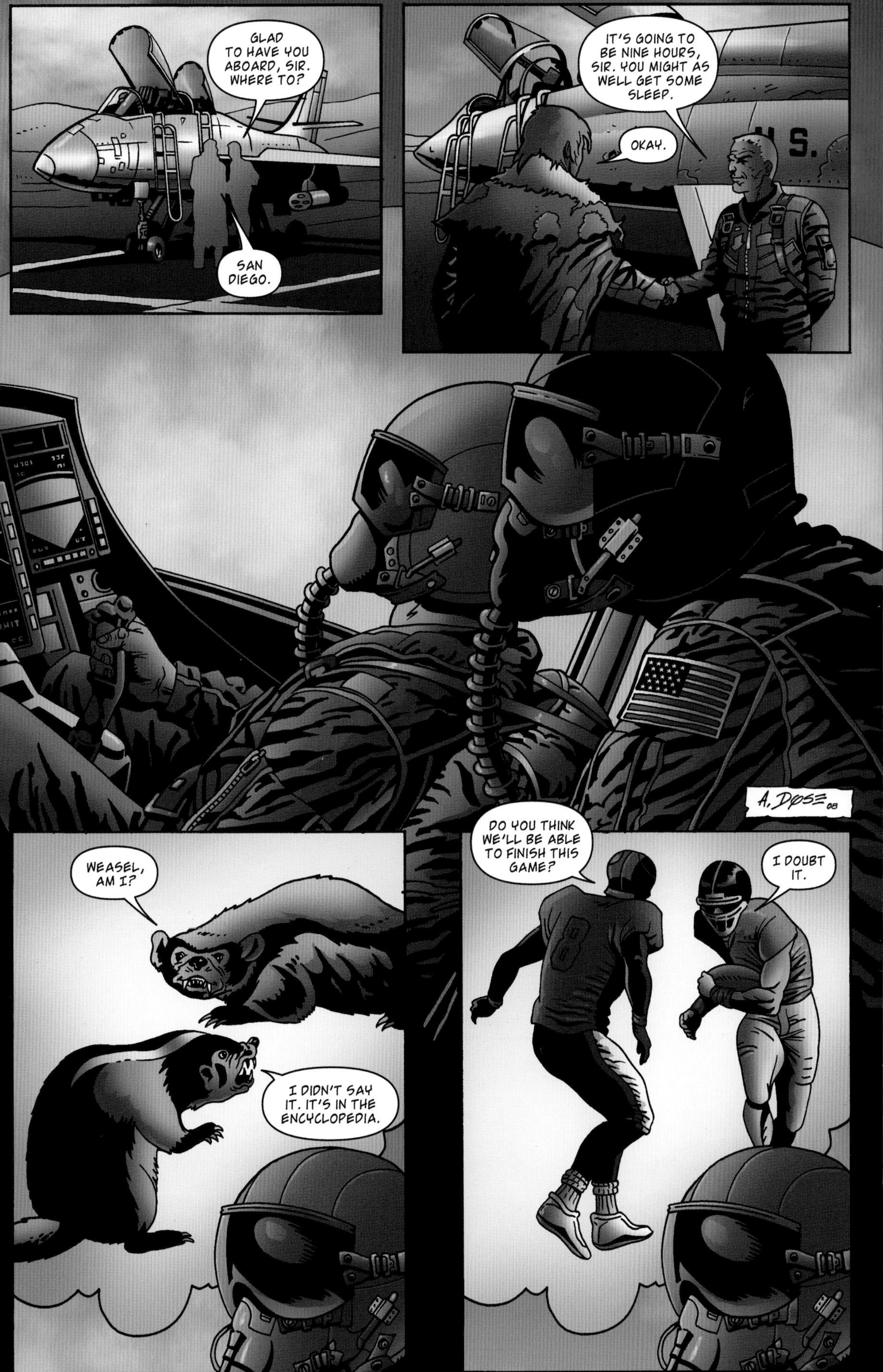
GLAD TO HAVE YOU ABOARD, SIR. WHERE TO?
SAN DIEGO.
IT'S GOING TO BE NINE HOURS, SIR. YOU MIGHT AS WELL GET SOME SLEEP.
OKAY.
A. DOSE 08
WEASEL, AM I?
I DIDN'T SAY IT. IT'S IN THE ENCYCLOPEDIA.
DO YOU THINK WE'LL BE ABLE TO FINISH THIS GAME?
I DOUBT IT.

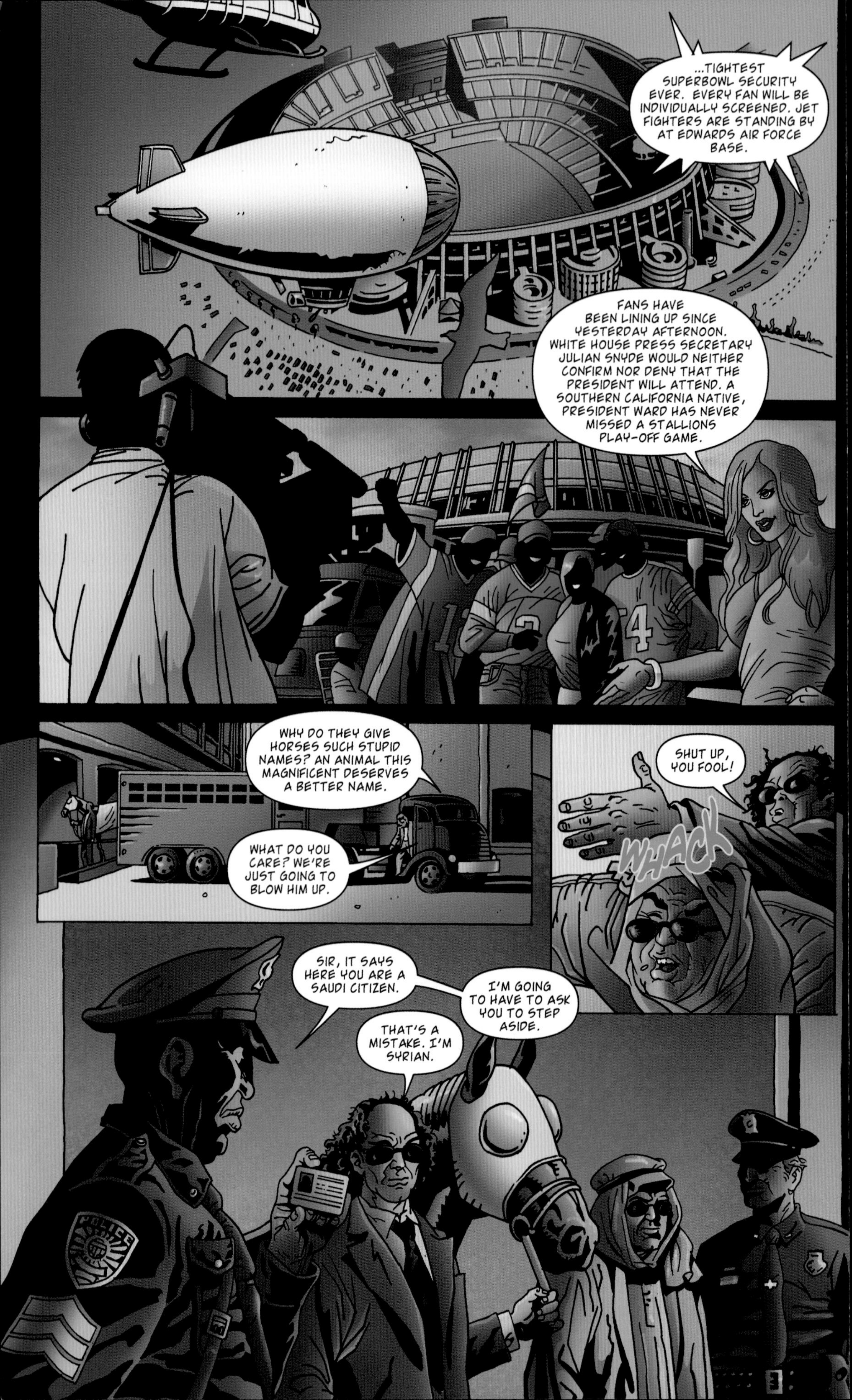
...TIGHTEST SUPERBOWL SECURITY EVER. EVERY FAN WILL BE INDIVIDUALLY SCREENED. JET FIGHTERS ARE STANDING BY AT EDWARDS AIR FORCE BASE.
FANS HAVE BEEN LINING UP SINCE YESTERDAY AFTERNOON. WHITE HOUSE PRESS SECRETARY JULIAN SNYDE WOULD NEITHER CONFIRM NOR DENY THAT THE PRESIDENT WILL ATTEND. A SOUTHERN CALIFORNIA NATIVE, PRESIDENT WARD HAS NEVER MISSED A STALLIONS PLAY-OFF GAME.
WHY DO THEY GIVE HORSES SUCH STUPID NAMES? AN ANIMAL THIS MAGNIFICENT DESERVES A BETTER NAME.
WHAT DO YOU CARE? WE'RE JUST GOING TO BLOW HIM UP.
SHUT UP, YOU FOOL!
WHACK
SIR, IT SAYS HERE YOU ARE A SAUDI CITIZEN.
I'M GOING TO HAVE TO ASK YOU TO STEP ASIDE.
THAT'S A MISTAKE. I'M SYRIAN.
POLICE

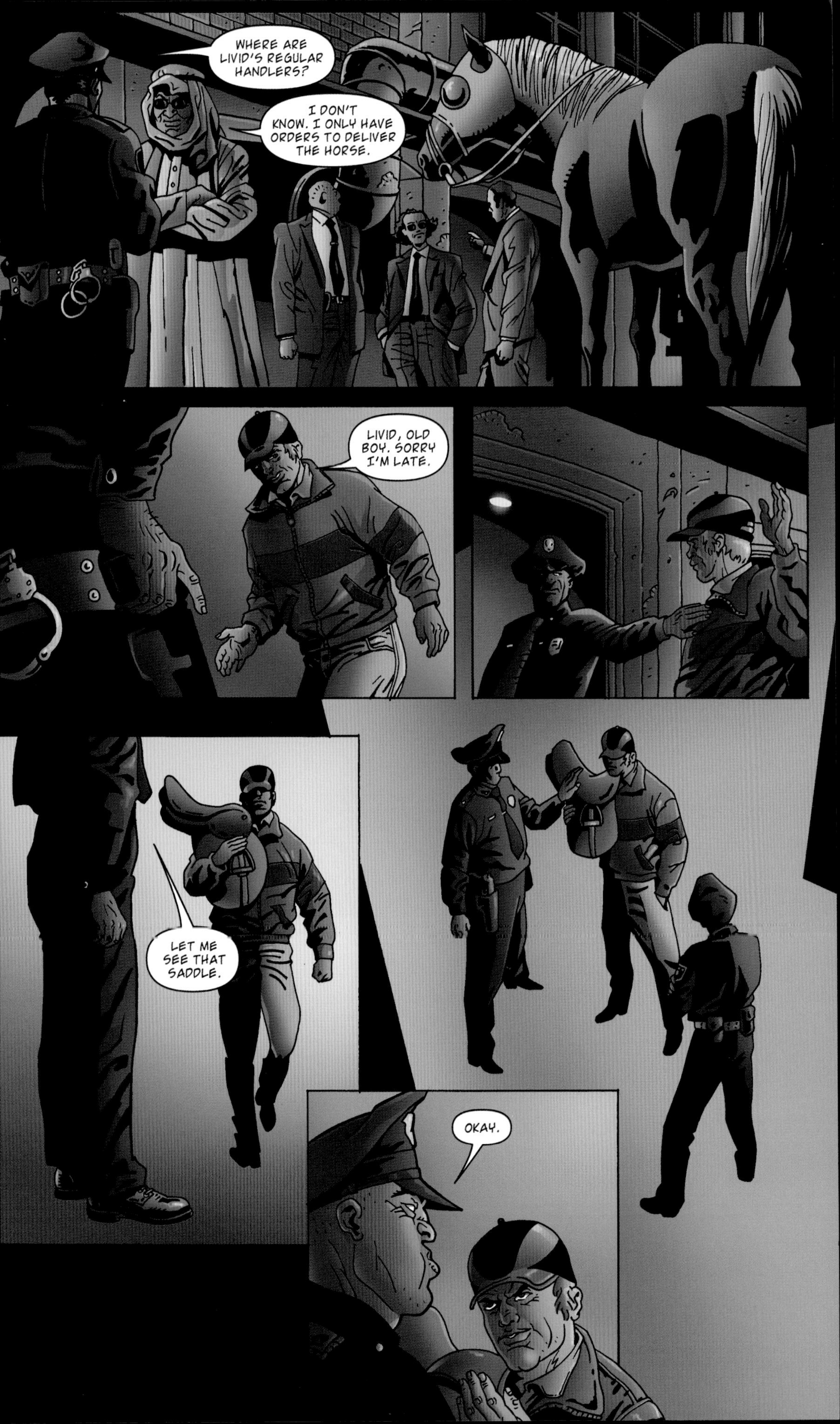
WHERE ARE LIVID'S REGULAR HANDLERS?
I DON'T KNOW. I ONLY HAVE ORDERS TO DELIVER THE HORSE.
LIVID, OLD BOY. SORRY I'M LATE.
LET ME SEE THAT SADDLE.
OKAY.

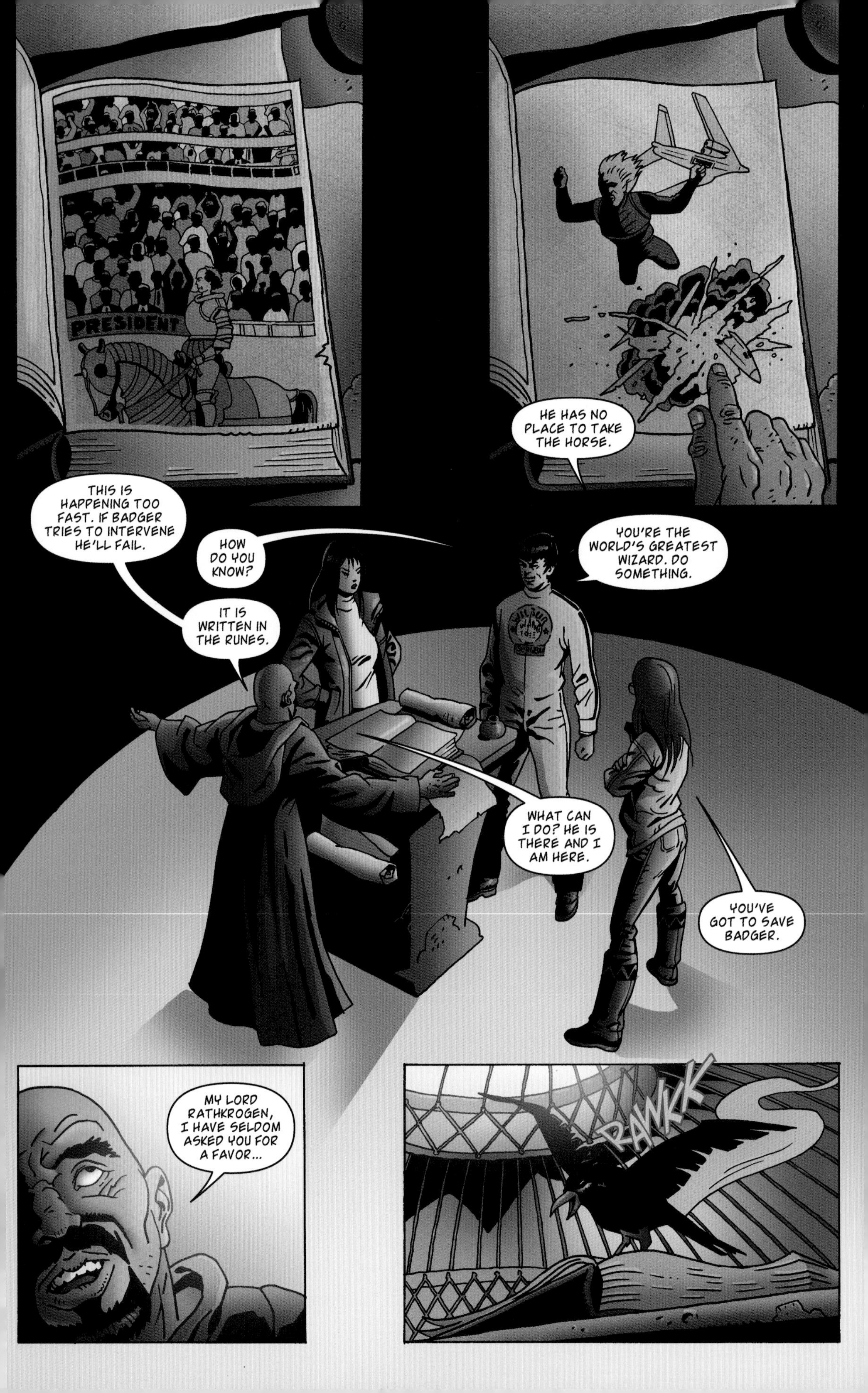
PRESIDENT
HE HAS NO PLACE TO TAKE THE HORSE.
THIS IS HAPPENING TOO FAST. IF BADGER TRIES TO INTERVENE HE'LL FAIL.
HOW DO YOU KNOW?
IT IS WRITTEN IN THE RUNES.
YOU'RE THE WORLD'S GREATEST WIZARD. DO SOMETHING.
WHAT CAN I DO? HE IS THERE AND I AM HERE.
YOU'VE GOT TO SAVE BADGER.
MY LORD RATHKROGEN, I HAVE SELDOM ASKED YOU FOR A FAVOR...
RAWKK

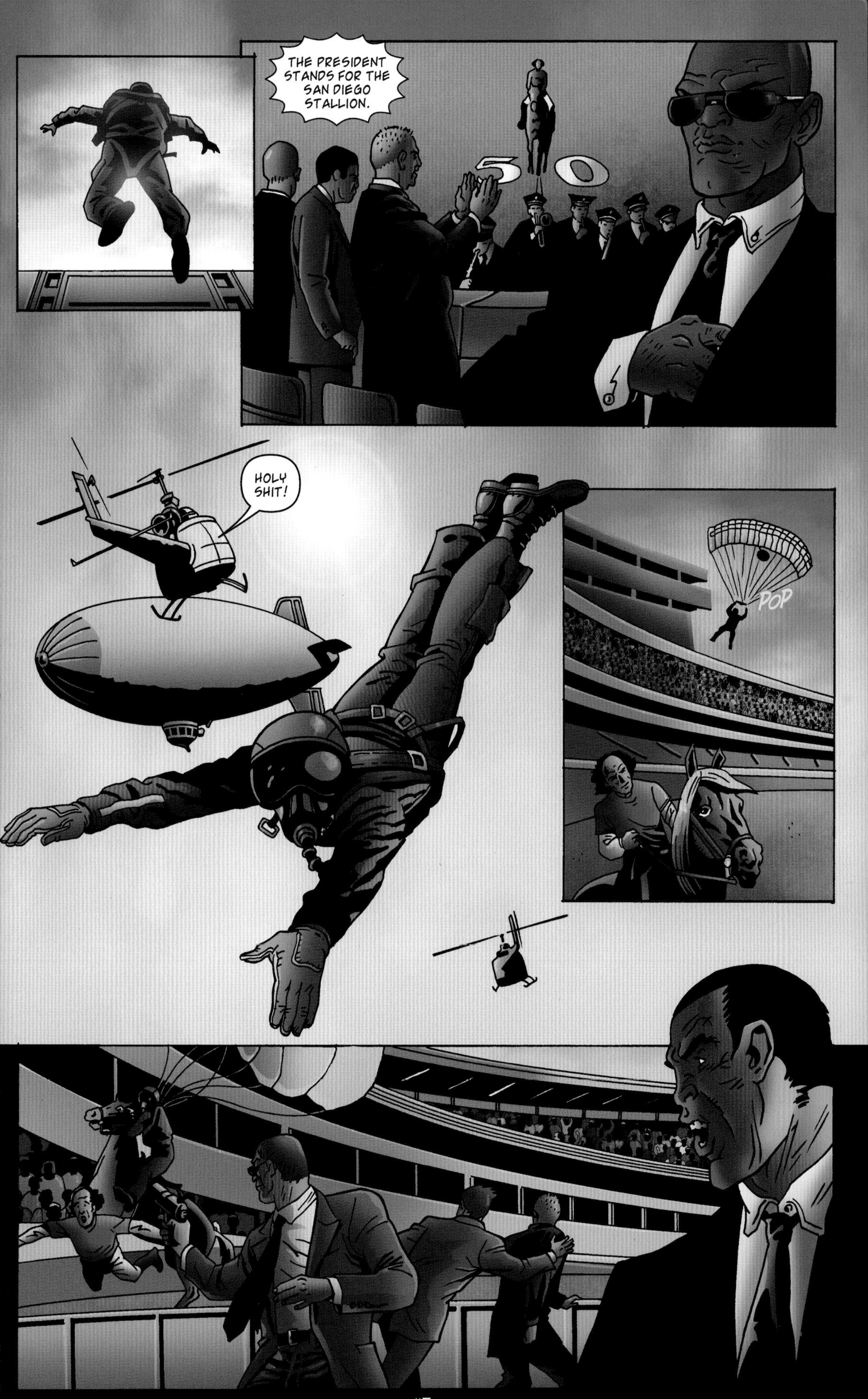
THE PRESIDENT STANDS FOR THE SAN DIEGO STALLION.
50
HOLY SHIT!
POP

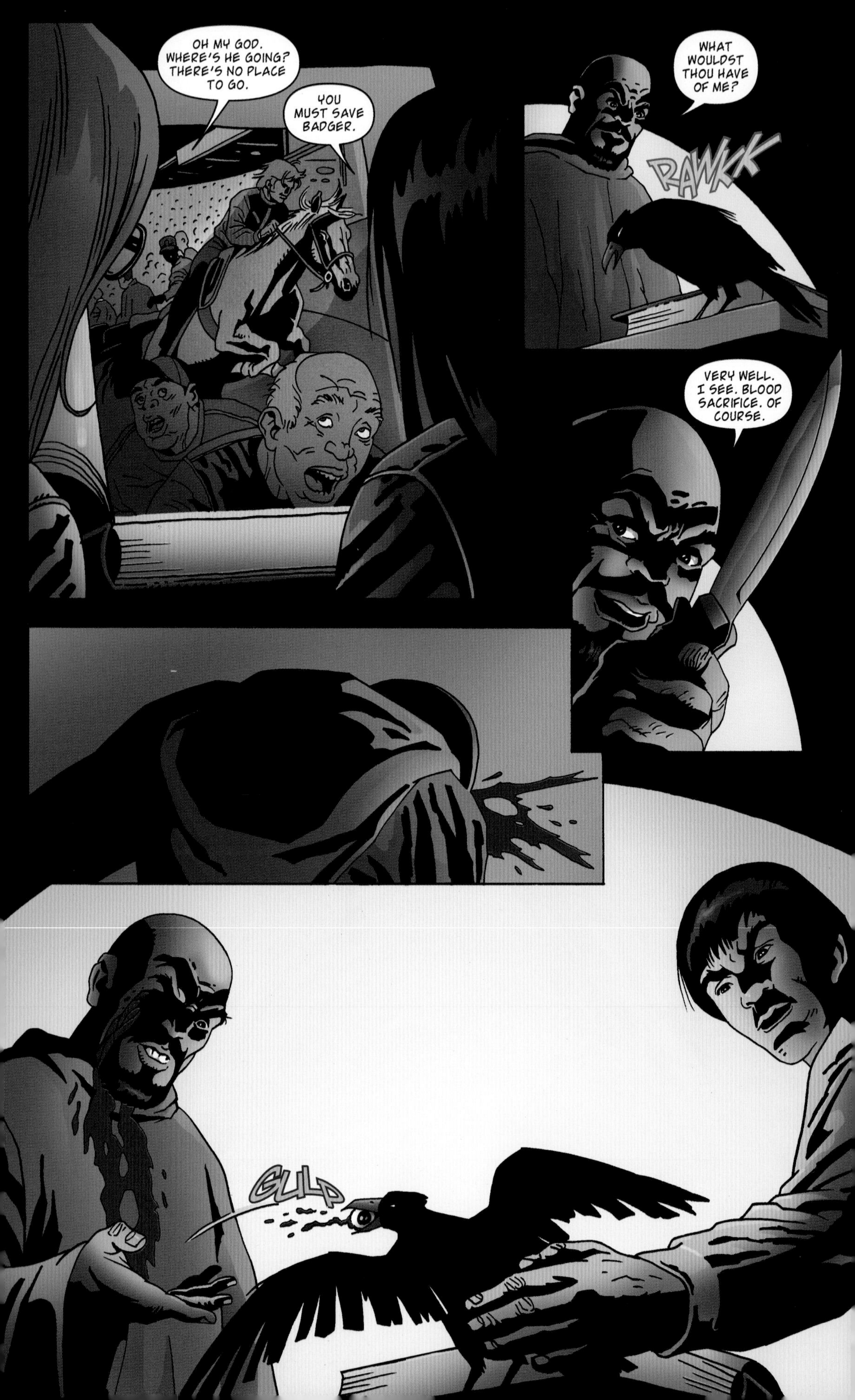
OH MY GOD. WHERE'S HE GOING? THERE'S NO PLACE TO GO.
YOU MUST SAVE BADGER.
WHAT WOULDST THOU HAVE OF ME?
RAWKK
VERY WELL. I SEE. BLOOD SACRIFICE. OF COURSE.
GULP

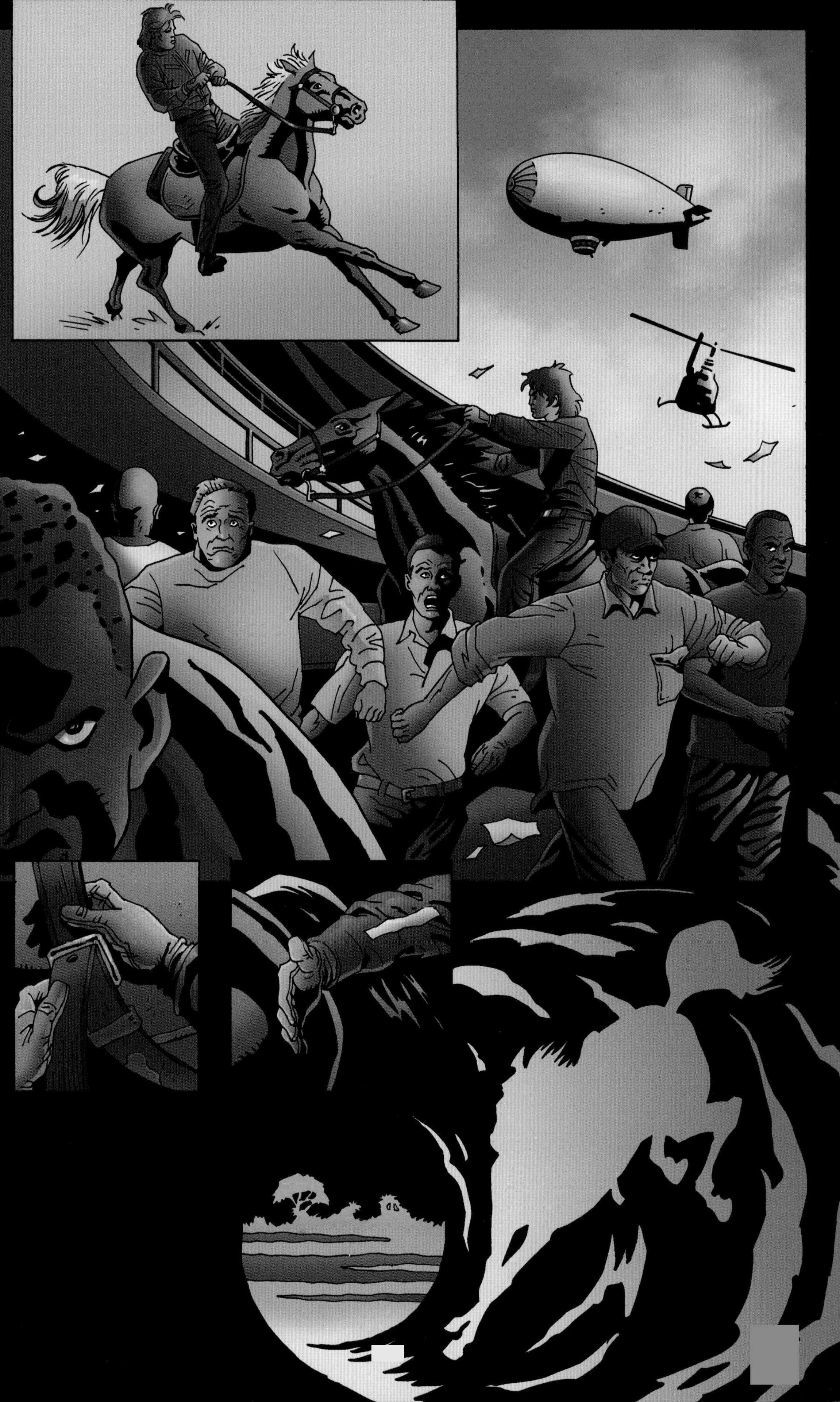

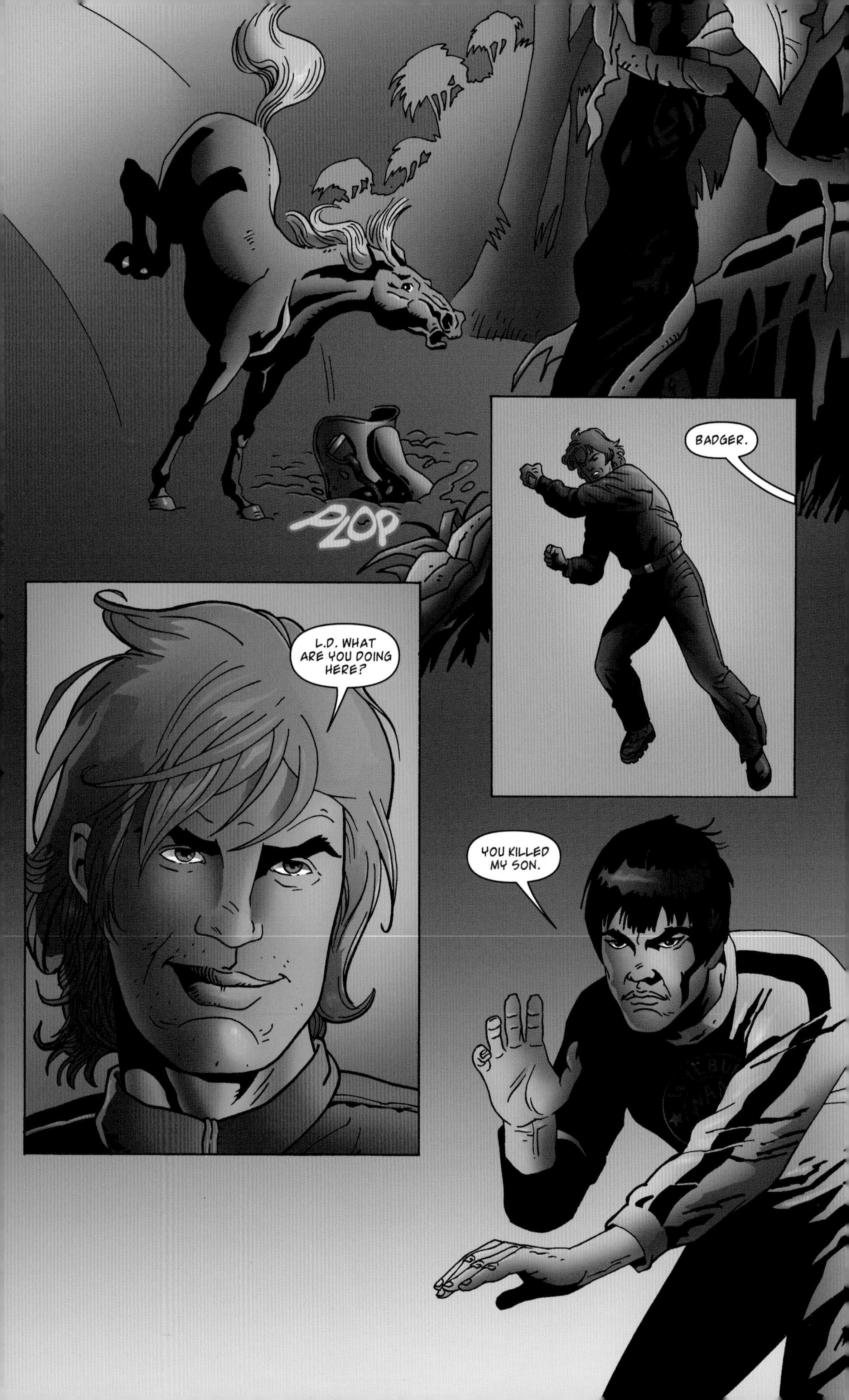
PLOP
BADGER.
L.D. WHAT ARE YOU DOING HERE?
YOU KILLED MY SON.

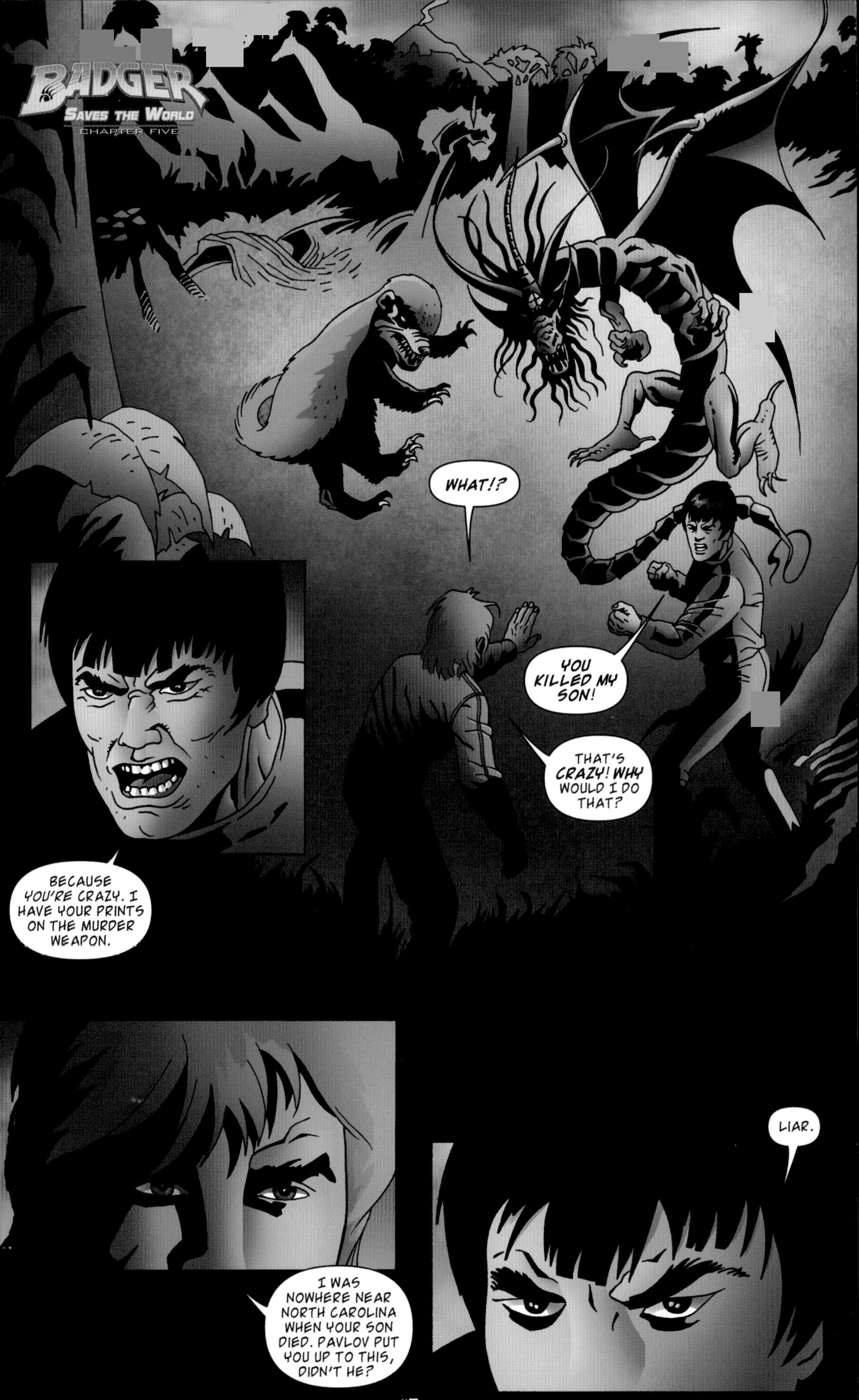
BADGER
SAVES THE WORLD
CHAPTER FIVE
WHAT!?
YOU KILLED MY SON!
THAT'S CRAZY! WHY WOULD I DO THAT?
BECAUSE YOU'RE CRAZY. I HAVE YOUR PRINTS ON THE MURDER WEAPON.
LIAR.
I WAS NOWHERE NEAR NORTH CAROLINA WHEN YOUR SON DIED. PAVLOV PUT YOU UP TO THIS, DIDN'T HE?

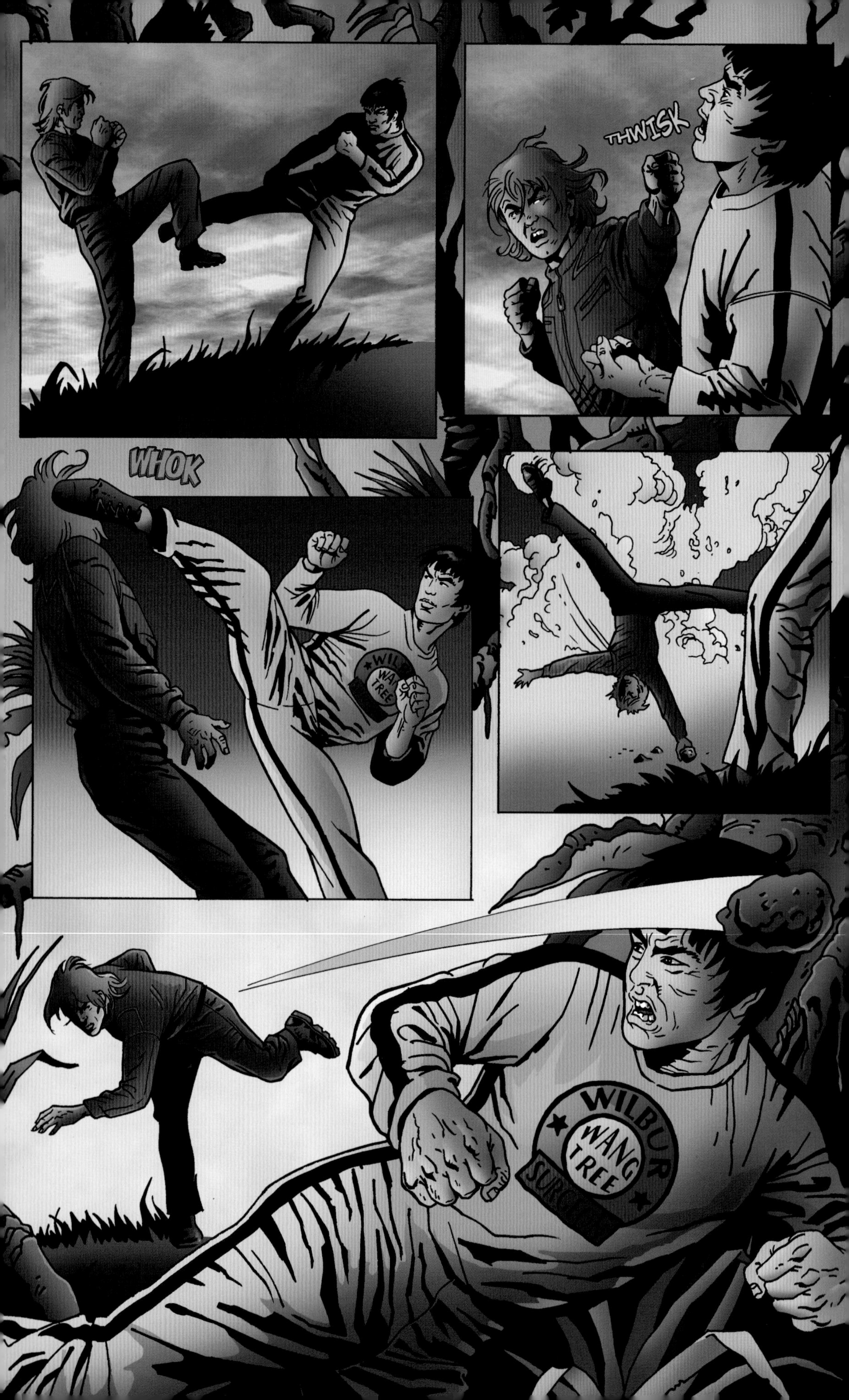
THWISK
WHOK
WILBUR
WANG
TREE
WILBUR
WANG
TREE

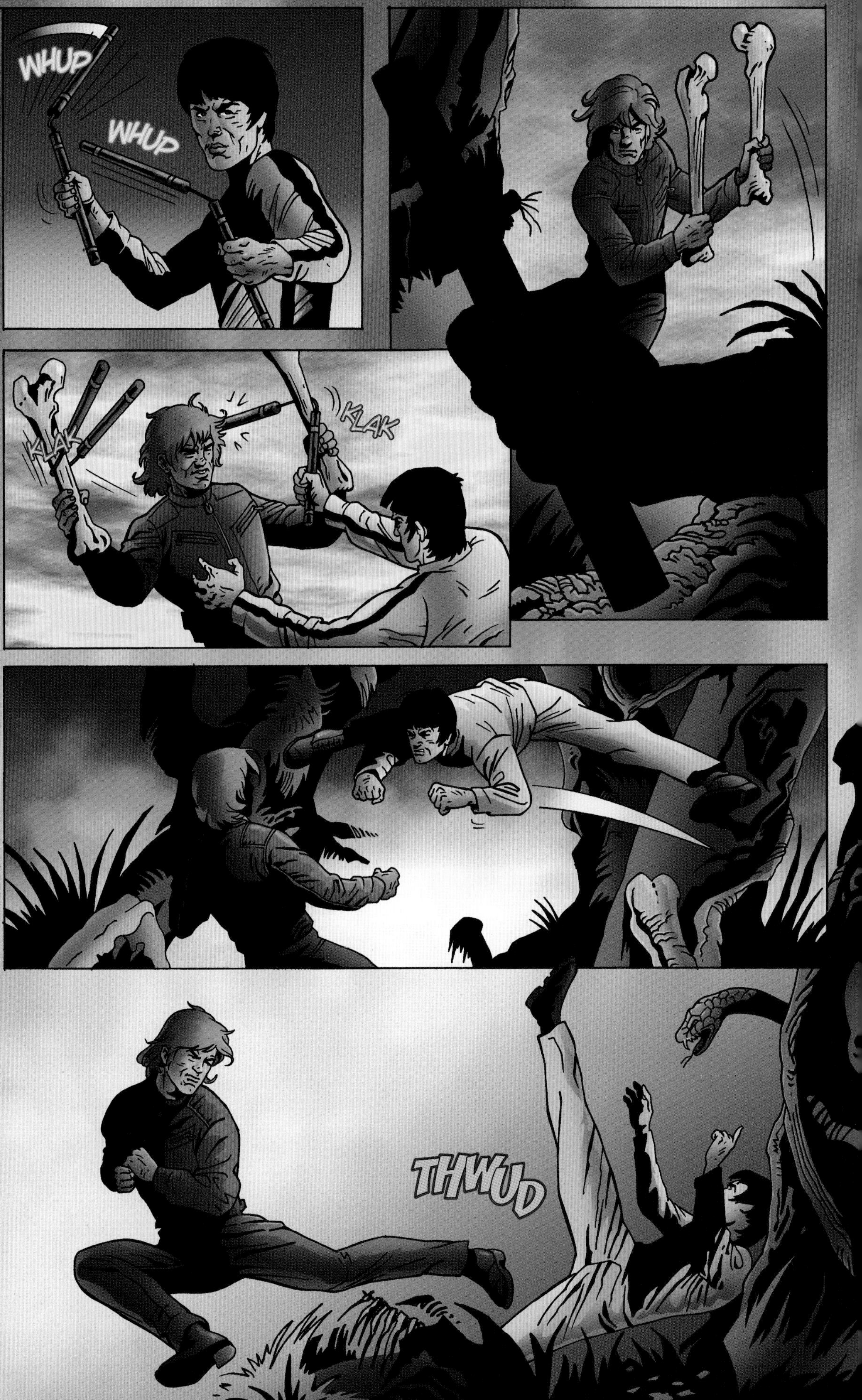
WHUP
WHUP
KLAK
KLAK
THWUD

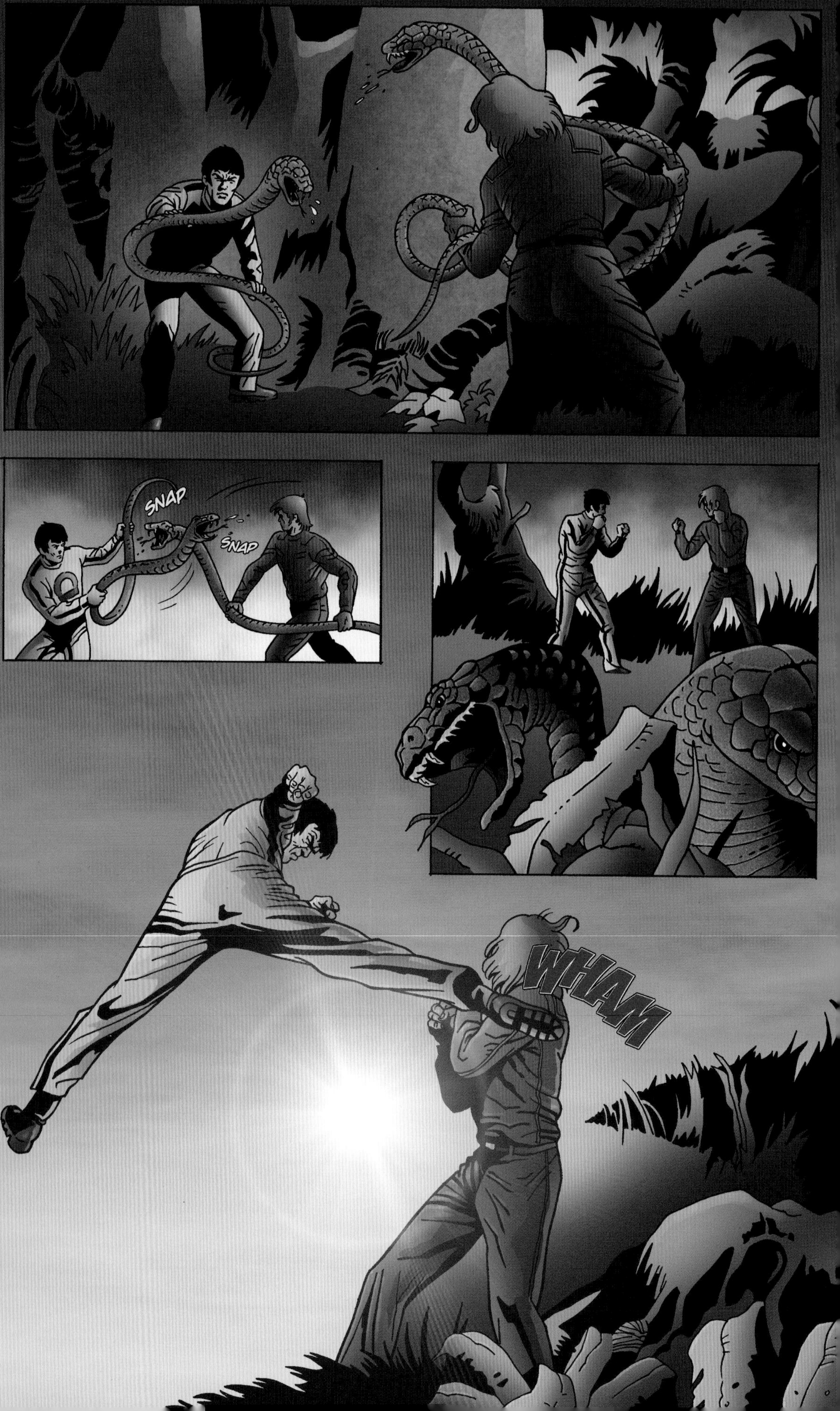
SNAP
SNAP
WHAM

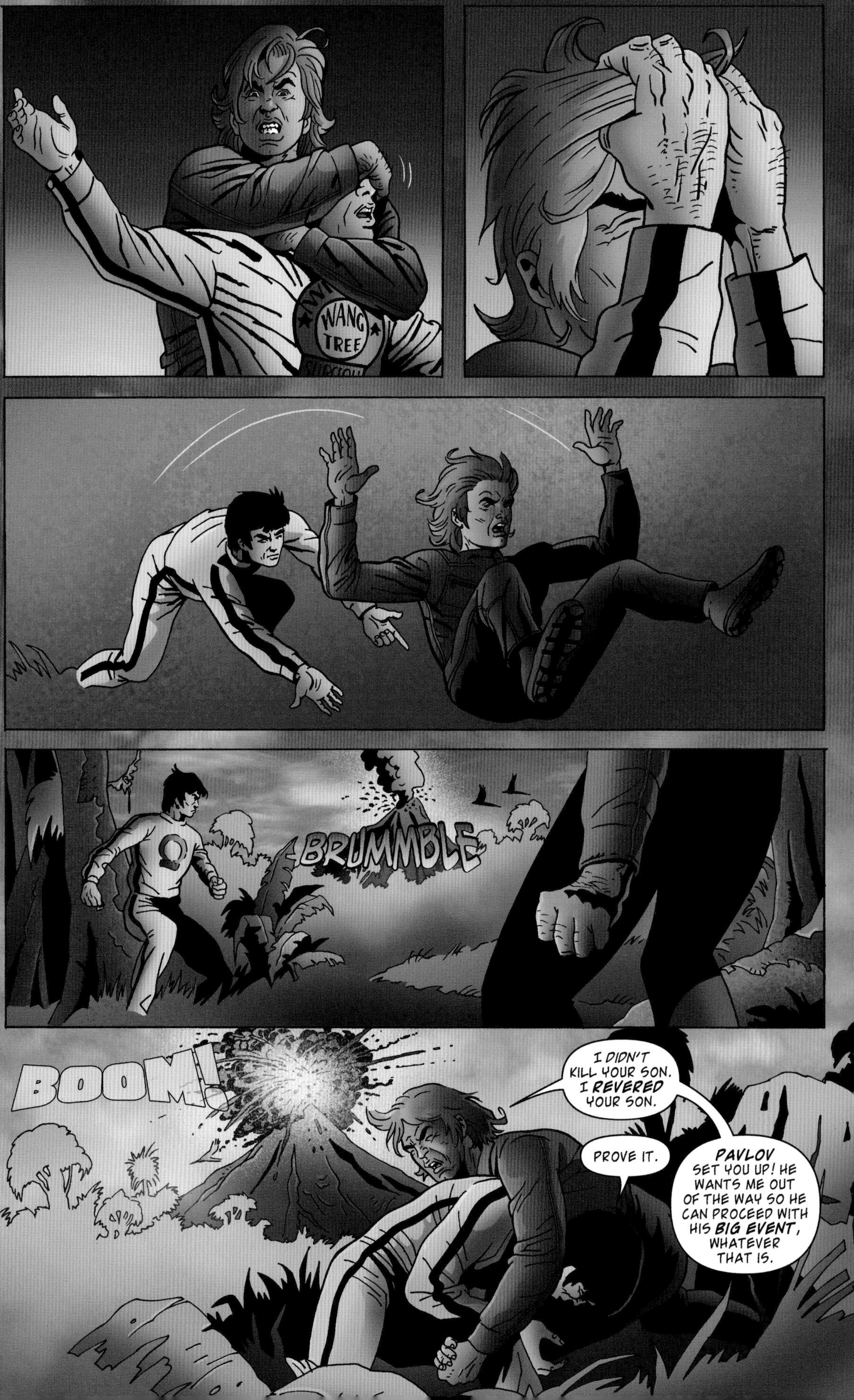
WANG TREE
BRUMMBLE
BOOM!
I DIDN'T KILL YOUR SON. I REVERED YOUR SON.
PROVE IT.
PAVLOV SET YOU UP! HE WANTS ME OUT OF THE WAY SO HE CAN PROCEED WITH HIS BIG EVENT, WHATEVER THAT IS.

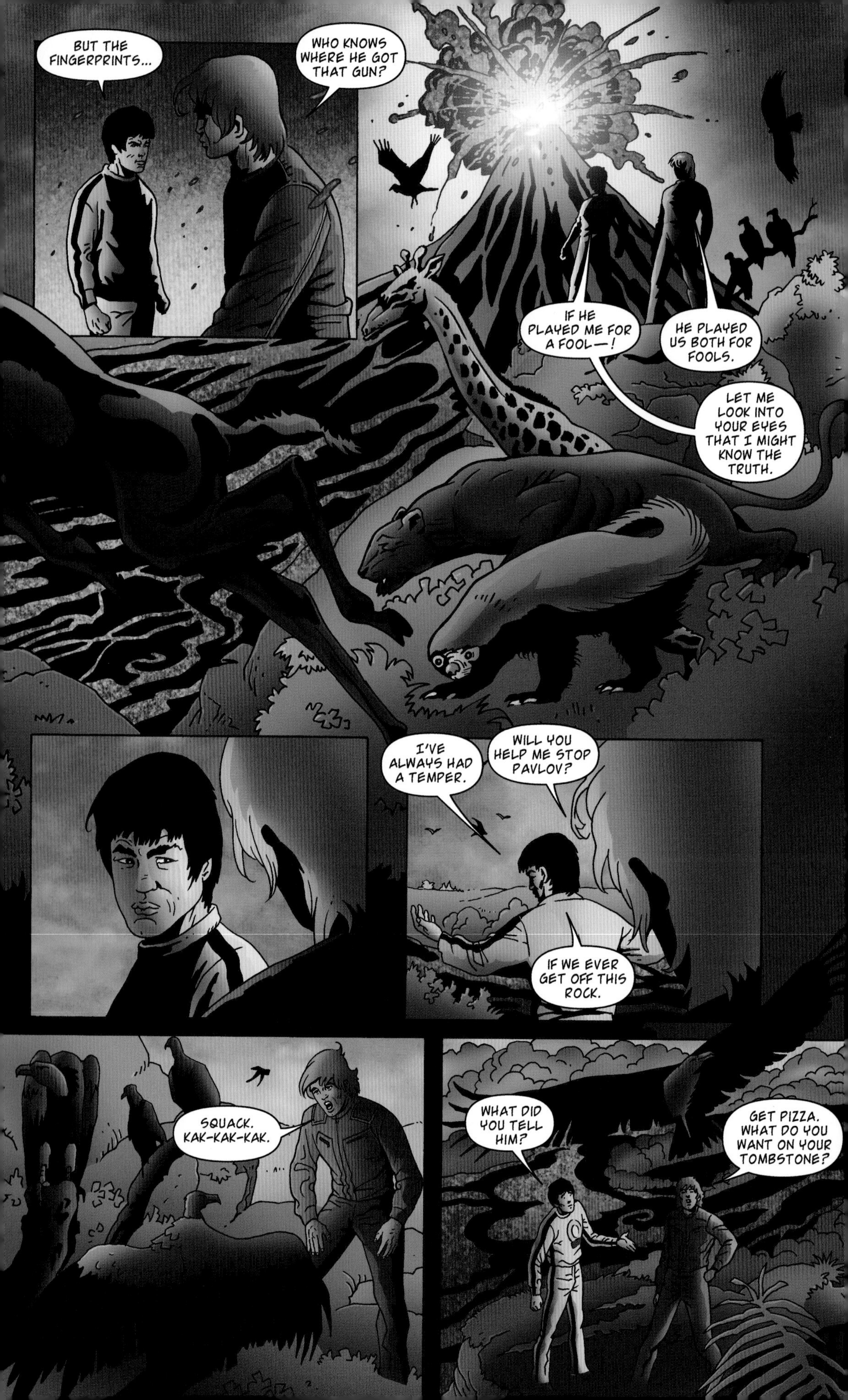
BUT THE FINGERPRINTS...
WHO KNOWS WHERE HE GOT THAT GUN?
IF HE PLAYED ME FOR A FOOL—!
HE PLAYED US BOTH FOR FOOLS.
LET ME LOOK INTO YOUR EYES THAT I MIGHT KNOW THE TRUTH.
I'VE ALWAYS HAD A TEMPER.
WILL YOU HELP ME STOP PAVLOV?
IF WE EVER GET OFF THIS ROCK.
SQUACK. KAK-KAK-KAK.
WHAT DID YOU TELL HIM?
GET PIZZA. WHAT DO YOU WANT ON YOUR TOMBSTONE?

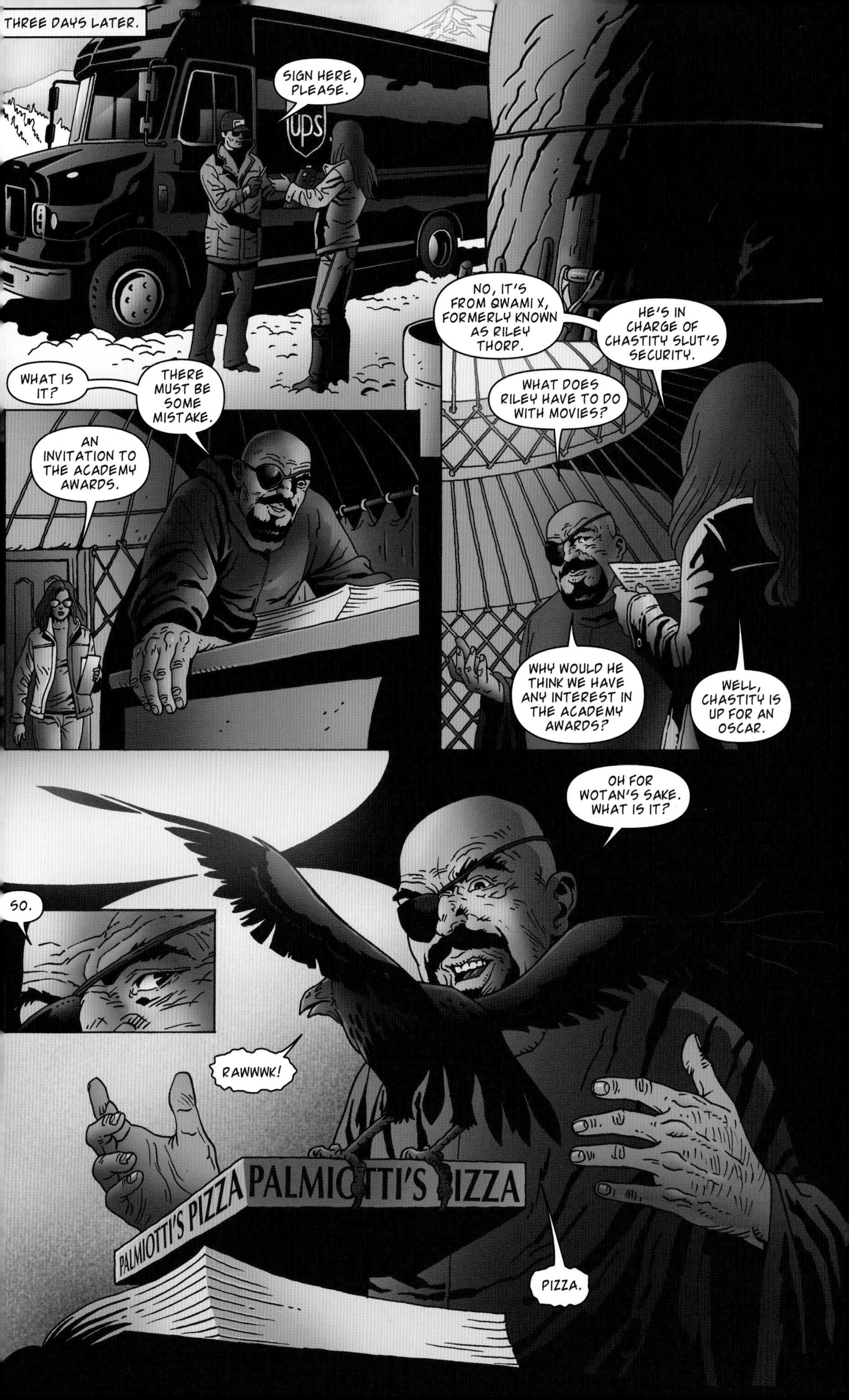
THREE DAYS LATER.
SIGN HERE, PLEASE.
UPS
WHAT IS IT?
THERE MUST BE SOME MISTAKE.
AN INVITATION TO THE ACADEMY AWARDS.
NO, IT'S FROM QWAMI X, FORMERLY KNOWN AS RILEY THORP.
HE'S IN CHARGE OF CHASTITY SLUT'S SECURITY.
WHAT DOES RILEY HAVE TO DO WITH MOVIES?
WHY WOULD HE THINK WE HAVE ANY INTEREST IN THE ACADEMY AWARDS?
WELL, CHASTITY IS UP FOR AN OSCAR.
OH FOR WOTAN'S SAKE. WHAT IS IT?
SO.
RAWWWK!
PALMIOTTI'S PIZZA
PALMIOTTI'S PIZZA
PALMIOTTI'S PIZZA
PIZZA.

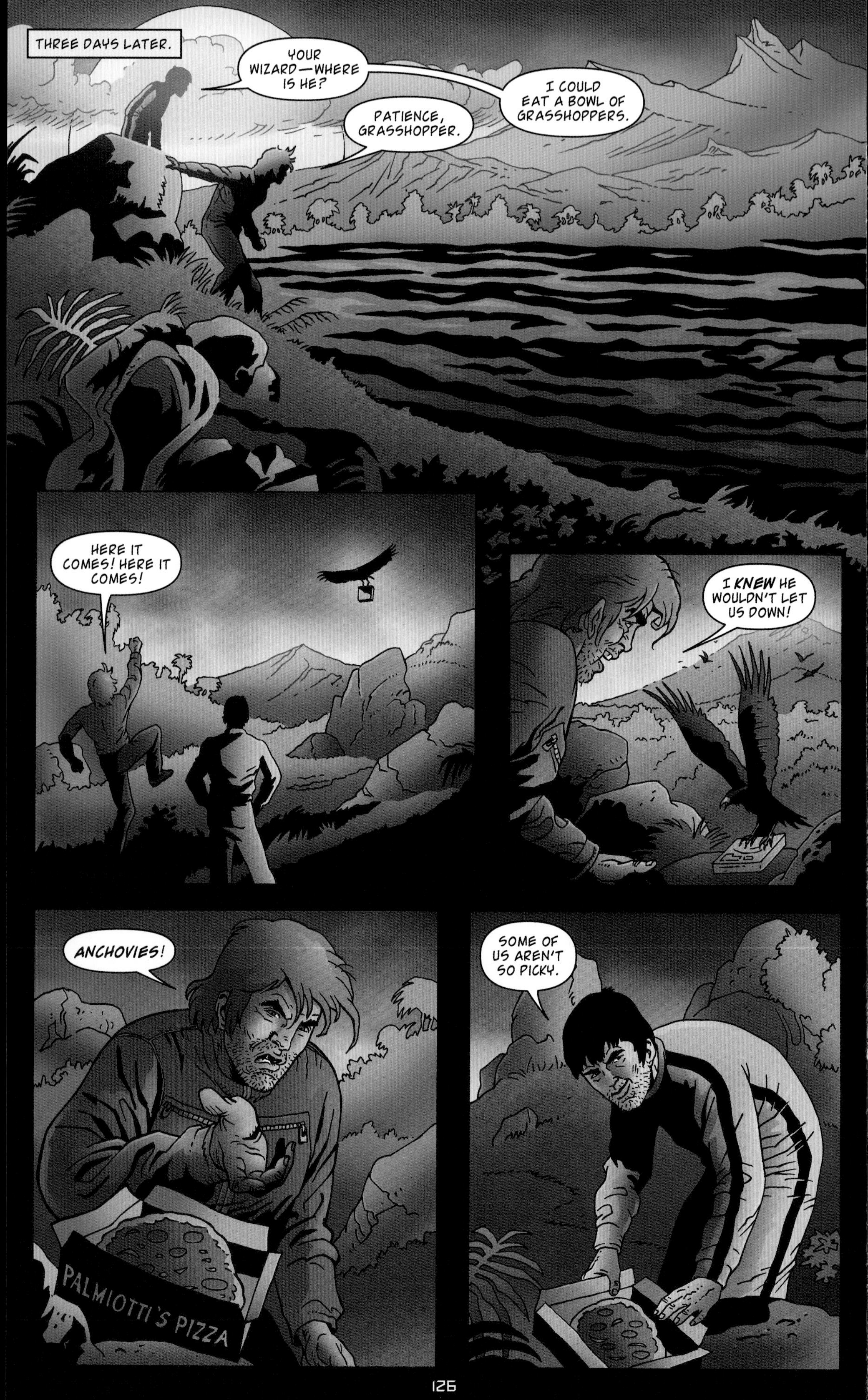
THREE DAYS LATER.
YOUR WIZARD—WHERE IS HE?
I COULD EAT A BOWL OF GRASSHOPPERS.
PATIENCE, GRASSHOPPER.
HERE IT COMES! HERE IT COMES!
I KNEW HE WOULDN'T LET US DOWN!
ANCHOVIES!
PALMIOTTI'S PIZZA
SOME OF US AREN'T SO PICKY.

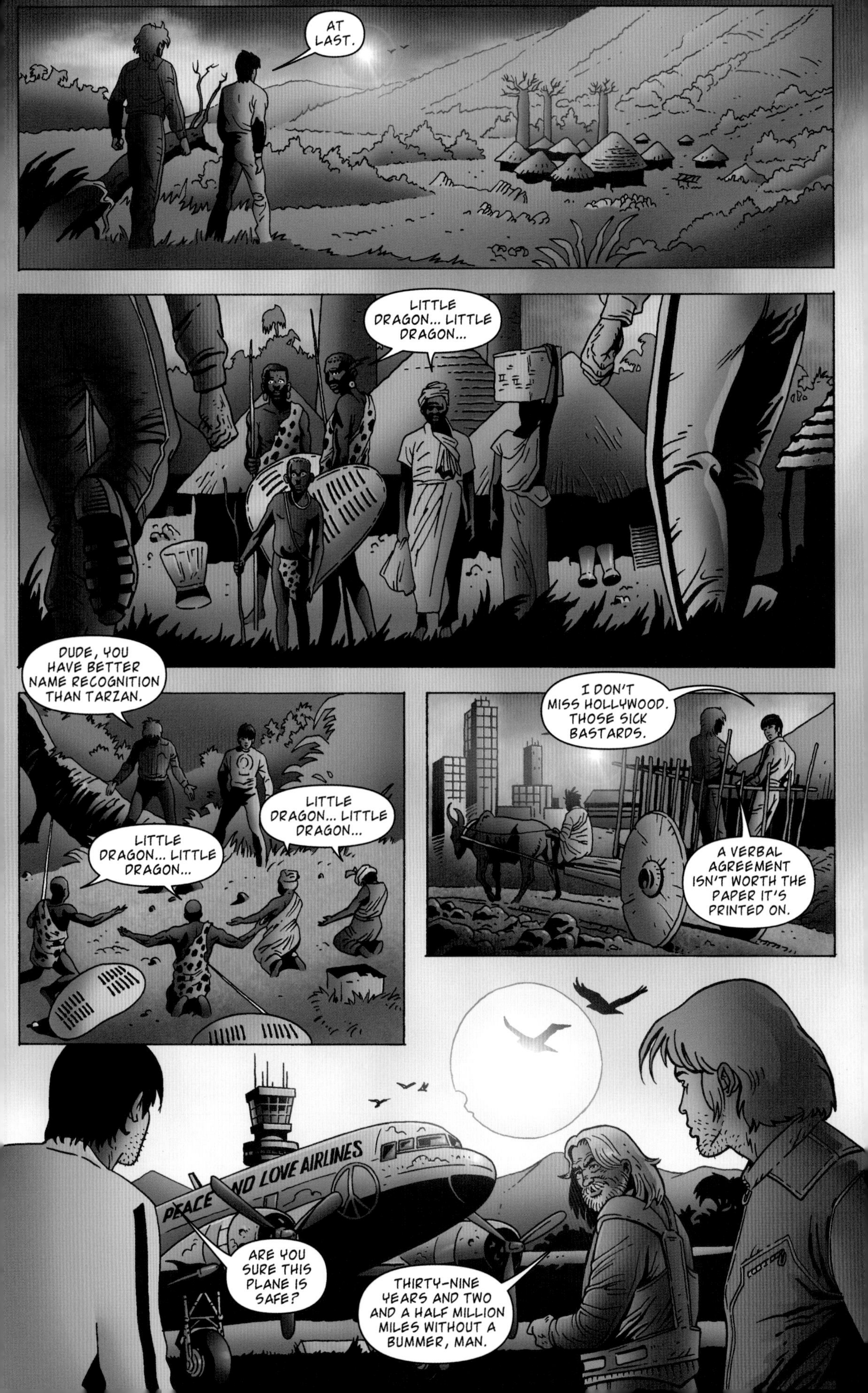

AT LAST.
LITTLE DRAGON... LITTLE DRAGON...
DUDE, YOU HAVE BETTER NAME RECOGNITION THAN TARZAN.
LITTLE DRAGON... LITTLE DRAGON...
LITTLE DRAGON... LITTLE DRAGON...
I DON'T MISS HOLLYWOOD. THOSE SICK BASTARDS.
A VERBAL AGREEMENT ISN'T WORTH THE PAPER IT'S PRINTED ON.
PEACE AND LOVE AIRLINES
ARE YOU SURE THIS PLANE IS SAFE?
THIRTY-NINE YEARS AND TWO AND A HALF MILLION MILES WITHOUT A BUMMER, MAN.

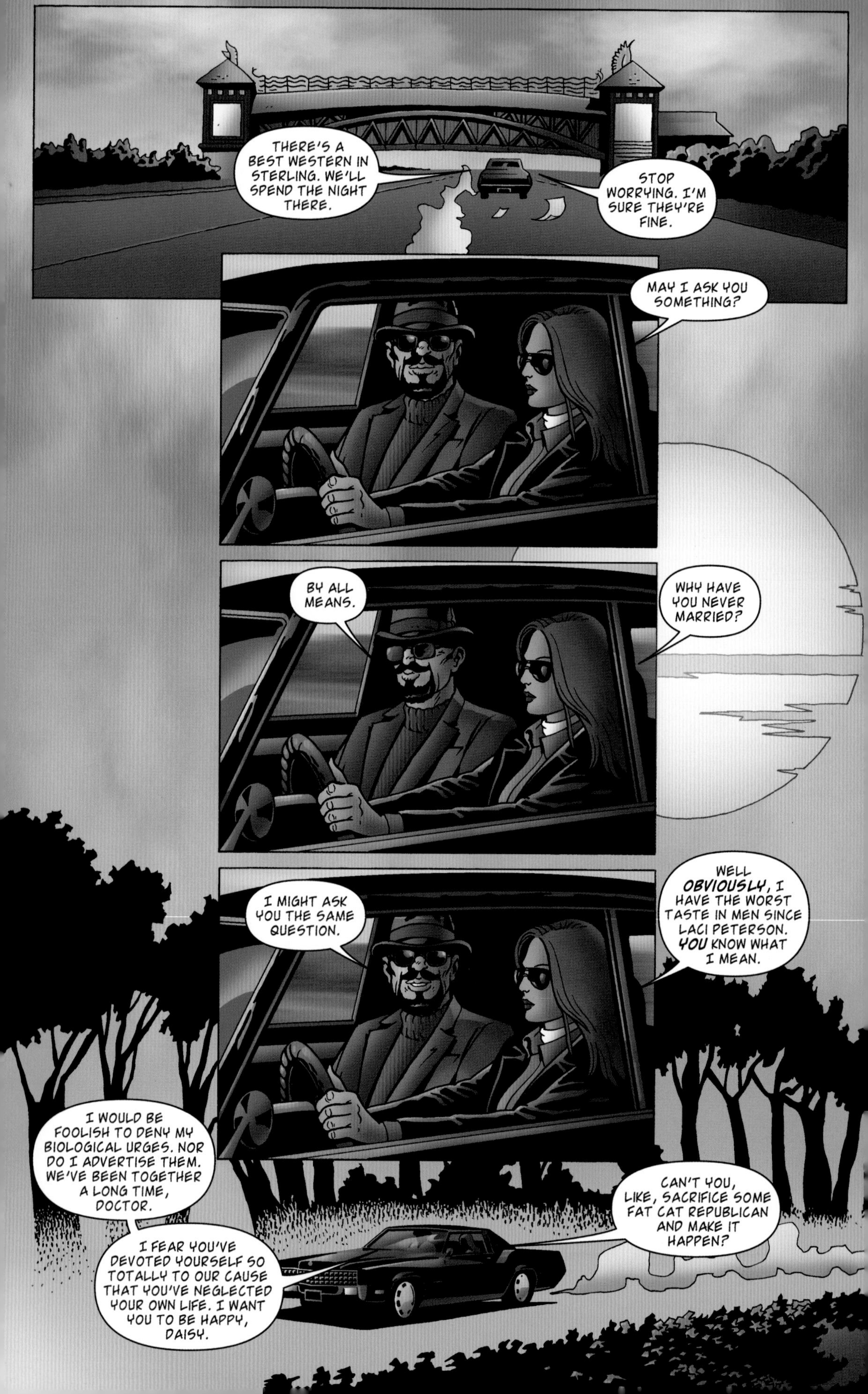
THERE'S A BEST WESTERN IN STERLING. WE'LL SPEND THE NIGHT THERE.
STOP WORRYING. I'M SURE THEY'RE FINE.
MAY I ASK YOU SOMETHING?
BY ALL MEANS.
WHY HAVE YOU NEVER MARRIED?
I MIGHT ASK YOU THE SAME QUESTION.
WELL *OBVIOUSLY*, I HAVE THE WORST TASTE IN MEN SINCE LACI PETERSON. *YOU* KNOW WHAT I MEAN.
I WOULD BE FOOLISH TO DENY MY BIOLOGICAL URGES. NOR DO I ADVERTISE THEM. WE'VE BEEN TOGETHER A LONG TIME, DOCTOR.
I FEAR YOU'VE DEVOTED YOURSELF SO TOTALLY TO OUR CAUSE THAT YOU'VE NEGLECTED YOUR OWN LIFE. I WANT YOU TO BE HAPPY, DAISY.
CAN'T YOU, LIKE, SACRIFICE SOME FAT CAT REPUBLICAN AND MAKE IT HAPPEN?

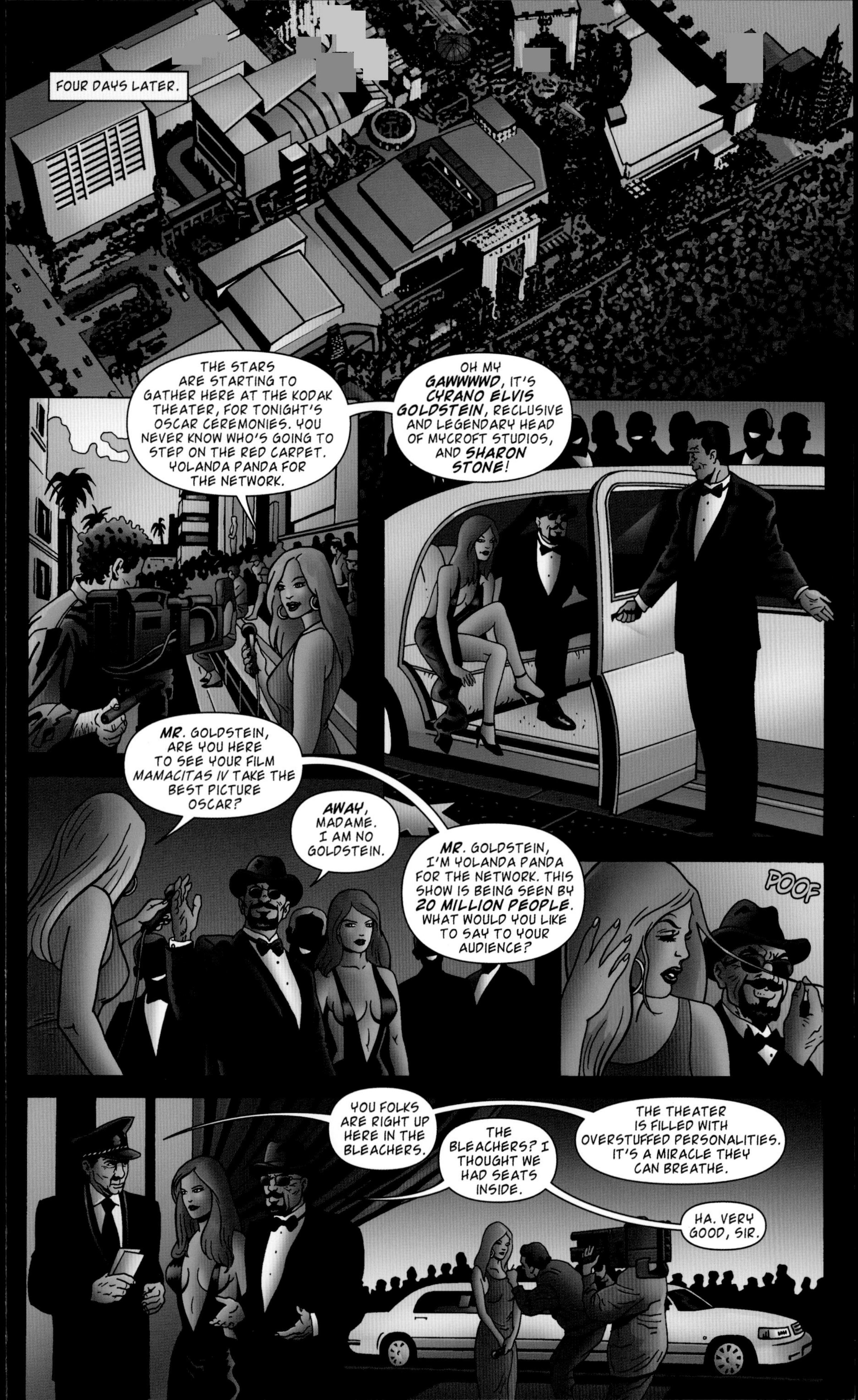
FOUR DAYS LATER.
THE STARS ARE STARTING TO GATHER HERE AT THE KODAK THEATER, FOR TONIGHT'S OSCAR CEREMONIES. YOU NEVER KNOW WHO'S GOING TO STEP ON THE RED CARPET. YOLANDA PANDA FOR THE NETWORK.
OH MY GAWWWWD, IT'S CYRANO ELVIS GOLDSTEIN, RECLUSIVE AND LEGENDARY HEAD OF MYCROFT STUDIOS, AND SHARON STONE!
MR. GOLDSTEIN, ARE YOU HERE TO SEE YOUR FILM MAMACITAS IV TAKE THE BEST PICTURE OSCAR?
AWAY, MADAME. I AM NO GOLDSTEIN.
MR. GOLDSTEIN, I'M YOLANDA PANDA FOR THE NETWORK. THIS SHOW IS BEING SEEN BY 20 MILLION PEOPLE. WHAT WOULD YOU LIKE TO SAY TO YOUR AUDIENCE?
POOF
YOU FOLKS ARE RIGHT UP HERE IN THE BLEACHERS.
THE BLEACHERS? I THOUGHT WE HAD SEATS INSIDE.
THE THEATER IS FILLED WITH OVERSTUFFED PERSONALITIES. IT'S A MIRACLE THEY CAN BREATHE.
HA. VERY GOOD, SIR.

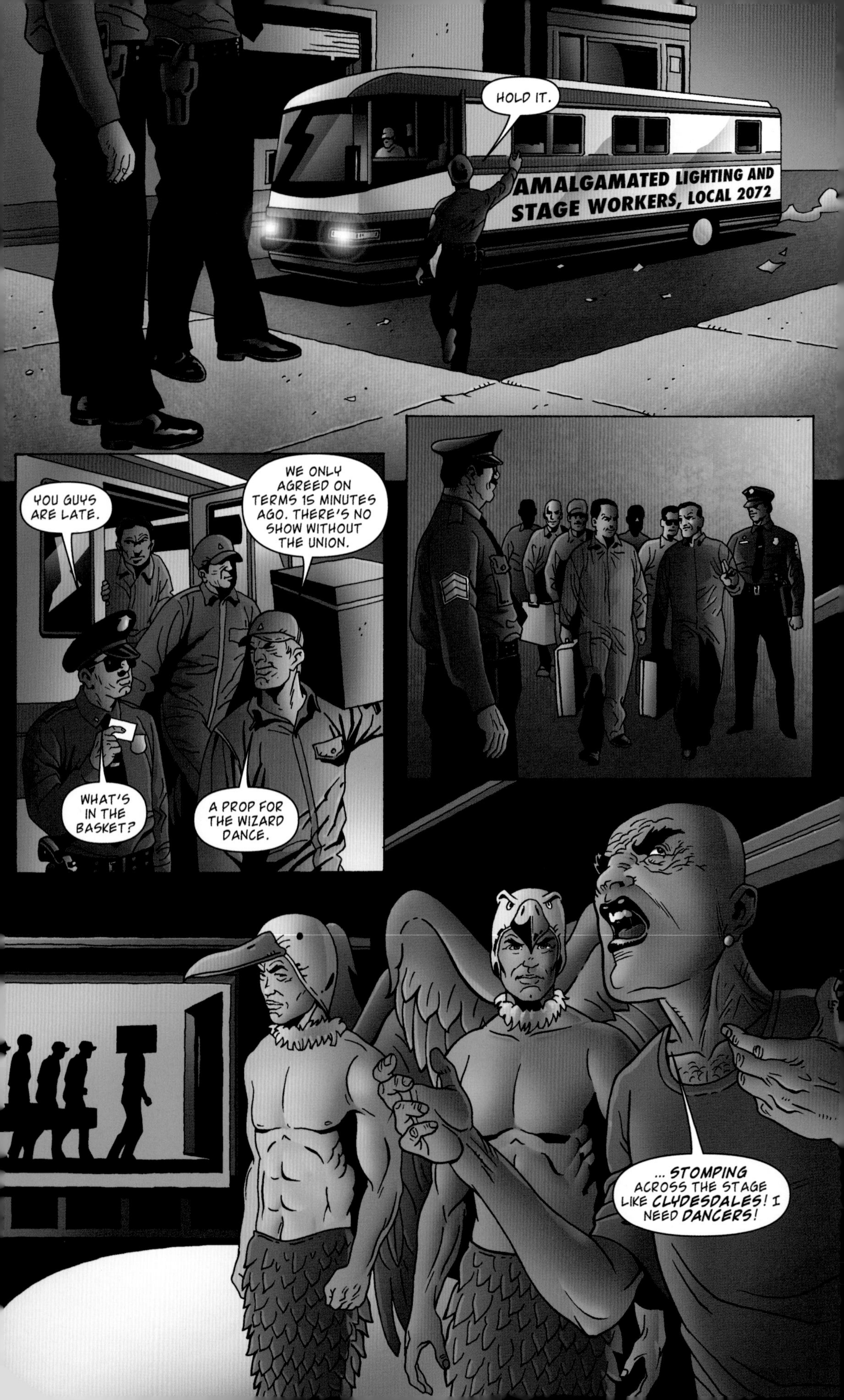
HOLD IT.
AMALGAMATED LIGHTING AND STAGE WORKERS, LOCAL 2072
YOU GUYS ARE LATE.
WE ONLY AGREED ON TERMS 15 MINUTES AGO. THERE'S NO SHOW WITHOUT THE UNION.
WHAT'S IN THE BASKET?
A PROP FOR THE WIZARD DANCE.
... STOMPING ACROSS THE STAGE LIKE CLYDESDALES! I NEED DANCERS!

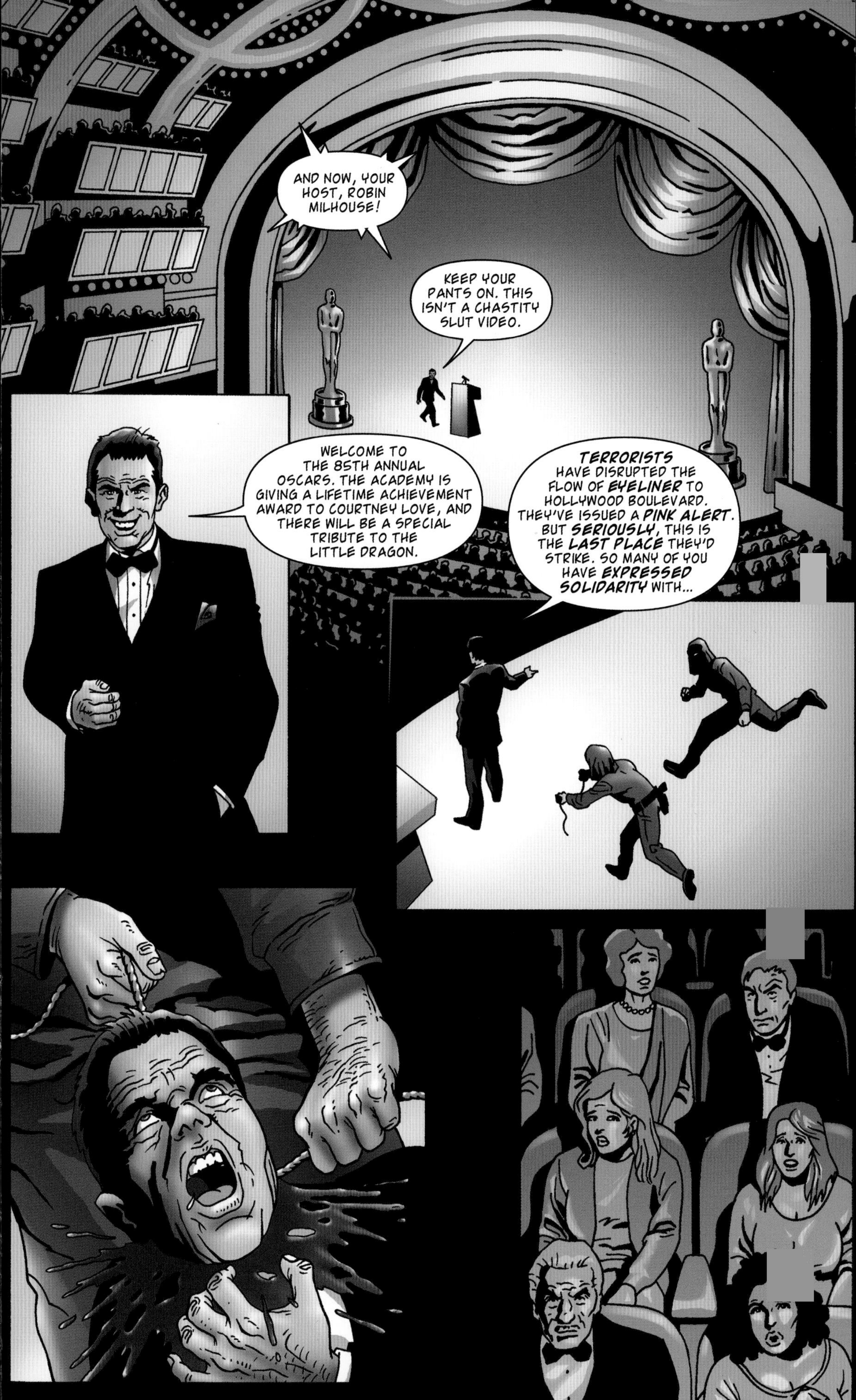
AND NOW, YOUR HOST, ROBIN MILHOUSE!
KEEP YOUR PANTS ON. THIS ISN'T A CHASTITY SLUT VIDEO.
WELCOME TO THE 85TH ANNUAL OSCARS. THE ACADEMY IS GIVING A LIFETIME ACHIEVEMENT AWARD TO COURTNEY LOVE, AND THERE WILL BE A SPECIAL TRIBUTE TO THE LITTLE DRAGON.
TERRORISTS HAVE DISRUPTED THE FLOW OF EYELINER TO HOLLYWOOD BOULEVARD. THEY'VE ISSUED A PINK ALERT. BUT SERIOUSLY, THIS IS THE LAST PLACE THEY'D STRIKE. SO MANY OF YOU HAVE EXPRESSED SOLIDARITY WITH...

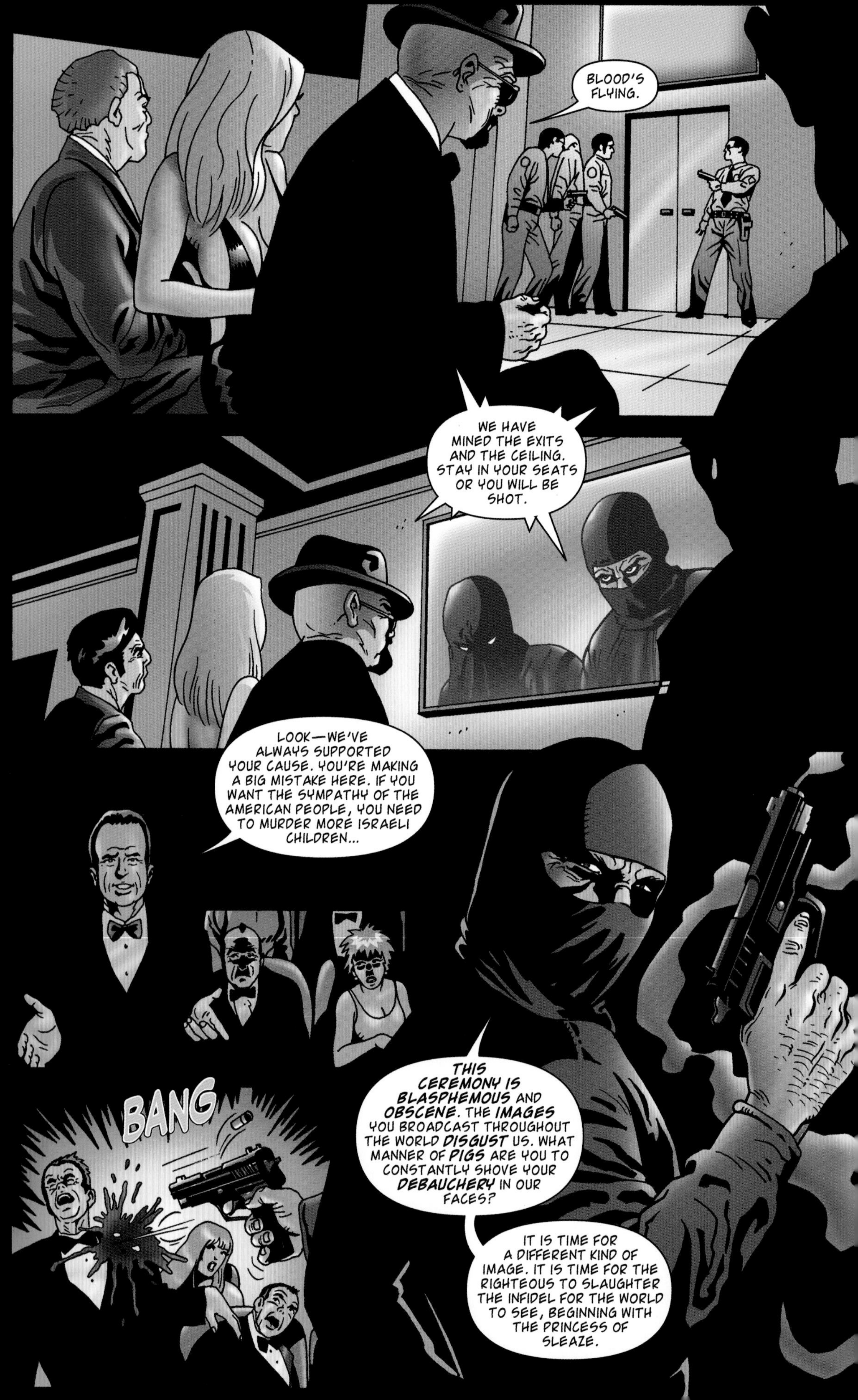
BLOOD'S FLYING.
WE HAVE MINED THE EXITS AND THE CEILING. STAY IN YOUR SEATS OR YOU WILL BE SHOT.
LOOK—WE'VE ALWAYS SUPPORTED YOUR CAUSE. YOU'RE MAKING A BIG MISTAKE HERE. IF YOU WANT THE SYMPATHY OF THE AMERICAN PEOPLE, YOU NEED TO MURDER MORE ISRAELI CHILDREN...
THIS CEREMONY IS BLASPHEMOUS AND OBSCENE. THE IMAGES YOU BROADCAST THROUGHOUT THE WORLD DISGUST US. WHAT MANNER OF PIGS ARE YOU TO CONSTANTLY SHOVE YOUR DEBAUCHERY IN OUR FACES?
IT IS TIME FOR A DIFFERENT KIND OF IMAGE. IT IS TIME FOR THE RIGHTEOUS TO SLAUGHTER THE INFIDEL FOR THE WORLD TO SEE, BEGINNING WITH THE PRINCESS OF SLEAZE.
BANG

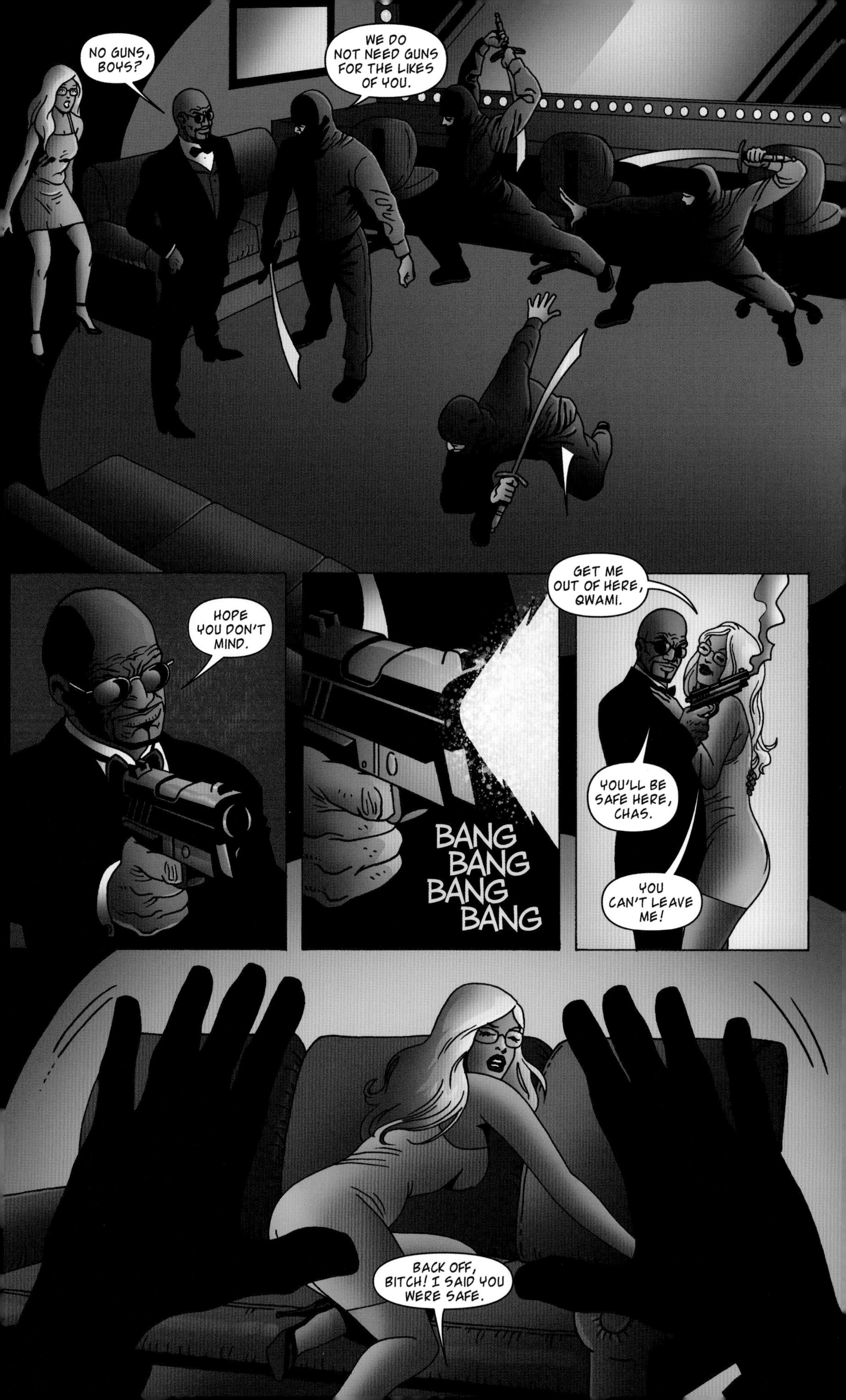
NO GUNS, BOYS?
WE DO NOT NEED GUNS FOR THE LIKES OF YOU.
HOPE YOU DON'T MIND.
BANG BANG BANG BANG
GET ME OUT OF HERE, QWAMI.
YOU'LL BE SAFE HERE, CHAS.
YOU CAN'T LEAVE ME!
BACK OFF, BITCH! I SAID YOU WERE SAFE.

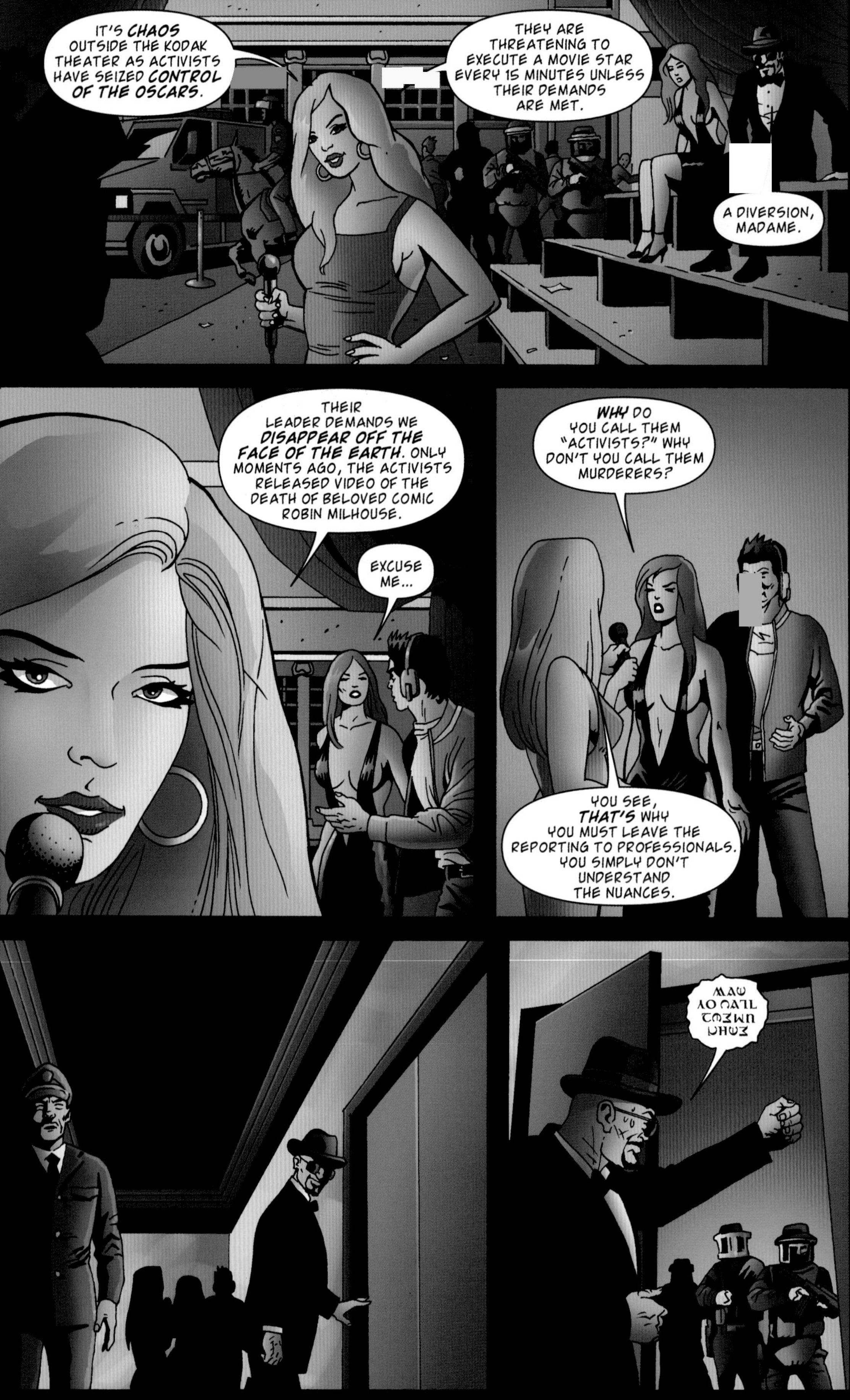
IT'S CHAOS OUTSIDE THE KODAK THEATER AS ACTIVISTS HAVE SEIZED CONTROL OF THE OSCARS.
THEY ARE THREATENING TO EXECUTE A MOVIE STAR EVERY 15 MINUTES UNLESS THEIR DEMANDS ARE MET.
A DIVERSION, MADAME.
THEIR LEADER DEMANDS WE DISAPPEAR OFF THE FACE OF THE EARTH. ONLY MOMENTS AGO, THE ACTIVISTS RELEASED VIDEO OF THE DEATH OF BELOVED COMIC ROBIN MILHOUSE.
EXCUSE ME...
WHY DO YOU CALL THEM "ACTIVISTS?" WHY DON'T YOU CALL THEM MURDERERS?
YOU SEE, THAT'S WHY YOU MUST LEAVE THE REPORTING TO PROFESSIONALS. YOU SIMPLY DON'T UNDERSTAND THE NUANCES.

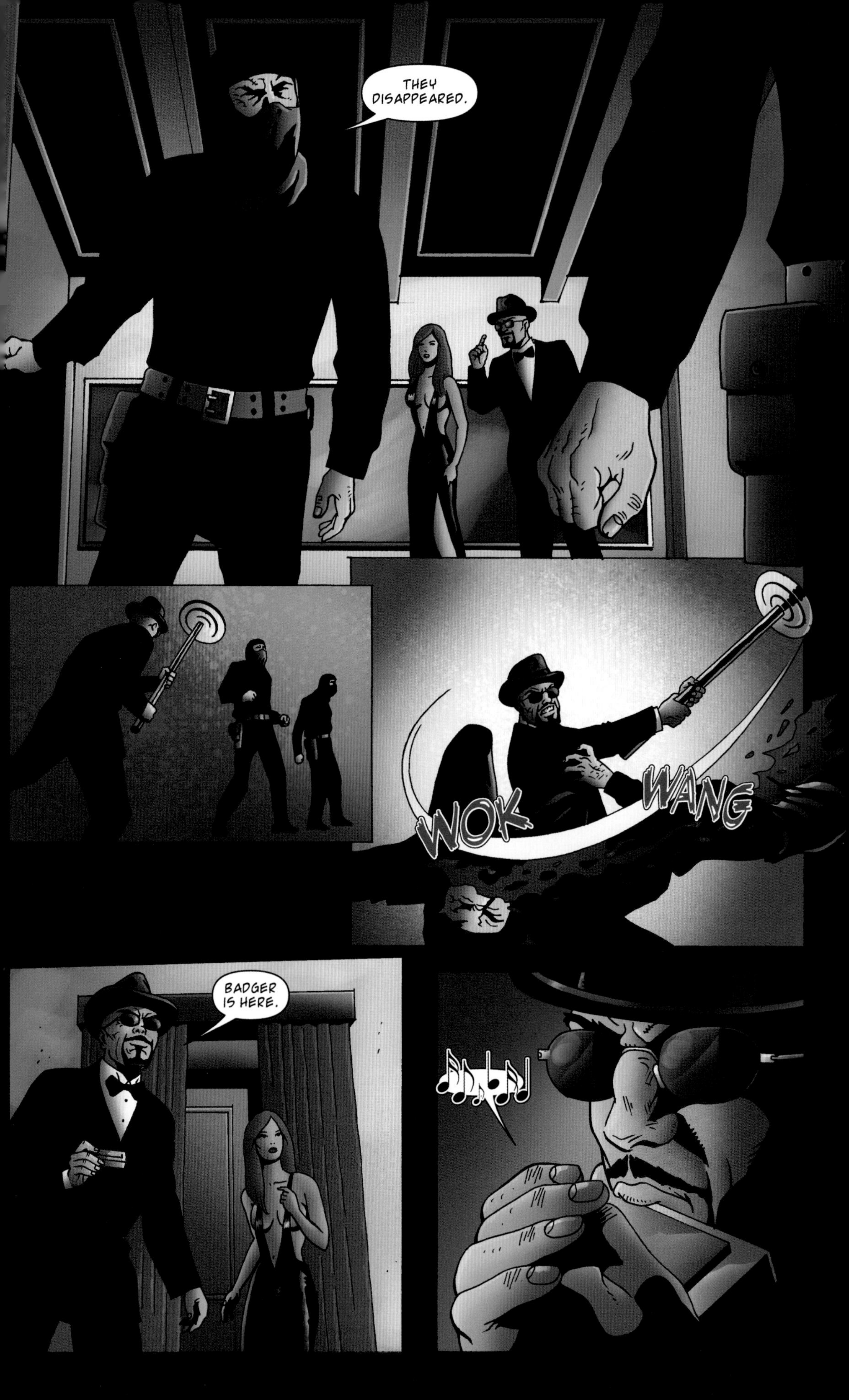
THEY DISAPPEARED.
WOK
WANG
BADGER IS HERE.

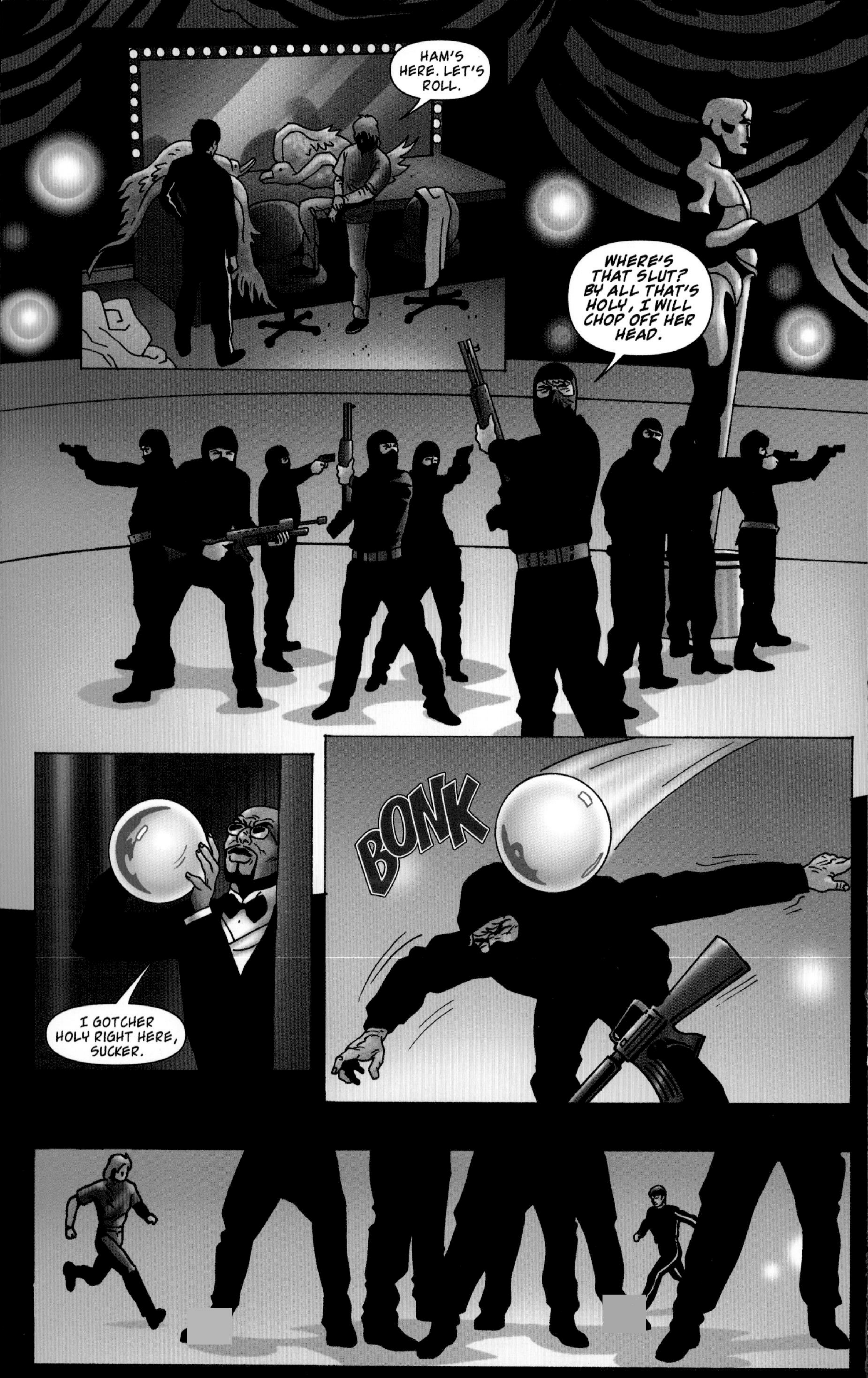
HAM'S HERE. LET'S ROLL.
WHERE'S THAT SLUT? BY ALL THAT'S HOLY, I WILL CHOP OFF HER HEAD.
I GOTCHER HOLY RIGHT HERE, SUCKER.
BONK

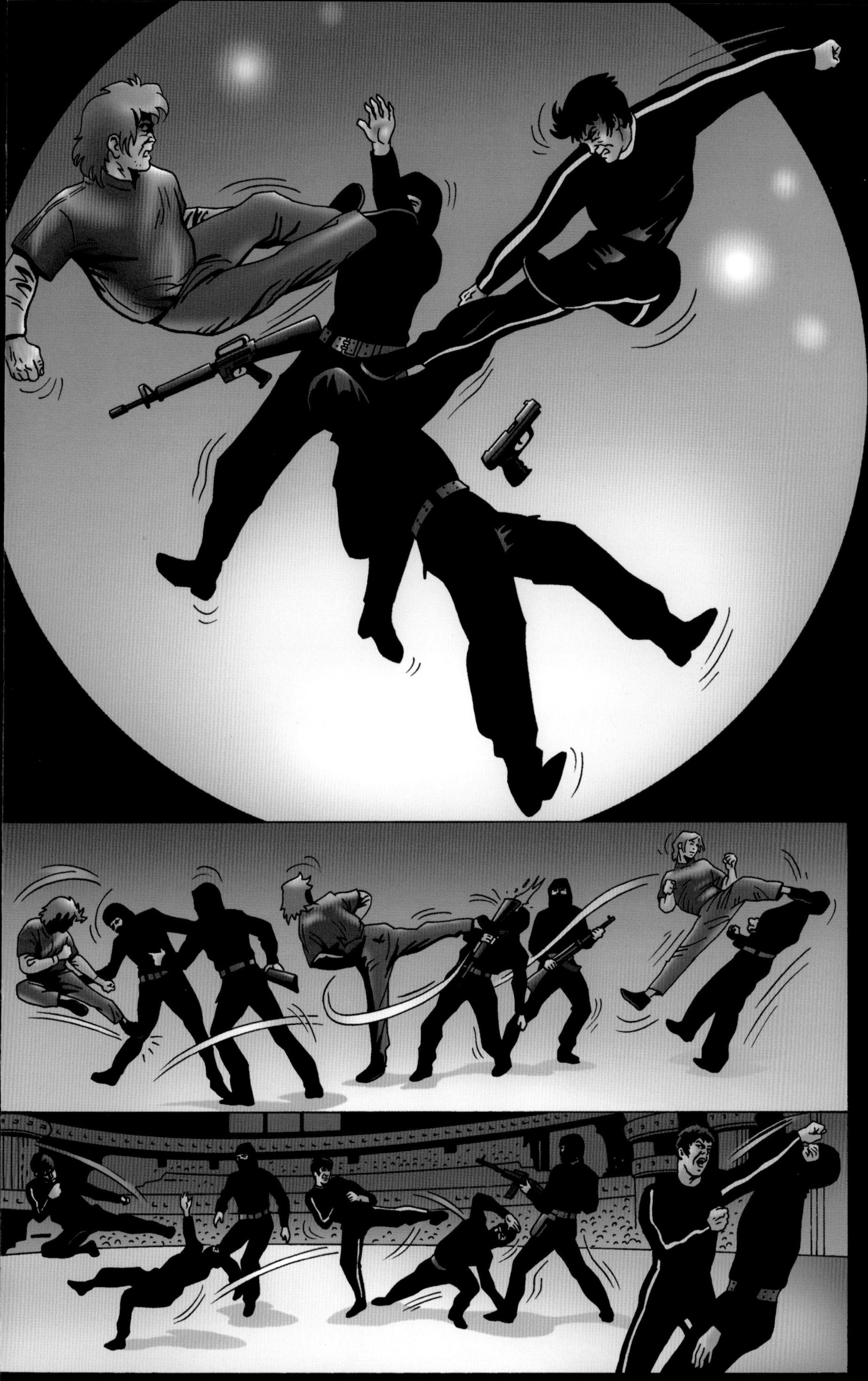

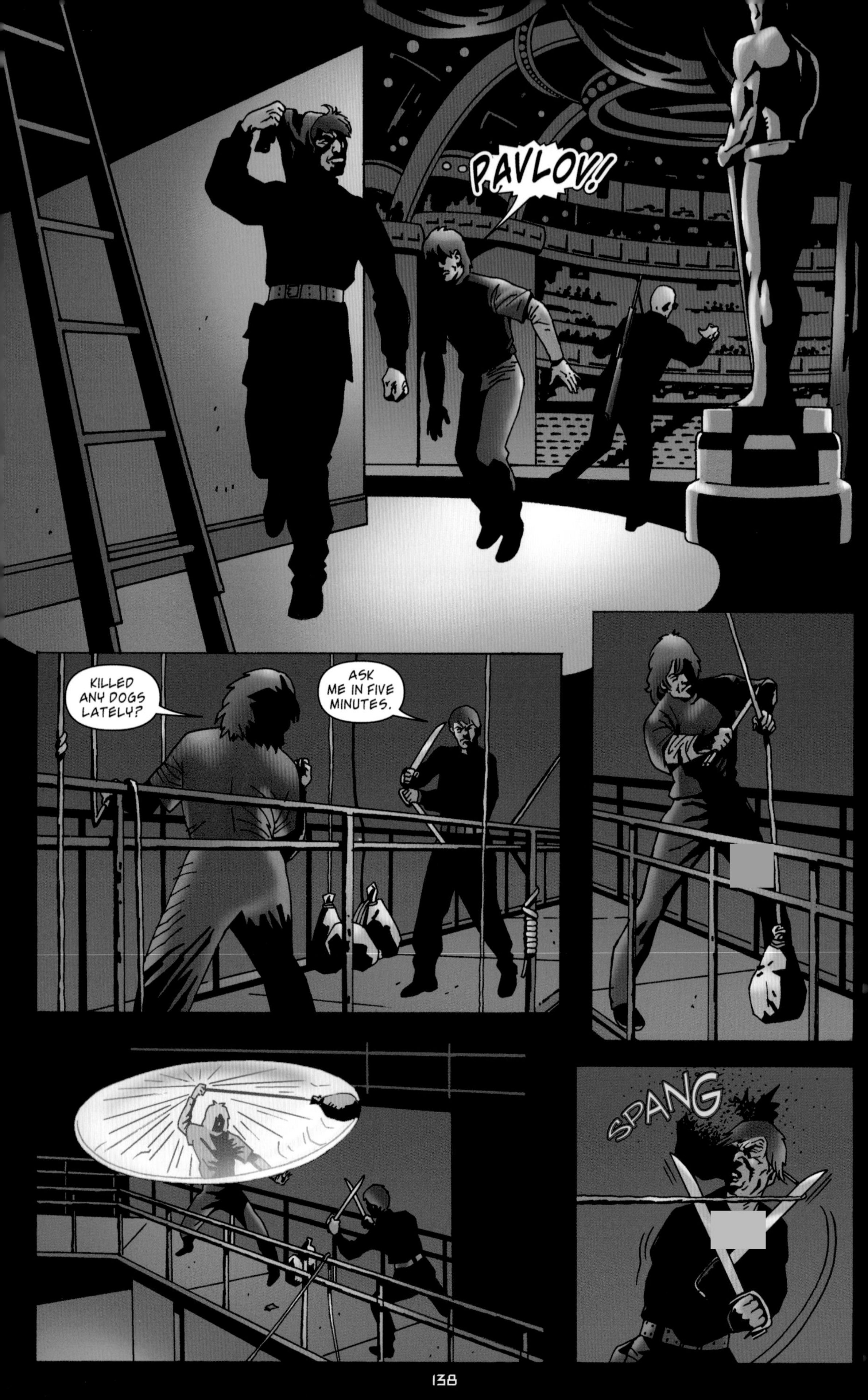
PAVLOV!
KILLED ANY DOGS LATELY?
ASK ME IN FIVE MINUTES.
SPANG

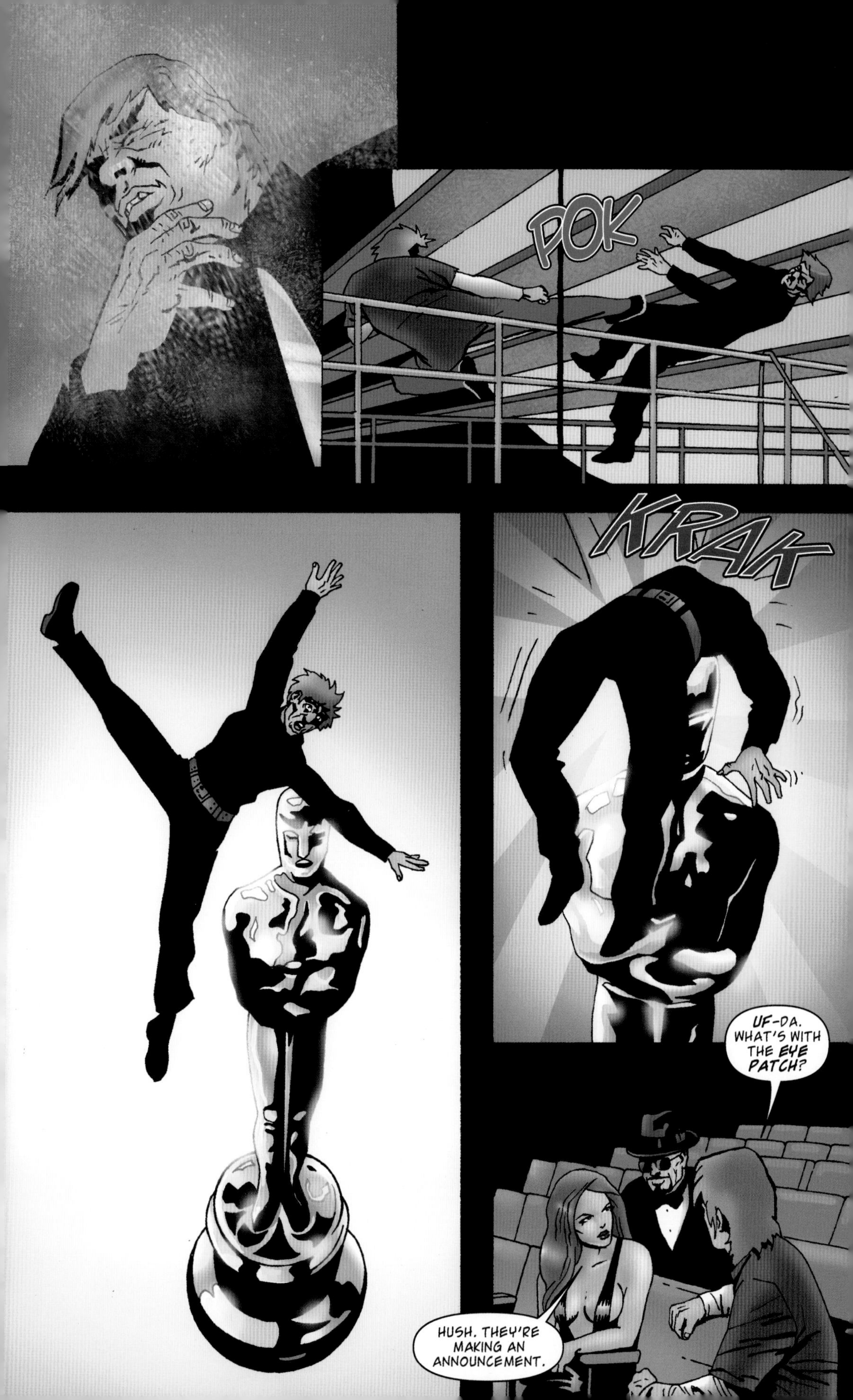
POK
KRAK
UF-DA. WHAT'S WITH THE EYE PATCH?
HUSH. THEY'RE MAKING AN ANNOUNCEMENT.

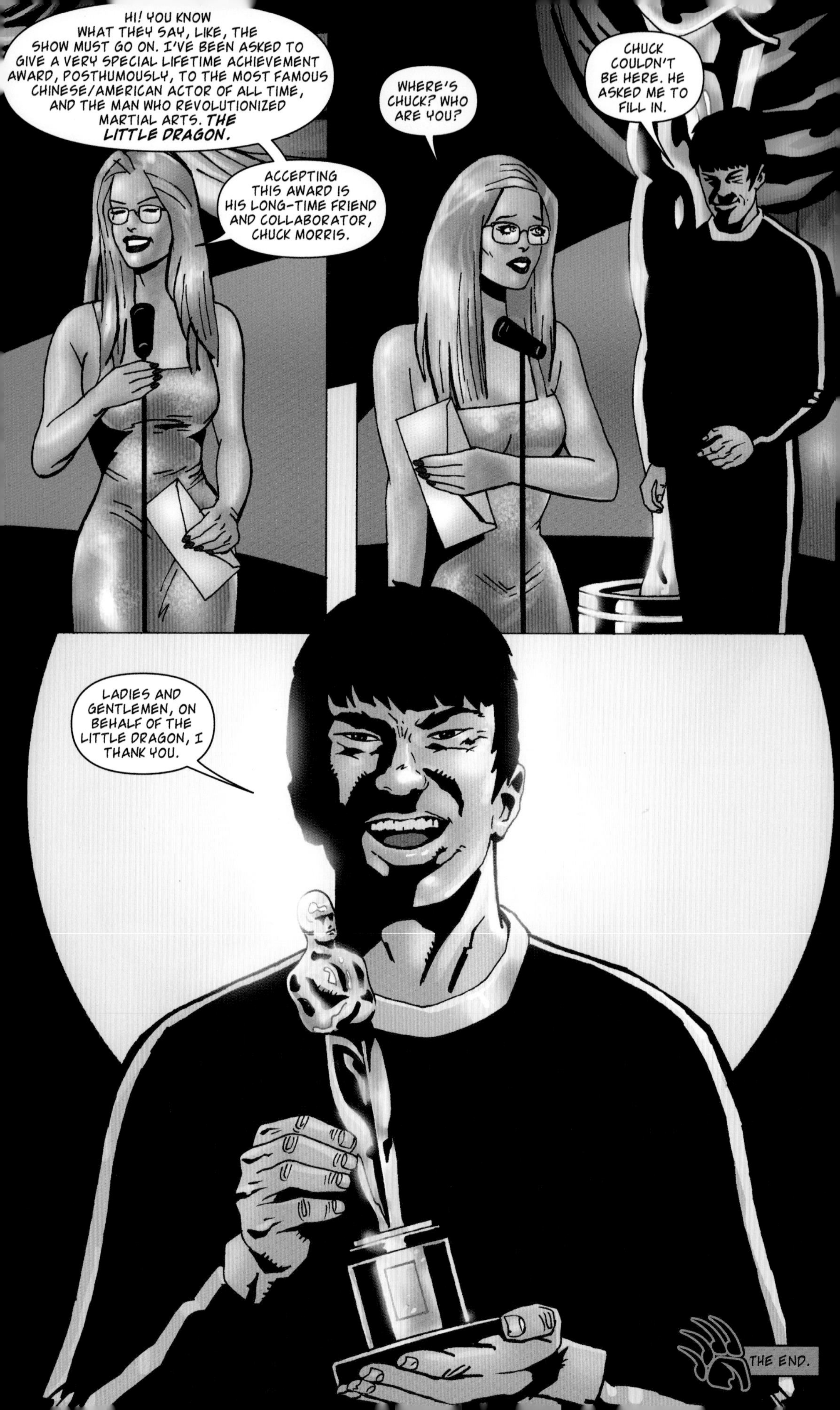
HI! YOU KNOW WHAT THEY SAY, LIKE, THE SHOW MUST GO ON. I'VE BEEN ASKED TO GIVE A VERY SPECIAL LIFETIME ACHIEVEMENT AWARD, POSTHUMOUSLY, TO THE MOST FAMOUS CHINESE/AMERICAN ACTOR OF ALL TIME, AND THE MAN WHO REVOLUTIONIZED MARTIAL ARTS. THE LITTLE DRAGON.
ACCEPTING THIS AWARD IS HIS LONG-TIME FRIEND AND COLLABORATOR, CHUCK MORRIS.
WHERE'S CHUCK? WHO ARE YOU?
CHUCK COULDN'T BE HERE. HE ASKED ME TO FILL IN.
LADIES AND GENTLEMEN, ON BEHALF OF THE LITTLE DRAGON, I THANK YOU.
THE END.

ART GALLERY

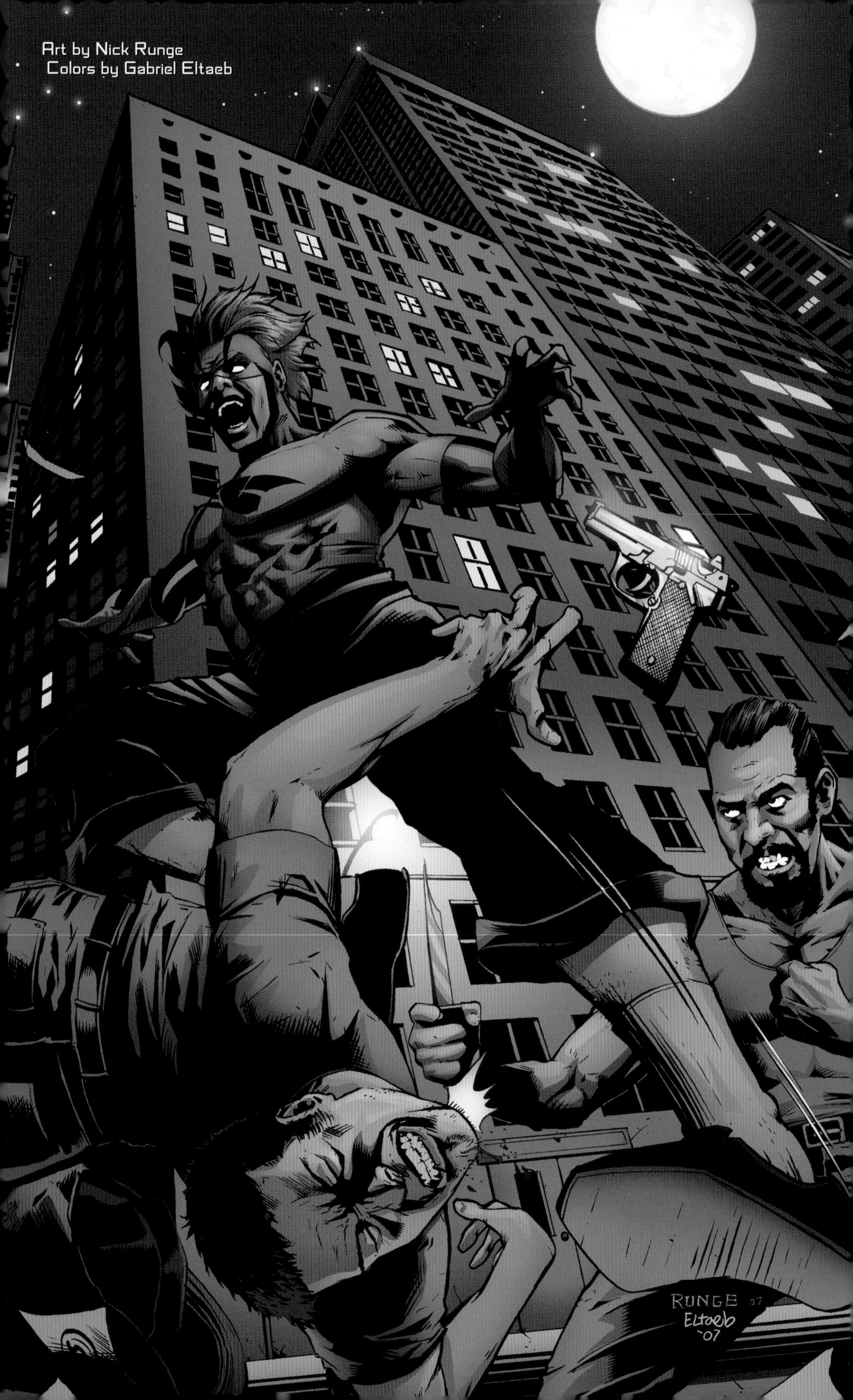
Art by Nick Runge
Colors by Gabriel Eltaeb
RUNGE 07
Eltaeb '07

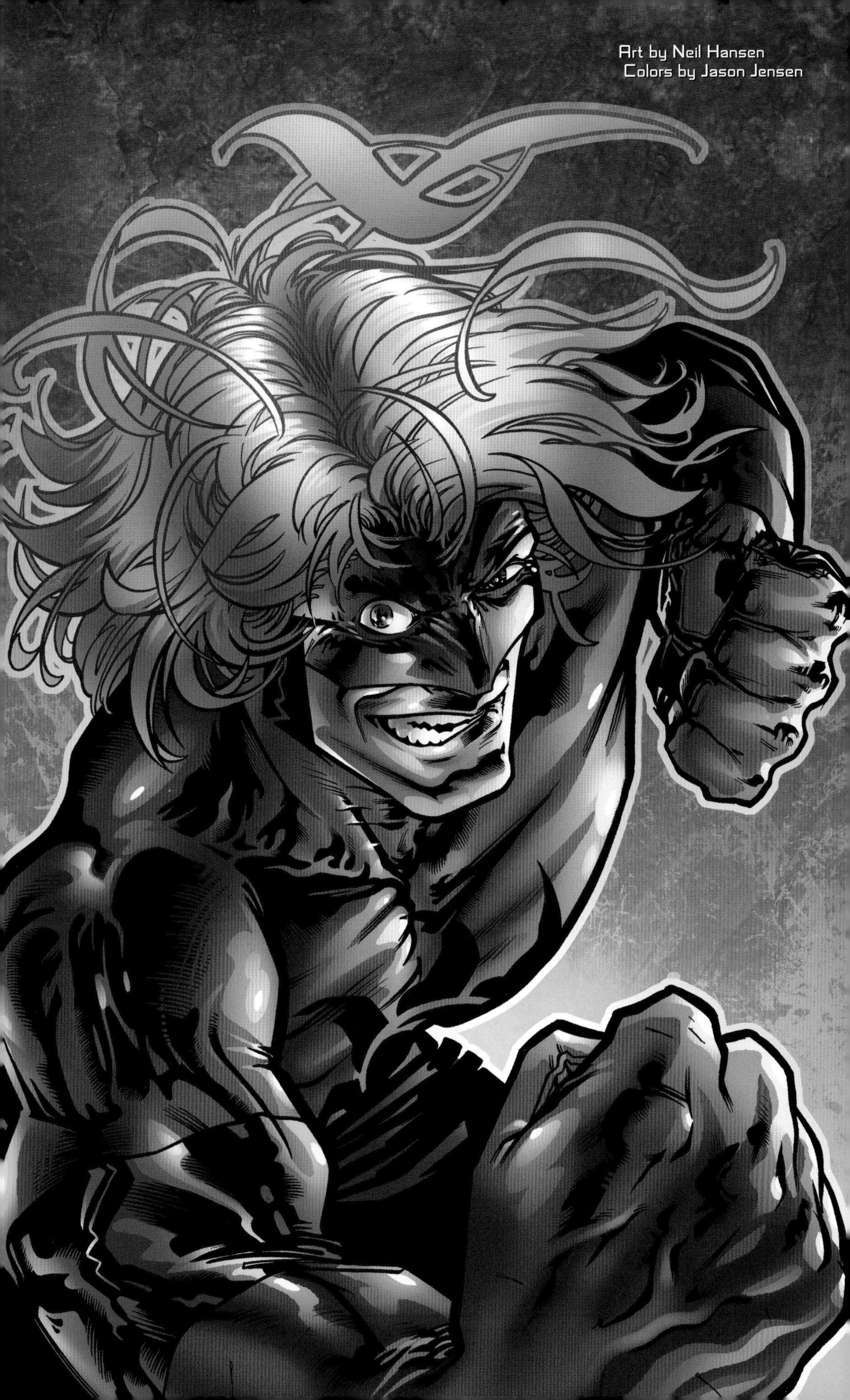
Art by Neil Hansen
Colors by Jason Jensen

Art by David Messina

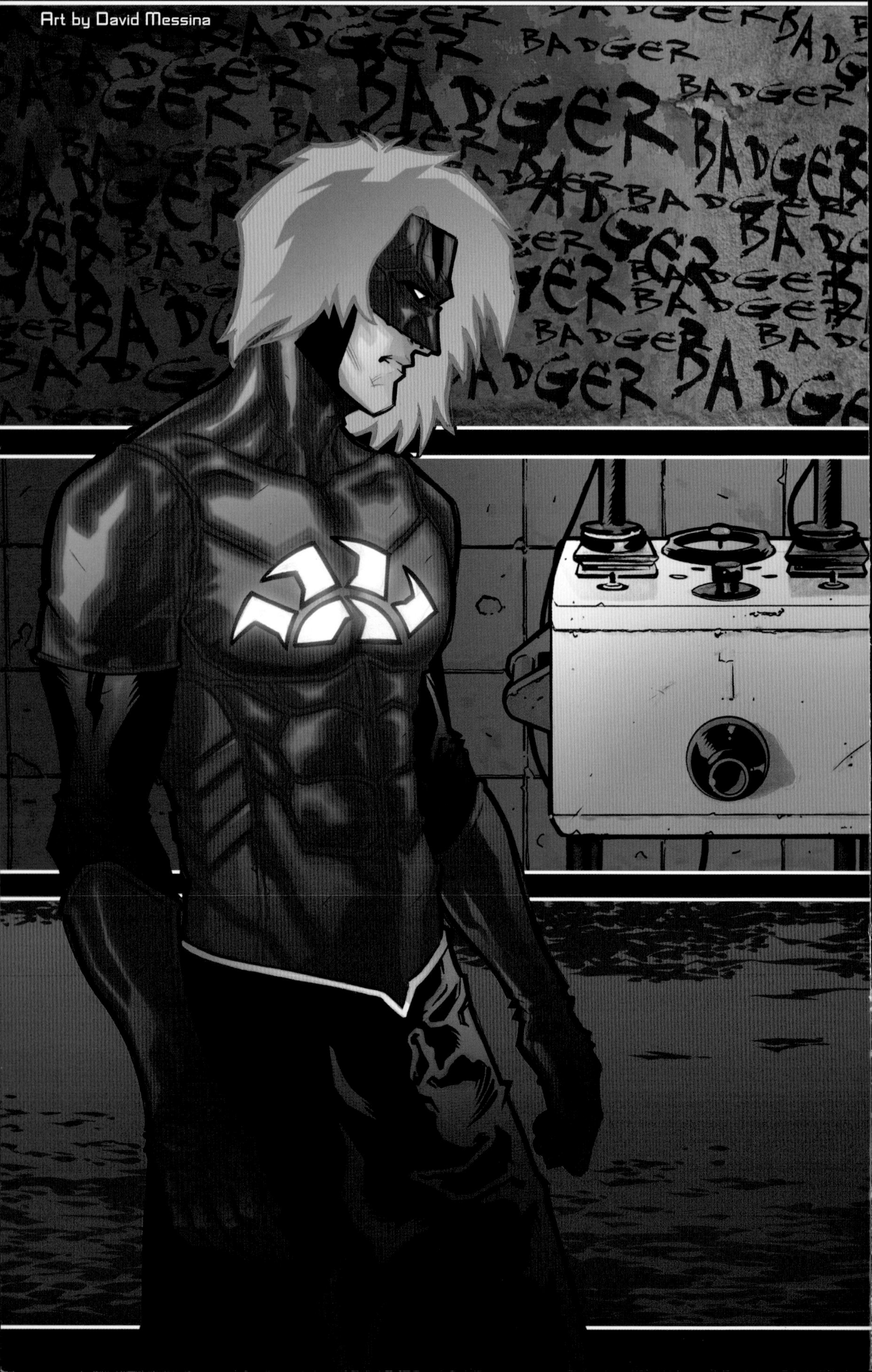
BADGER
BADGER
BADGER
BADGER
BADGER

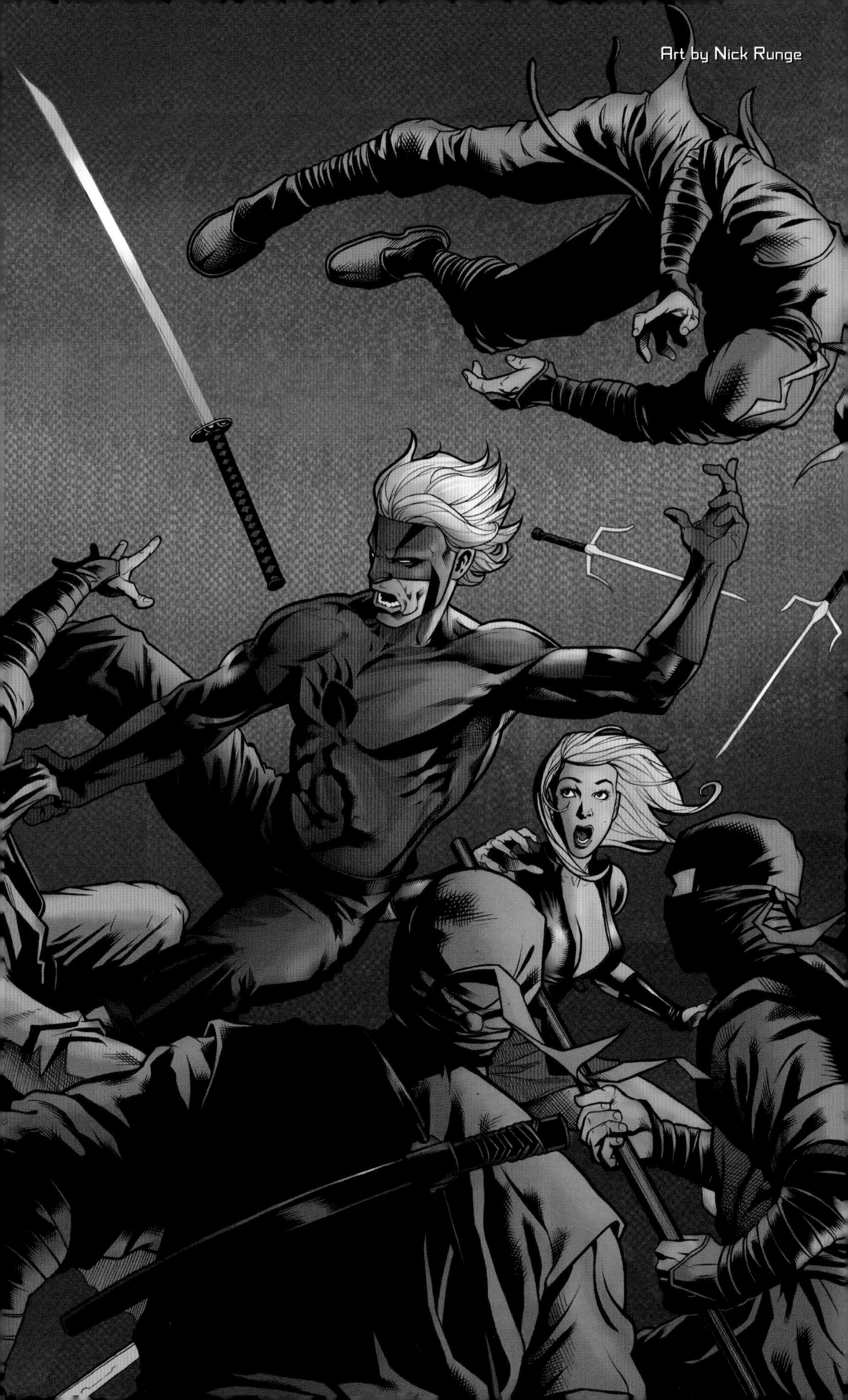
Art by Nick Runge

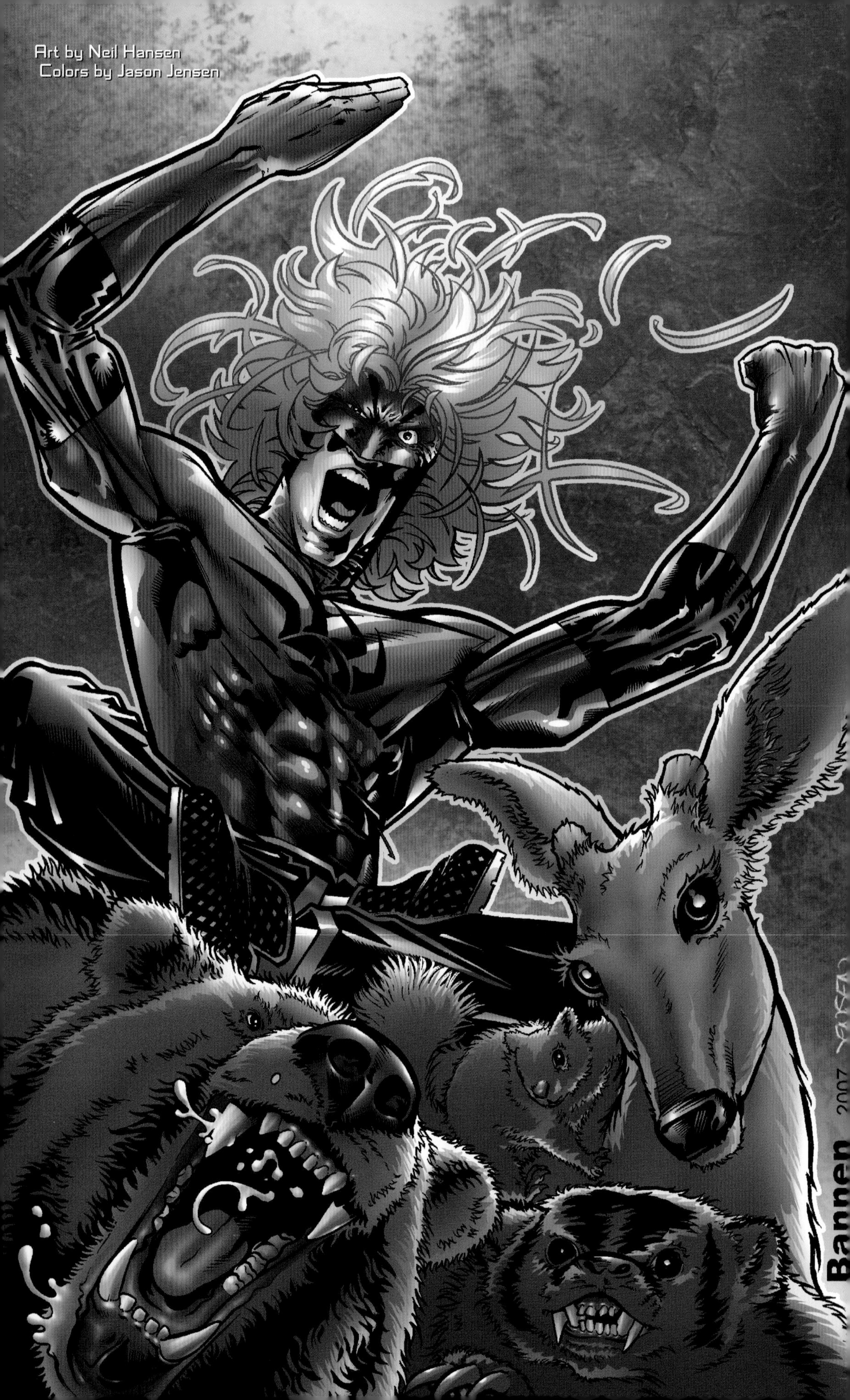
Art by Neil Hansen
Colors by Jason Jensen
Bannen 2007

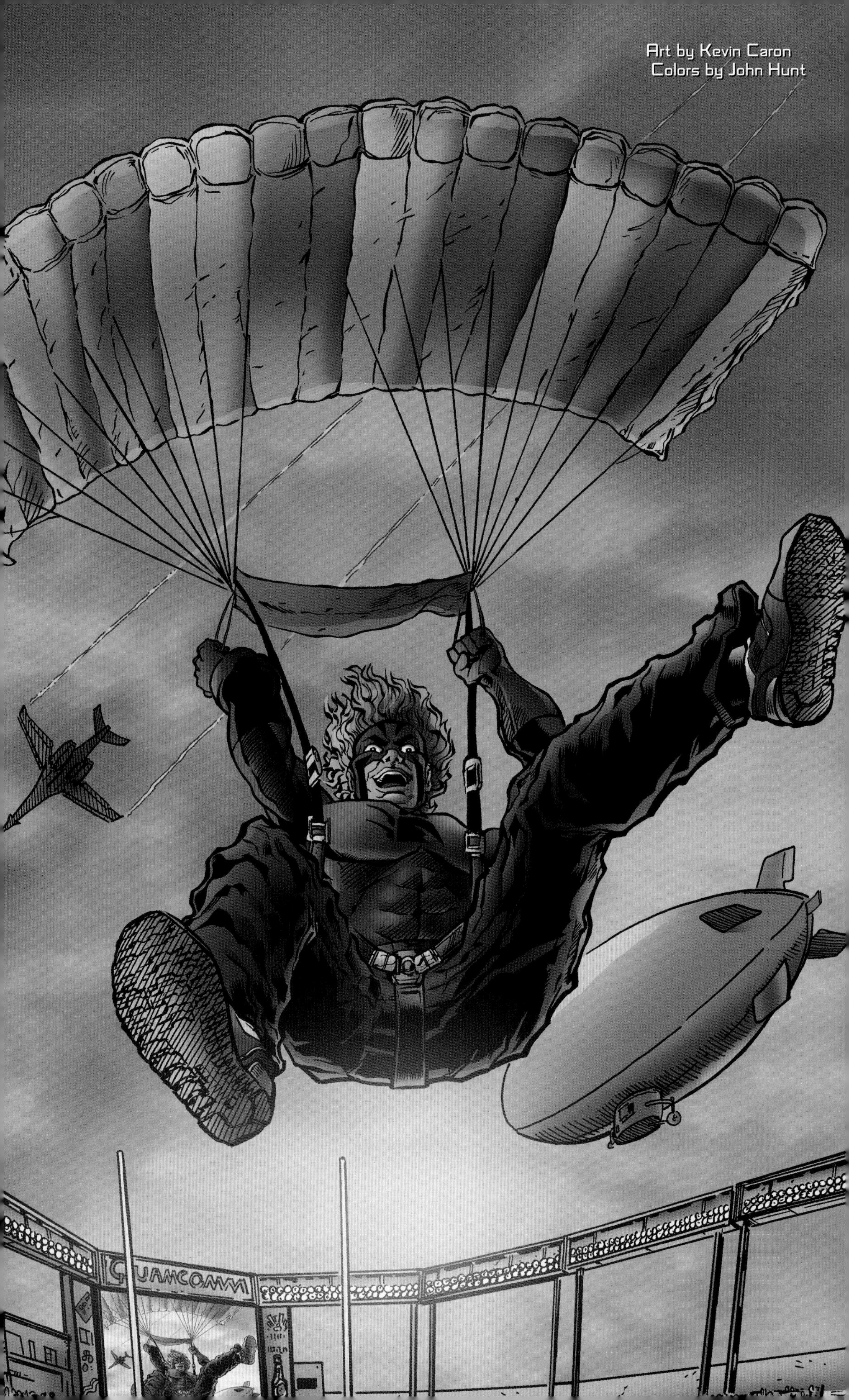
Art by Kevin Caron
Colors by John Hunt
QUAMCOMM

Art by Mike Oeming
Colors by Nick Filardi

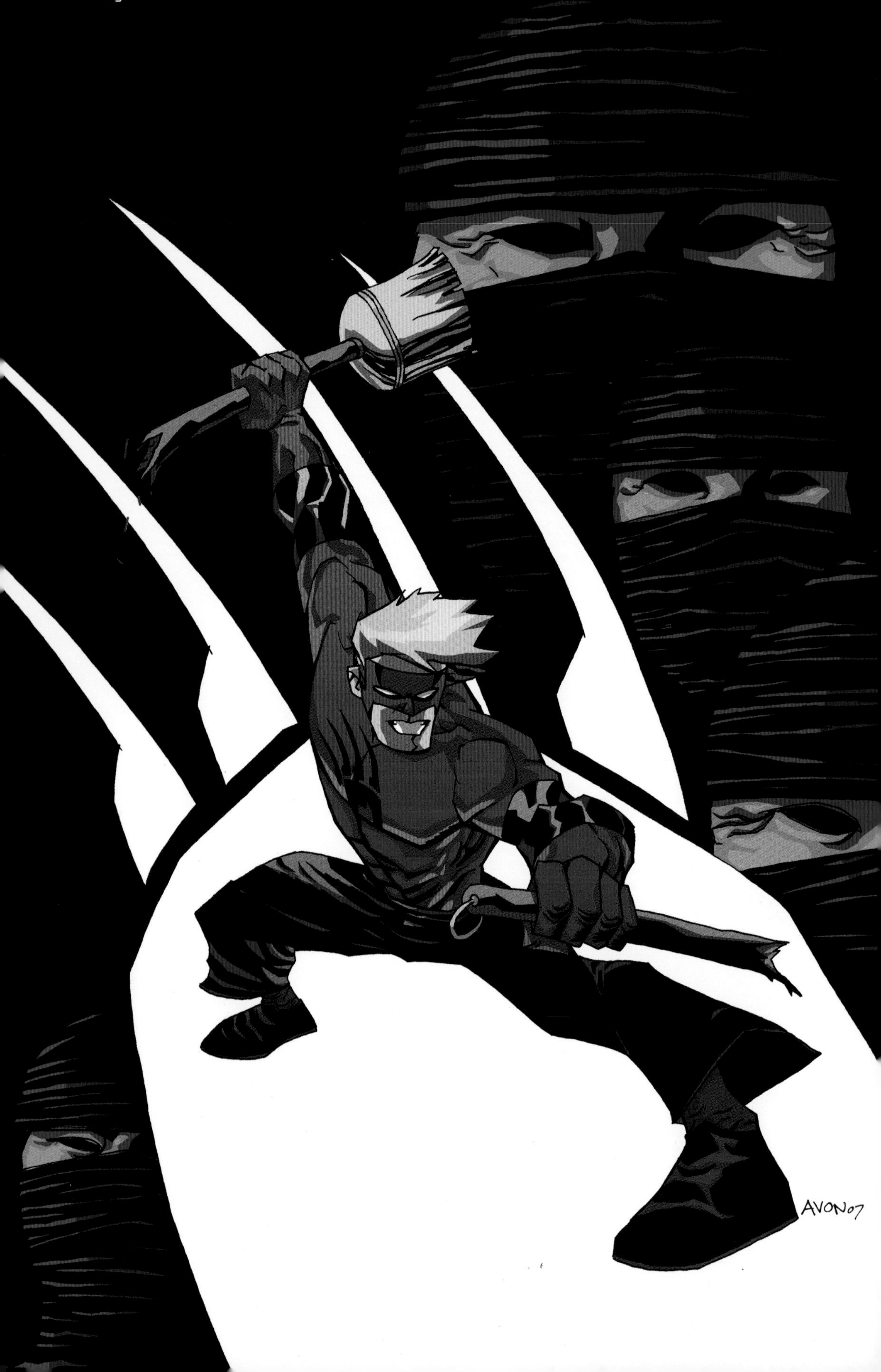
AVON07

SKUNK!

BY MIKE BARON
PENCILLED BY JEFF T. CRUZ

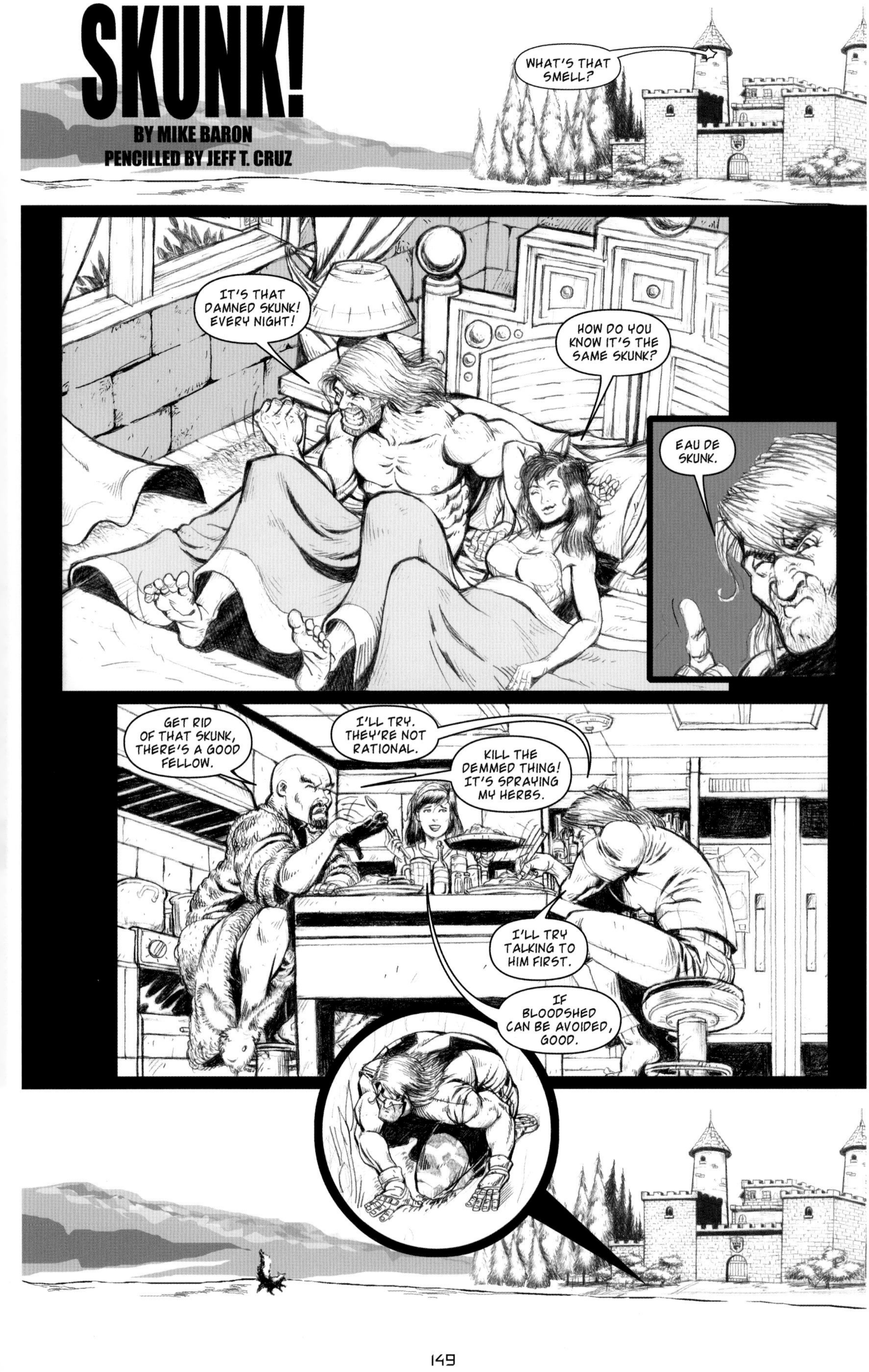
WHAT'S THAT SMELL?
IT'S THAT DAMNED SKUNK! EVERY NIGHT!
HOW DO YOU KNOW IT'S THE SAME SKUNK?
EAU DE SKUNK.
GET RID OF THAT SKUNK, THERE'S A GOOD FELLOW.
I'LL TRY. THEY'RE NOT RATIONAL.
KILL THE DEMMED THING! IT'S SPRAYING MY HERBS.
I'LL TRY TALKING TO HIM FIRST.
IF BLOODSHED CAN BE AVOIDED, GOOD.

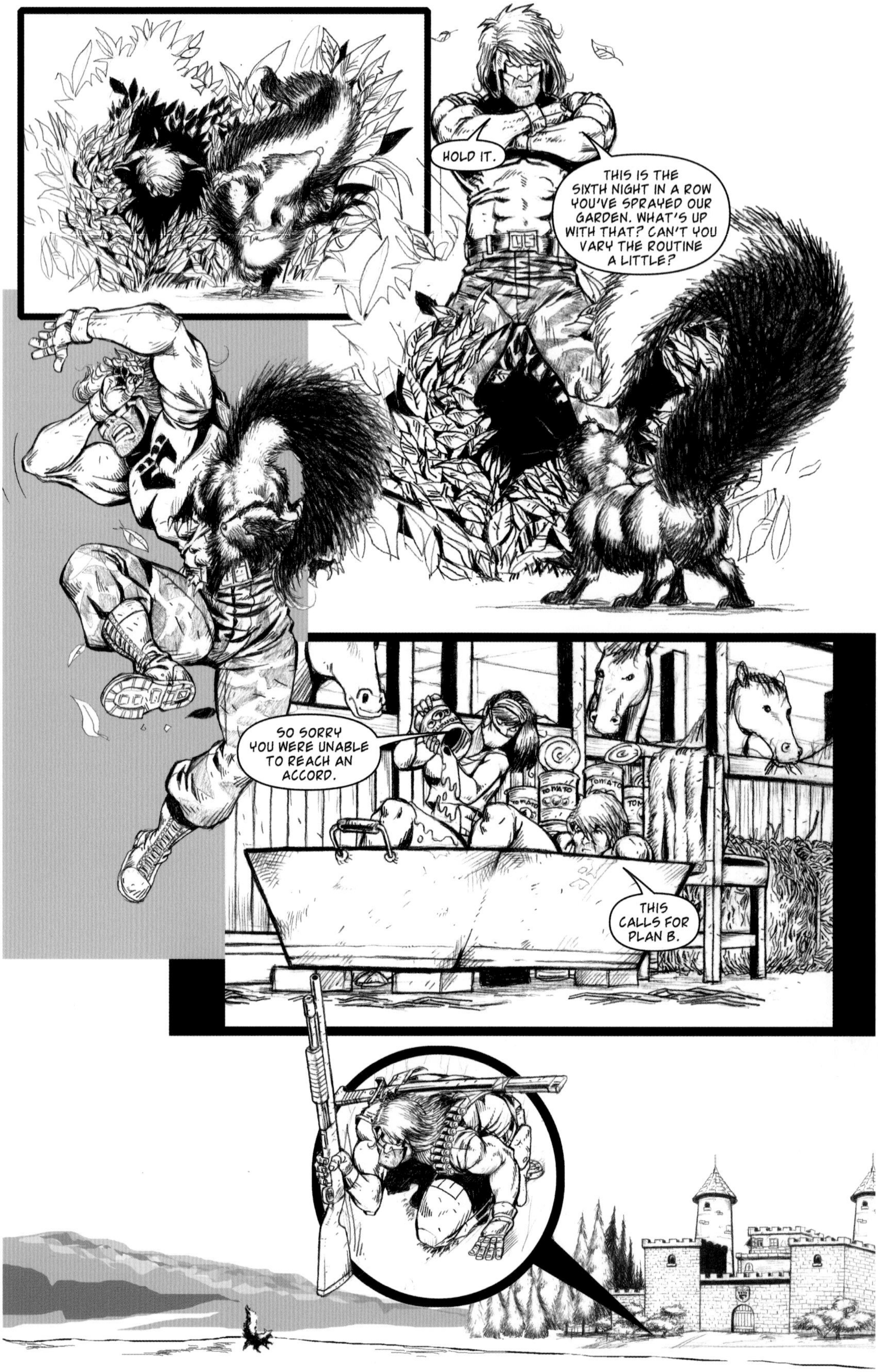
HOLD IT.
THIS IS THE SIXTH NIGHT IN A ROW YOU'VE SPRAYED OUR GARDEN. WHAT'S UP WITH THAT? CAN'T YOU VARY THE ROUTINE A LITTLE?
SO SORRY YOU WERE UNABLE TO REACH AN ACCORD.
THIS CALLS FOR PLAN B.

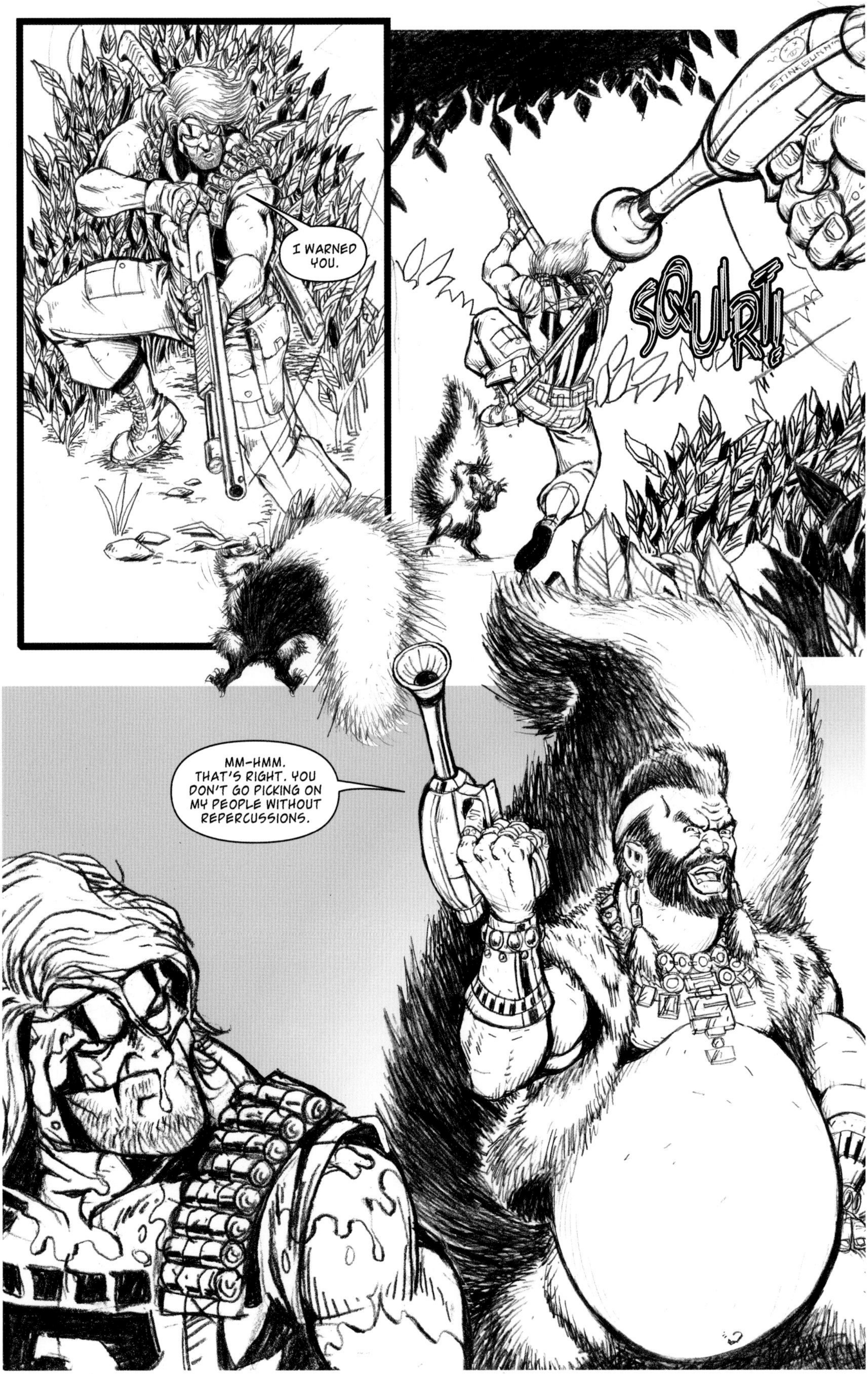
I WARNED YOU.
SQUIRT!
MM-HMM. THAT'S RIGHT. YOU DON'T GO PICKING ON MY PEOPLE WITHOUT REPERCUSSIONS.